Globalization and Women in the Japanese Workforce

Japan's position as an affluent, industrialized liberal democracy with a distinctive national model of capitalism means that Japanese women's experiences of globalization differ from those of women elsewhere in Asia and in other First World countries. The Japanese state and Japanese companies have been instrumental in the globalization of production, which is now having reciprocal effects domestically. Japan's national model of capitalism is undergoing profound changes, which affect men and women differently, as liberalizing processes associated with globalization interact with specific local institutions, including the ideal of the three-generation family and the position of women in the Japanese workforce.

Globalization and Women in the Japanese Workforce contributes to the debate about the impact of globalization upon women. It examines the impact of restructuring upon women's employment in Japan and describes the actions women are taking individually and collectively to campaign for change in their working environment and the laws and practices regulating it.

Beverley Bishop is a Senior Analyst in the Older and Working Age People Research and Evaluation Unit of the Ministry of Social Development in New Zealand. In 2003 she was awarded a PhD at Sheffield University for research on the impact of globalization on women working in Japan.

Sheffield Centre for Japanese Studies/ RoutledgeCurzon Series

Series Editor: Glenn D. Hook
Professor of Japanese Studies, University of Sheffield

This series, published by RoutledgeCurzon in association with the Centre for Japanese Studies at the University of Sheffield, both makes available original research on a wide range of subjects dealing with Japan and provides introductory overviews of key topics in Japanese Studies.

Globalization and Women in the Japanese Workforce

Beverley Bishop

RoutledgeCurzon
Taylor & Francis Group

LONDON AND NEW YORK

First published 2005
by RoutledgeCurzon
2 Park Square, Milton Park, Abingdon, Oxon OX14 4RN

Simultaneously published in the USA and Canada
by RoutledgeCurzon
270 Madison Ave, New York, NY 10016

RoutledgeCurzon is an imprint of the Taylor & Francis Group

© 2005 Beverley Bishop

Typeset in Baskerville by
Florence Production Ltd, Stoodleigh, Devon
Printed and bound in Great Britain by
Antony Rowe Ltd, Chippenham, Wiltshire

British Library Cataloguing in Publication Data
A catalogue record for this book is available from the British Library

Library of Congress Cataloging in Publication Data
A catalog record for this book is available from the Library of Congress

ISBN 0–415–34249–X

To my mum and dad, who have always encouraged me, but never pushed

Contents

Figures and tables

Figures

Tables

Acknowledgements

I have been very fortunate in receiving a great deal of support, as well as thought-provoking comments and suggestions, from many people during the process of researching this book and the PhD on which it is based.

I owe an enormous debt of gratitude to my PhD supervisors, Georgina Waylen, Jenny Roberts and Glenn Hook. I would also like to thank all connected with the Political Economy Research Centre, particularly Sylvia McColm for making it a lovely place to be, as well as my friends and fellow PERCies, Rajiv Prabhakar, Jonathan Perraton and Peter Wells, who all took the time to read drafts and make useful and pertinent comments. Peter Wells deserves special recognition, since, as my landlord, he had to live with me when I was writing up my thesis.

I could not have conducted fieldwork in Japan without the generous assistance of Usui Yuki, Komatsu Makiko, Koedou Shizuko, Morishita Miwa, Miwa Kyoko, and Nakura Yoshie, who have acted as key informants, vital links to activist networks, translators and interpreters, but who, most of all, have been great people to have as friends.

I learnt much from access to the meetings, actions and internal papers of Working Women's Network, Working Women's International Network, Women Helping Women, Shosha ni Hataraku Josei, Tokyo Josei Union and Women's Messages. Reasons of space stop me acknowledging by name all the other women who kindly took the trouble to take part in interviews, fill out questionnaires and send me documents.

I am also grateful to the Economic and Social Research Council (ESRC), the University of Sheffield, the University of Shiga, the International Research Centre for Japanese Studies, the International Studies Association, the Anglo-Japanese Academy and the Nordic Institute for Asian Studies for providing me with grants and other resources to enable me to carry out my research and attend seminars and conferences.

I would like to thank the Working Women's PAW, the Organisation for Economic Co-operation and Development (OECD), the Ministry of Economy, Trade and Industry (METI), the Japanese Ministry of Education, Culture, Sport and Technology and the Statistics Bureau of the Ministry of Public Management, Home Affairs, Posts and Telecommunications for allowing me to reproduce their work to illustrate this book.

Marina Lee-Cunin and Shannon Frances have been truly (practically and emotionally) supportive friends, as have Ashley Hyde, Peter Holcroft and Roger Ashman – I am incredibly lucky to know them. Throughout the process of turning the thesis into a book, my partner, Peter North, was, as always, unfailingly kind, patient and helpful.

Abbreviations

ANA	All Nippon Airlines
APEC	Asia-Pacific Economic Cooperation
APWLD	Asia Pacific Forum on Women, Law and Development
ASEAN	Association of Southeast Asian Nations
AWA	Asian Women's Association
BBC	British Broadcasting Corporation
Beijing JAC	Beijing Japan Accountability Caucus
CEDAW	Convention on the Elimination of All Forms of Discrimination Against Women
CGE	Council for Gender Equality
CONAMUP	Coordinadora Nacional de Movimiento Urbano Popular
CONGO	Conference of Non-Governmental Organizations
EEOL	Equal Employment Opportunities Law
EMOSA	Exportadora de Mano de Obra S. A.
EOMC	Equal Opportunity Mediation Commission
EU	European Union
EZ	export zone
FDI	foreign direct investment
FY	fiscal year
GATT	General Agreement on Tariffs and Trade
GDP	gross domestic product
ICFTU	International Confederation of Free Trade Unions
ILO	International Labour Organization
IMF	International Monetary Fund
JAIWR	Japan Association of International Women's Rights
JCP	Japan Communist Party
JETRO	Japan External Trade Organization
JNR	Japan National Railways
LDP	Liberal Democratic Party
LSL	Labour Standards Law
M&As	mergers and acquisitions
MBA	Master of Business Administration
METI	Ministry of Economy, Trade and Industry

MIT	Massachusetts Institute of Technology
MITI	Ministry of International Trade and Industry
NAFTA	North American Free Trade Agreement
NAO	National Administrative Office (Department of Labor, US)
NHK	Nippon Hoso Kyokai (Japan Broadcasting Corporation
NIC	newly industrialized country
NIE	Newly industrialized economy
NGO	non-governmental organization
NOW	National Organization for Women
NPO	non-profit-making organization
NTT	Nippon Telegraph and Telephone Public Corporation
ODA	Overseas Development Assistance
OECD	Organisation for Economic Co-operation and Development
OL	'office lady', woman working in administrative or secretarial position
PAW	Part-timers Analysis and Watch
PBS	Public Broadcasting Service
SAP	Structural Adjustment Programme
SCAP	Supreme Commander for the Allied Powers
SDP	Social Democratic Party
SEAPAT	South-East Asia and the Pacific Multidisciplinary Advisory Team
TNC	transnational corporation
UN	United Nations
UNCTAD	United Nations Conference on Trade and Development
WIEGO	Women in Informal Employment Globalizing and Organizing
WTO	World Trade Organization
WWIN	Working Women's International Network
WWN	Working Women's Network

Glossary of Japanese terms

Ajia no onnatachi no kai	Association of Asian Women
appaku mensetsu	'oppressive interview'; method of interview likely to discourage female job applicants
arubaito	Part-time job carried out by a student
Burakumin	Disadvantaged outcaste group
Dai Nippon Aikoku Fujin Kai	Greater Japan Women's Patriotic Association
danjou kyoudou sankaku	joint participation of men and women
danjyou byoudou	gender equality
duburu sukuru	attending a vocational course at the same time as taking a bachelor's or associate degree ('double school')
eikyuu shuushoku	lifetime employment
endaka	the rising value of the Japanese yen
fujin kaikan	women's centre
Fujin Kouwakai	discussion group on 'the woman question'
Fujin Roudousha mondai kenkyuukai	Women Workers Research Group
furita 'freeter'	someone who is working at one or more part-time jobs and moves between jobs freely
gaiatsu	foreign pressure
gaishikei	foreign-affiliate firm
gakureki shugi	educational credentialism
girichoko	(lit. 'obligation chocolates') – chocolates given on Valentine's Day by female workers to male co-workers
gurobaruka	globalization
gyoumushoku	business operations track
gyousei	administrative body
hakenkaisha	worker dispatching agency

haken/hakensha	dispatched work/worker
hishain	non-regular worker
ie	family/household
ippanshoku	general track
japayuki-san	(lit. Ms Going to Japan) women who go to Japan from foreign countries to work in the sex trade
jimu shoku	clerical track
Josei no waakinguraifu wo kangaeru paata kenkyuukai	(lit. Study Group to Consider Part-time Working and Women's Working Life) – known in English as Working Women's PAW (Part-timers Analysis and Watch)
josei sentaa	women's centre
joseigaku	women's studies
kaggiko	latchkey child
kaizen	continuous improvement
kanban	'just-in-time' production aimed at eliminating waste
kazuko kokka	literally 'family state', the idea of all Japanese people are one family under the Emperor
keiretsu	corporate grouping characterized by large firms heading a subcontracting chain of smaller firms
kekkon taishoku	retirement upon marriage
kikan ga paato kokusaika	'key' part-timers internationalization
Kokusai Fujin-nen Renraku-kai	International Women's Year Conference on Japan
kokusaika	internationalization
koshikake	temporary seat
kouwakai	discussion group
kudouka	'hollowing out'
minikomi	newsletter, often produced by activist groups
naishoku	homeworking
naiyo no ko	domestic labour
nenko	system of payment according to seniority
Nikkeijin	non-Japanese of Japanese heritage
Nihon Joseigaku Kai	The Women's Studies Association of Japan
Nikkeiren	Japan Federation of Employers' Associations
o-bento	lunchbox

Onna kara Onnatachi e: *Ichinichi Juen no Kai*	From Woman to Women: Ten-Yen a Day group
Onna no Nettowakingu	Women's Networking
onnarashii	feminine or womanly
paato	part-time work/employee
paato no obachan	middle-aged women carrying out *paato* work
ryosai kenbo	good wife and wise mother
sanbetsu kaigi	industrial union
Sangyou Houkoku Kai	Industrial Patriotic Society
seiri kyuuka	menstrual leave (literally physiological leave)
seishain	regular worker
seku hara	sexual harassment
senmonka	specialist
senmonshoku	specialist track
shain	company employee
shakai kengaku	(lit. a study trip in society) – the idea that it is useful for women to work for a short while so that they might understand more about the world
Shiba Shinkin	Shiba Credit Association
shokuba no hana	'office flowers' – young (and attractive) female white collar workers
Shougyou Rouren	Japan Federation of Commercial Workers' Union
sogoshoku	management track
tokusei	special character
uuman ribu	'women's lib'
yakuza	Japanese mafia
zaibatsu	large family-owned banking or industrial combine associated with the pre-1945 era
Zenkoku Ippan	National Union of General Workers
Zenroren	National Confederation of Trade Unions

Notes on style

Citations and websites

Where the full names of Japanese individuals are cited in this work, the given name is written before the family name in accordance with Japanese convention.

Where websites are quoted in the text, only the date and author are given. Website addresses can be found in the Bibliography.

Figures in tables

Where columns in tables do not exactly total 100 percent, this is due to rounding.

1 Introduction

Aims, methodology and structure of the book

This book argues that globalization is a real, but not an immutable, force which is producing profound changes in national models of capitalism and national socio-economic institutions, and is affecting men and women within these national models in different ways. I shall put forward an analysis of the relationship between gender and globalization using women workers in Japan as a case study. Japan was chosen because its distinctive model of capitalism is being transformed by the processes associated with globalization. As men and women have had very different positions within that model, this transformation is having different impacts upon male and female workers.

The last few decades have seen growing cultural, economic and political interconnections and interdependencies between countries. Globalization results from flows of people, flows of images and information through the mass media, flows of central ideas, terms and images, flows of ideologies, flows of technology and increasingly rapid flows of international capital between national economies (Appadurai, 1990). While these flows influence all countries to a greater or lesser extent, this book will argue that the *way* in which globalization impacts upon nations, and on groups within nations, depends upon cultural or institutional factors. The impact of globalization on a nation will depend on its previous economic, political and social structure, and the effect of globalization on any individual will be mediated by, among other things, gender, age, ethnicity and social class.

Japan was chosen as a case study because of its distinctive national model of capitalism, which is characterized by a clearly gendered division of labour, and by a government which long resisted adopting the neo-liberal model associated with globalization. This chapter defines the Japanese national model of capitalism and sets out the relationship of the institutions of the Japanese national model of capitalism to globalization. It shows how Japanese government and business reactions to globalization are interacting with changes in the roles and expectations of women in the Japanese labour force. Specifically, it shows that, faced with the pressures of globalization, the Japanese state and other key economic actors are attempting to deregulate the Japanese labour market. At the same time the development of the ideal of equality of opportunity and of a nascent global legal standard of sex equality within the workplace has resulted in the Japanese government increasing the regulation of women's labour rights.

This chapter will put the research into its academic context and explain its central aims. It will then describe the methods that have been used, before setting out the structure of the book and outlining the contribution made by each chapter to the overall argument of the book, and to meeting the book's central aims.

Context

The rate of economic growth of Japan in the 1950s and 1960s,[1] its consequent increased importance in the world economy and its apparently low level of industrial strife have attracted considerable attention from Western theorists since the late 1950s. The focus of much industrial relations literature in English about the Japanese model has been the organization of work for core workers within large companies. Abegglen and Stalk (1985) wrote of the way workers traded a guarantee of lifetime employment for loyalty to the firm. Dore (1986) attributed the success of the Japanese model to 'flexible rigidities': the tendency towards oligopoly, tenured job security for core workers and state underwriting of capital actually made the Japanese system more flexible in that they engendered co-operativeness, functional flexibility, the ability to negotiate sensible compromises between capital and labour, and thoroughness of planning. Political economists examined the idea that we were witnessing a 'global Japanization' of the labour process (Jessop *et al.*, 1987; Elger and Smith, 1994). Japan's recent economic decline has again focused business and academic opinion on Japan. The focus now, however, is on how the Japanese model is changing to respond to the exigencies of globalization (Boyer and Drache, 1996; Hasegawa and Hook, 1998; Dore, 2000; Hook and Hasegawa, 2001).

Theorists such as Abegglen (1958) and Dore (1973, 1986) largely neglected the role of women in the Japanese workforce. The classical Japanese 'model' that they described was one that was mainly relevant to male workers (Wakisaka, 1997: 31), despite the fact that female workers have constituted a significant part of the workforce. In 1945, the proportion of working women in the total population was arguably the highest of all developed nations (Iwao, 1993: 154). However, Japan was the only industrialized country in which a decline in the number of women working outside the home was observed for the years following the Second World War. Today, Japanese women participate in the workforce in numbers comparable to those of women in other modern industrial societies.[2] This reversal in participation trends can be attributed to a number of factors including an increase in longevity, a decline in the fertility rate,[3] an increase in housing and education costs, the return of 'baby boom' wives to the labour market, and changing social attitudes to women's place in society (Whittaker, 1990). Furthermore, the Equal Employment Opportunities Law (EEOL), which came into effect in 1986 and was revised in 1997 (with the revisions coming into effect in April 1999), has been enacted with the ostensible aim of giving women equal opportunities in the workplace. These social and legal changes, which are, as this book will show, also partially attributable to globalization, are interacting with government and company attempts to restructure the Japanese model of employment in the face of economic globalization.

In Japan, as in other countries, women earn less, on average, than men and tend to be vertically and horizontally segregated from men in the workforce (Gelb and Palley, 1994: 9). This trend is becoming even more marked as the labour shortage resulting from demographic change, i.e. a shortage of young people entering the labour market, draws more women into the paid workforce, particularly into poorly rewarded 'non-core' jobs, as I shall demonstrate. This process is being facilitated by legal change (Sugeno and Suwa, 1997) and the planned and actual reorganization of the Japanese labour force, which intensified in the wake of the East Asian economic crisis of the late 1990s (*Economist*, 1998). The changing regional political economy of East Asia has had particular consequences for Japan. The intense competitiveness of other East Asian economies, the international reaction to the high value of the yen, and the relocation of a substantial proportion of Japanese manufacturing to other countries have led to predictions that Japan's distinctive labour practice will be radically restructured (Ministry of Labour, 1999). Despite obvious similarities with trends in Western industrialized economies, there is a tendency for the deeply gendered division of labour in Japan to be seen as either rooted in national culture (Stockman *et al.*, 1995) or as an epiphenomenon resulting from Japan's relatively late industrialization (Brinton, 1993). I shall show that, although affected by the Japanese family model, a gendered division of labour was established in the specific conditions of the post-war international political economy. This division of labour is changing in response to a changing global political economy.

The structural transformation of other developed economies has had particularly far-reaching effects for women in all 'core' areas of the world economy. The growth of the service sector, the leisure industry and the use of information technology have affected several aspects of the organization of work, including the proportions of men and women in the workforce, the types of employment available, the number of temporary and part-time jobs, work and leisure-related aspirations, and the place of work in women's life course (Dex, 1988: 1). Globalization is accelerating structural change in developed and developing countries. However, most mainstream theoretical work about globalization does not emphasize the particular effects that such structural change has for women. As Chapter 3 will show, feminist researchers working within gendered political economy have added gendered perspectives to mainstream theories of globalization. However, these perspectives have been of limited applicability to Japan. The characteristics of Japan's national model of capitalism have influenced the patterns of women's participation in the workforce throughout the post-war period. Furthermore, unlike other First World countries, Japan has maintained the tradition of the three-generation household.[4] This family structure impacts on demand for migrant domestic workers; it means that highly educated women tend to leave the workforce upon becoming mothers, then re-enter the workforce at rather lower levels than they left; and it informs government assumptions about welfare provision and the appropriate legal framework for non-regular work. The patterns of resistance to neo-liberal globalization and activism in support of equal labour rights for women are also informed by Japan's normative homosocial order.

Central aims of this book

The central aims of this book are as follows:

- to contribute to the debate about the impact of globalization upon women by bringing in insights from the case of Japan into the wider academic discourse;
- to examine the impact of restructuring upon women's employment in Japan;
- to describe the actions women are taking individually and collectively to resist or campaign for change in their working environment and the laws and practices regulating it.

Methodology

The book draws on both quantitative and qualitative data. Most statistical information in this book comes from the wealth of data published by Japanese government agencies, trade unions and research organizations, as well as that produced by activists. These data are complemented by material from semi-structured interviews with working women, in-depth interviews with trade union representatives, plaintiffs in court cases about gender and employment, and Japanese academics, as well as primary data from reports and surveys. This mixture of research methods is often recommended as a way to achieve triangulation, i.e. when the same explanation can be obtained from different sources then the explanation is more plausible. Mason's (1994) rationale for combining quantitative and qualitative methods is also persuasive. This was not so much to permit triangulation but to allow the quantitative component to map general patterns and the qualitative stage of the research to reveal the processes and perspectives of those actually involved in the situation under investigation. This is particularly important in conducting cross-cultural research, where it is necessary to search for 'meanings within a social context where people act according to the rules of the social setting' (May, 1997: 190).

To examine the extent to which women's experience of work is changing as the Japanese national model of capitalism adapts to the exigencies of globalization, it was first necessary to gain an understanding of the experiences of women within that model. For this purpose, I conducted a pilot study in 1996 and 1997, using semi-structured interviews and written questionnaires. This provided useful background material and informed some of the research questions which I later composed. More information about this, the demographic and employment status of respondents and the text of questionnaires can be found in Appendix A, while Appendix B lists the types of employment carried out by the face-to-face interviewees.

I returned to Japan to conduct more focused fieldwork at the International Research Centre for Japanese Studies in Kyoto from October 1999 to March 2000. This fieldwork was focused on the specific effects of globalization upon women's employment and on women's agency in using some of the trends induced by globalization to improve their position. I consulted Japanese academics who were working in the field of gender studies and labour studies. I was also an active participant in two grassroots campaigning groups, Working Women's Network (WWN) and Women Helping Women, taking part in meetings and attending protest actions and court hearings in support of women bringing cases of sexual discrimination against different branches of the Sumitomo Corporation. These interviewees are listed in Appendix C. Through taking part in protest actions, I was able not only to gain an understanding of the range of methods employed by Japanese women activists but also to build relationships with some of the plaintiffs. Being involved in activism did, however, raise some ethical questions.[5]

Feminist researchers, particularly, have raised the question of the ethics of power imbalance in the relationship between researcher and researched in the research process. Wolf (1996) notes three areas of potential power imbalance:

- power differences stemming from the different positions of the researcher and researched (race, class, nationality, life chances);
- power exerted during the research process – defining the research process, unequal exchange and exploitation;
- power exerted during the post-fieldwork process – writing and representing.

I do not believe that there were significant intrinsic power differences between my informants and myself. To the best of my knowledge all were from the majority Japanese community,[6] and few were of a significantly different economic or educational status from myself.

This work does not address in any depth how globalization has resulted in an increased flow of female migrant workers into Japan. Increasing migration is an important effect of globalization, and takes very gendered forms, as I shall discuss in Chapter 3. Furthermore, non-Japanese women are recruited to Japan to fill very specific niches in the labour market, which have arisen because of globalization. These niches include carrying out sex work and being recruited to be wives of Japanese male farmers. However, conducting primary research about female migrants such as these would have raised significant ethical problems. It would have involved using a group of people with comparatively fewer life chances than I have had, in order to further my career, without being able to offer them any reciprocal benefits of participating in research. It would also have raised issues of 'race', sexuality and colonialism that are not core to my central argument. I therefore address female immigration to Japan only in so far as it affects or does not affect the productive and reproductive work of Japanese women.

As far as power exerted in the research process was concerned, although I was genuinely supportive of the cause of WWN and Working Women's International Network (WWIN), my primary goal in coming to Japan, and in joining these groups was to conduct research, the parameters of which I had defined in advance. Many of the activists were also experienced researchers and were therefore well aware of the research process, advising me on useful seminars and court hearings to attend, and on Japanese texts to consult. These women agreed to be interviewed and loaned me materials that they had used in support of their case. The organizations in question were keen to attract foreign members. They used strategies such as hosting websites in English, advertising their meetings in an English language magazine and sending out regular updates of their activities to an international mailing list. This was an overt attempt to employ a 'boomerang' strategy such as that described by Keck and Sikkink (1998).[7] Nonetheless, I am acutely aware that the exchange was not equal, and their contribution to my work was far greater than my contribution to theirs.

During the fieldwork process, and afterwards, I took steps to avoid falsely representing the groups with whom I was working. I showed draft papers to activists, gave talks to women's groups and asked questions of WWIN and Shosha ni Hataraku Josei to check whether they believed I was accurately representing their actions and opinions.[8] I also conducted a focus group meeting with an organization of women who had worked together to produce an English-language book about the situation of women in Japan, and exchanged ideas with members of Japan Women's Messages, and provided them with a copy of the resulting research.

Initially, the majority of questionnaires and semi-structured interviews were carried out with the aid of interpreters and translators. When my Japanese language proficiency improved after auditing MA Japanese language classes at the University of Sheffield, I began to carry out interviews without an interpreter present, but using a translator to help me transcribe interviews. Some respondents wished to carry out interviews in English, because they had lived in English-speaking countries, they met to discuss women's issues in English, or they produced a bilingual magazine. In these cases, I have used verbatim transcripts of the interviews (with omissions or additions for clarification in square brackets) when quoting these respondents in this book. While I believe the meaning of the quotations to be sufficiently clear, the wording of some quotations may seem unconventional.

During my fieldwork, I frequently attended lectures and seminars organized at the Dawn Centre (Osaka women's centre). These events were not only extremely informative in their own right but also enabled me to gain contact with, and subsequently interview, representatives of both trade unions and organizations for professional women. The Dawn Centre has an extensive collection of journals and press cuttings about the situation of women in Japan. This material, and material supplied by the Tokyo Josei Union and two other unions (which remain anonymous in this book), provided concrete examples of recent case studies of legal changes as well as changes in company employment practice. The Japan Institute of Labour, the Ministry of Labour, the Gender Equality Bureau of the Prime Minister's Office and Japanese think tanks and business organizations also provide a considerable amount of statistical data about the gender composition of different parts of the labour force and detailed information about changes in laws and policies in the face of globalization.

As the diversification of employment resulting from restructuring is often presented by proponents of restructuring as enabling diverse women to fulfil their potential in different ways (Koike, 1995), it is important to gauge whether women feel this to be the case. Using the snowball technique used in the 1996–7 survey, I carried out further semi-structured interviews with female agency workers, part-time and full-time employees and women who had chosen or attempted to enter the management track of firms. Initial contacts were made through my membership of the grassroots organization, Women Helping Women.

Structure of the book

The book is divided into three sections. Chapters 2 and 3 review the theoretical insights which have informed my research. Chapter 2 summarizes insights from theories of globalization, and Chapter 3 critically reviews the attempts that have been made to 'gender' globalization. Chapters 4 and 5 are an essential background to the analysis by setting out conditions specific to Japan, namely the position women have traditionally held in the Japanese labour force since 1945 and the pressures of globalization on the Japanese economy. Chapters 6 and 7 present empirical evidence to show the changes that are occurring for women working in the regular and non-regular workforces in Japan. The final substantive chapter, Chapter 8, examines women's activism, describing both the struggle against the effects of globalization that these women perceive as negative as well as the use

feminist campaigners are making of transnational networking and transnational organization to change their work situations.

Chapter 2 provides the theoretical background to my aim of showing
how the secondary effects of globalization on the Japanese workforce are
mutable and are shaped by the responses of the Japanese state and other
actors and institutions. It does so by providing a synthesis of insights from
mainstream debate about globalization and the state. The chapter begins
by summarizing the main theoretical perspectives surrounding globalization,
defining globalization and discussing whether it is a real phenomenon.
It examines the work of hyperglobalizers, who argue that globalization is a
real condition which has rendered the nation state irrelevant. However,
as the chapter illustrates, closer analysis shows that the nation state is still a
salient feature of an increasingly globalized international political economy.
The chapter then examines the work of sceptics and shows that, while some
of their reservations about the triumph of globalization are valid, globalization is a phenomenon that is qualitatively different from international trade
and is a process that has been increasing in momentum in recent decades.
The transformationalist thesis is found to be the most convincing in that it
recognizes that globalization is a progressive phenomenon, and that its effects
are mutable, because they are refracted through the institutions of different
states. As evidence will be presented about how the Japanese state has
been implicated in facilitating the reorganization of employment in Japan as
a response to globalization, the next part of this chapter will examine the
role of the state in an increasingly globalized political economy. Examples
are provided to show that, while the state remains highly relevant in an
age of globalization, and indeed is a necessary enabler of the project of
globalization, the role and the capacity of the state are changing. Even in
a globalizing world, the development of states will tend to be 'path dependent'. This means that, although individuals and groups within a society,
and ideas that gain acceptance within that society, can have an impact, the
institutions of a society, ranging from its laws to its normative social order,
will tend to influence the way it develops and reacts to external shocks (such
as globalization). Chapters 6, 7 and 8 will discuss how Japan's laws, company
practice and gender order have affected the positions open to Japanese working women and how these institutions have accommodated the changes
wrought by globalization, thereby showing how the secondary effects of
globalization on the Japanese workforce are mutable and are shaped by the
responses of the Japanese state and other actors and institutions.

As the focus of this research is the impact of globalization upon women
in Japan, Chapter 3 will critically review attempts to 'gender' the analysis
of globalization. This is in order to contribute to the feminist debate about
the impact of globalization upon women by bringing in insights from the
case of Japan. The chapter sets out major strands of feminist debate about
the impact of globalization upon women, showing how an understanding
of feminist ideas greatly enriched the theoretical framework outline in

Chapter 2. The chapter identifies areas where the Japanese case exemplifies or runs counter to existing hypotheses, and lists general hypotheses about gender and globalization, the validity of which in the case of Japan will be examined in Chapters 6, 7 and 8.

Feminist analyses of globalization can be divided into three main areas: two theoretical and one empirical. First, feminist critiques of neo-liberal economic globalization are an extension of more general critiques of the gender blindness of neo-classical economics, which has been heavily drawn upon by promoters of neo-liberal economic globalization. Second, feminist writers have also perceptively discussed the gendered nature of the *discourse* surrounding globalization, that is, the way that hegemonic discourse constructs globalization as a natural and irresistible force, to which feminized national cultures must submit. Third, feminist researchers have conducted empirical case studies which show that the actual effects of global restructuring on women are complex and contradictory. Some educated and/or middle-class women in most countries are gaining job positions that were not previously open to them. There is also some disputed evidence that women in developing countries experience economic gains as their countries become integrated into the global economy. However, such change does not necessarily mean a rise in social status, and views about how globalization affects the status of women within families and societies are mixed. In states where women's social and economic rights have been well established, a move towards economic liberalism can lead to job losses. Although little has been written on how the social and economic processes associated with globalization affect Japanese women in particular, drawing out key observations about the impact of such processes upon women globally provides a basis for comparison. The relative wealth of Japan means that it is in some ways difficult to draw parallels with studies of the impact of globalization upon women elsewhere in Asia. However, women's increasing incorporation into the workforce, the use of women as flexible labour, women's reproductive work filling the gaps left when states withdraw from the provision of welfare, grassroots mobilization loosening the bonds of custom and the use of transnational networking are all observable phenomena in Japan, as elsewhere. The pre-existence of a distinctive national model of capitalism, Japanese gender roles and the persistence of the three-generation household, however, differentiate Japan from other First World countries.

Following reviews of the general theoretical literature about gender and globalization, Chapter 4 provides more country-specific information about the role key economic actors in Japan have played in facilitating neo-liberal economic globalization. It also explains the reciprocal effects this has had on the Japanese national model of capitalism and on the institutions of Japanese society. The chapter situates the 'Japanese economic miracle' in the context of the Cold War, and shows how US security considerations enabled Japan to develop a very distinctive and economically successful model of production, which was nonetheless dependent upon women being largely confined to peripheral positions in the workforce.

Japan's own security considerations, trading relations, and economic pragmatism encouraged the Japanese government and Japanese companies to invest overseas. The globalization of Japanese production followed on from the globalization of Japanese capital investment, as economic change encouraged companies to locate more and more production overseas. The collapse of the Bretton Woods system in 1970, the 1985 Plaza Accord and the 1996–7 East Asian financial crisis were key discontinuities, which fuelled the outflow of capital and production. This 'hollowing out' of Japanese industry has resulted in the steady erosion of the capacity of the Japanese state to influence Japanese corporations. Japanese policy-makers have experienced pressure from sources both inside and outside Japan to allow Japanese firms to produce overseas and to allow entry of foreign companies into the Japanese domestic market. However, while imports have entered Japan, Japan has seen very little foreign direct investment. Consequently, it appears that the net flows of jobs and finance are out of Japan.

Japanese industry has tried to counter this challenge by attempting to cut the costs of domestic production, by reducing labour costs and making the workforce more numerically flexible. The chapter goes on to explain how the impact of globalization upon Japan is not only economic but also social and cultural. Japanese managers and students today have more diverse work experiences, which are altering their attitudes about social relations within the workplace, including gender relations.[9]

Chapter 5 describes how the institutions of Japanese state regulation and company practice in Japan, in combination with pre-existing gender relations in Japan, have played a large part in constructing a gender order in which men and women experience employment very differently. In general, since the Second World War, young Japanese women have been confined to routine jobs with little or no training and have been expected to leave paid employment upon marriage or childbirth. However, even before the acceleration of the process of globalization, gender relations in the post-war Japanese model of capitalism were evolving. Societal and demographic change, educational advance and the increased acceptance of the ideology of equal labour rights have resulted in a gradual increase in the determination of Japanese women to continue to work. A minority of determined women have succeeded in establishing themselves as professionals and a larger number of women have re-entered the workforce as non-regular employees. Both as short-term regular employees and as non-regular workers, Japanese women have enabled Japanese companies to maintain secure and well-rewarded employment for most male company employees. As shown in Chapter 4, the Japanese national model of capitalism emerged in the very specific conditions of the immediate post-war period. As Japan becomes ever more integrated into a very different international economy, this model is undergoing changes, which will both impact upon and be affected by the actions and choices of Japanese men and women. The chapter will examine the extent and nature of women's participation in both the non-regular workforce and the different sectors of the restructured regular workforce. This aim will be further developed in Chapters 6 and 7.

Chapter 6 examines the role that the Japanese state has played in changing the regulations governing the employment of regular women workers. It goes on to explain how this interacts with the desire of Japanese companies to reduce labour costs to compete more effectively in an increasingly global economy. In particular, the chapter shows how the promulgation of the Equal Employment Opportunities Law (EEOL) and the repeal of protective legislation have institutionalized a dual labour market. The chapter examines the extent to which, and the way in which, the regular workforce is being reorganized, through studying how firms have adopted tripartite recruitment and employee organization. The vast majority of women work in less skilled jobs than their male counterparts, and leave the workforce to raise children. For a minority of highly skilled specialists, professionals, and extremely dedicated *sogoshoku* (management track) employees, legal changes and restructuring are shown to provide some labour rights, despite frequent violations of the spirit of the law. However, historical institutionalists recognize the importance of ideas, as well as institutions, in politics. For society in general, the EEOL seems also to have contributed to changing attitudes about working women, and has given activists for women's labour rights a tool to use in the courts to fight against sexism in the workplace.

Most women who leave the workplace to raise children return as 'non-regular', part-time, temporary or agency workers. The regular and non-regular workforces in Japan are strictly differentiated. Non-regular workers can expect to receive lower wages, fewer fringe benefits and less legal protection than their full-time regular co-workers, and to be excluded from trade union membership. Chapter 7 details the growth of the non-regular workforce in Japan, and the characteristics associated with part-time work, agency workers and homeworking. This growth is particularly apparent in sectors such as the airline and banking industries, which have become more subject to foreign competition, or are vulnerable to capital flight. The affected industries have, therefore, attempted to restructure their workforces to cut costs and increase flexibility. The Japanese government has facilitated this restructuring through legal change. This restructuring not only makes use of the skills and experience of Japanese women in the workplace, but also enables the government to keep spending on welfare to a minimum, because, as shown in Chapter 3, women's reproductive work fills gaps left by state cutbacks. However, as the non-regular workforce has grown, it has also diversified. Chapter 7 also details the development of 'regular' part-timer jobs and the number and types of job that may be filled by dispatched workers. Chapters 6 and 7 also determine the characteristics of women who typically participate in different sections of the labour force, examining the effect of labour market and household structures. Taken together, these two chapters demonstrate that the impact of globalization has had complex and contradictory effects on the situation of working women in Japan.

Chapter 8 describes how campaigners in Japan are raising the global profile of Japanese women workers in order to describe the actions women are taking individually and collectively to resist or campaign for change in their working environment and the laws and practices regulating it. The institutions of the parliamentary system and mainstream trade union movement have largely excluded women. As a result, female activists have tended to concentrate their efforts in community groups or women's networks (cf. Chapter 3). Ironically, women are now gaining more national political representation, as national state capacity is decreasing (cf. Chapters 2 and 4). However, as the powers of the state are devolved to the sub-national level or being lost to supranational organization (cf. Chapter 2) some feminist activists are proving to be successful political actors at the local, transnational and international levels. A case study of Working Women's Network exemplifies the characteristics of feminist activist groups in Japan: a high degree of commitment from members; longevity; a combination of research and protest; and effective use of institutional facilities for women.

The final chapter summarizes the main findings of my research on the relationship between globalization and the situation of working women in Japan and examines these findings in the context of claims made about the relationship between gender and globalization.

Summary

Globalization is a multi-faceted process, which impacts differently upon different states and upon different groups within those states. Although globalization generally results in a reduction of the sovereignty of the nation state, the effects of economic globalization are mediated by state action and by national economic, political, social and cultural institutions. This work examines the impact of globalization upon women working in Japan, using a theoretical framework that draws on literature about globalization, the state and historical institutionalism. An explanation of this theoretical framework and insights from literature about gender and globalization form the first major section of the book. The second section describes Japan's role in promoting globalization and the role that women have played in the Japanese labour force during the post-war period. The third section shows how this role is changing with the impact of state re-regulation of Japanese employment, and company attempts to 'flexibilize' the workforce. It then goes on to describe and assess the effectiveness of women's activism under these changing conditions. The final chapter summarizes the main arguments of this book, and contextualizes these arguments in debates about gender and globalization.

Part I
Analytical framework

2 A critical analysis of globalization

Introduction

The central thesis of this book is that the Japanese model of capitalism is becoming less economically competitive in an increasingly globalized international economy, and that the Japanese elites and other key economic actors are attempting to counter this by deregulating the Japanese labour market and restructuring the Japanese workforce. Simultaneously, changing social attitudes and an emerging global standard of sexual equality of opportunity have created a momentum in favour of legal change and the 're'-regulation of women's work in Japan. Both deregulation and re-regulation are taking place in a specific national context. The changes being made are interacting with pre-existing social and political institutions in Japanese society, particularly the Japanese national model of capitalism, and the gender norms of Japanese society. In addition, workplace practices are being affected by the responses of workers and campaigners. Some advocates of sexual equality have also adapted their responses to the organization of labour in Japan to changes in the global political economy. The outcome of this complex interaction between the forces of globalization, national socio-economic and political institutions and the actions of, and reactions to, activists is that globalization impacts differently upon men and women in the Japanese workforce. To fully understand the wider process within which these processes operate, and to situate the impact of globalization and restructuring upon women in Japan, it is therefore appropriate to draw from the literature about globalization and reactions to it. This chapter critically reviews the literature in so far as it is relevant in the Japanese case. Although the main theoretical perspectives cited here are Anglophone sources, they are all pertinent to the Japanese case and are the foundation for much of the later Japanese work on the phenomenon of globalization.

'Globalization' describes the exponential growth in recent decades of transnational interdependencies and interconnections. Globalization has been particularly significant in the economic sphere. Trade flows have increased, the world's core economies have significantly increased their foreign direct investment (FDI), and the processes of production, exchange, distribution and consumption of goods and services are increasingly being organized on a transnational basis. The export of capital from First World economies to developing countries led to the rapid development of the newly industrializing countries (NICs). Consequently, many manufacturing jobs were 'exported' to the Third World, a process known as 'hollowing out' (or *kudouka* in Japanese). From the mid-1970s, there was also an increased flow of migrants who came to work in the rapidly developing Asian economies, particularly Taiwan and Singapore. This re-ordering of the international division of labour had reciprocal effects on production in First World economies. Globalization is therefore a *structural* phenomenon. However, in addition, the world economy is increasingly subject to *cyclical* forces (Dicken, 1998: 429). The collapse of the Bretton Woods system, state withdrawal from economic demand management and the liberalization of capital flows have together increased the likelihood of cyclical fluctuations, and, moreover, reduced the capacity of states to act in concert to implement counter-cyclical policies. These fluctuations result in periodic recession, a consequent decline in the demand for goods and services, and hence corresponding decline in the demand for the workers who produce them. In response, employers have attempted to cut back production costs and to make labour more flexible (to be examined in later chapters). Firms that have not gone overseas have invested in machinery to compete with low-cost labour, with a consequent reduction in job opportunities for unskilled and semi-skilled workers.

As well as being associated with profound economic change, globalization is also associated with the transformation of the political sphere through institutional innovations, and the internationalization of control and surveillance, such as global regulations upon trade and the international policing and law. Furthermore, the cultural sphere is being transformed through the representation of 'facts, affects, meanings, beliefs, preferences, tastes and values' (Waters, 1995: 8). As a consequence of these changes, advocates of a 'strong' globalization thesis, such as Ohmae (1995), argue that we now live in a 'borderless world', where states are irrelevant. Others argue that globalization is a 'myth' (Hirst and Thompson, 1996) or at least a large overstatement (Ruigrok and van Tulder, 1995). Those termed 'transformationalists' (Held *et al.*, 1999) accept that globalization is a genuine 'transformation of social geography marked by the growth of supraterritorial spaces' (Scholte, 2000: 8), albeit they accept that this transformation is an uneven process, and that globalization has not (yet) rendered territoriality redundant.

The next section in this chapter begins by defining globalization and then critically reviews the main theoretical perspectives on globalization. It argues that globalization is a concrete phenomenon, which is qualitatively different from internationalization. In addition, this section introduces the idea that globalization is not a phenomenon driven purely by technological change and economic logic. The changes associated with globalization are the result of human agency. Globalization is also a *project*: the goal of states, companies and individuals.

The section goes on to explain why theorists believe that the processes of economic globalization are having, and will continue to have, a significant impact on the labour forces of modern industrialized countries, and is impacting differently on different groups within those labour forces, but note that the *way* in which these processes impact upon groups or nations is mediated by cultural and institutional factors. In other words, there is a complex interaction of global and local forces.

The following section presents and critically analyses literature about the role of the state under these new conditions. The section examines the extent to which globalization has led to a decline in the *de facto* power of the state, or, according to the alternative thesis, the extent to which states have merely changed their policies and reformed their institutions to better cope with increasing internationalization. Both of these perspectives have shortcomings. The state is not powerless, but the nature of governance is constantly changing in a globalizing world undergoing globalization: power is exercised at supra- and sub-state levels; the state is serving different constituencies; and new actors are being incorporated into the governance process. Furthermore, the cultural, social and technical changes associated with globalization are permitting new forms of political participation, by non-state actors, to become more salient.

Globalization

Globalization has been described as 'a key idea by which we understand the transition of human society into the third millennium' (Waters, 1995: 1). The hegemonic nature of this discourse of globalization can be accounted for by both market-led trends in the organization of production and changes in policies resulting in a normative preference for neo-liberal economic globalization among influential policy-makers. It is important in any discussion of globalization to distinguish the reality of globalization from the discourse surrounding it. This is particularly so when discussing the Japanese case, where elite discourse often presents globalization as an exigency.

The concept of globalization does not only encompass increased economic integration and increased flows of capital but also social, political and cultural change. Appadurai (1990) identifies five increasingly strong 'flows' that produce globalization. *Finanscapes* are the increasingly rapid flows of international capital between national economies. *Ethnoscapes*, or flows of people such as tourists or guest workers, are impacting upon domestic and international politics to an unprecedented extent. *Mediascapes* are flows of images and information through the mass media, disseminating central ideas, terms and images central to *ideoscapes*, the international dissemination of the ideologies of freedom, welfare, rights, sovereignty, representation and democracy. *Technoscapes* are flows of technology. These processes reinforce each other. For example, ethnoscapes are facilitated by the spread of technology in the form of the increased accessibility of air travel. This multiplicity of flows implies that the process of globalization has social and cultural, as well as economic, impacts.

As technology permits the flow of ideology and information, societies become much more *reflexive* and aware of the precarious and contingent nature of their own structures and institutions (Giddens, 1984). This phenomenon of reflexivity resulting from flows of ideas, ideologies and practices is relevant both to the liberalization of Japanese economic management and changes in the Japanese gender order. First, neo-liberal economic globalization is also overtly linked to this reflexivity about hitherto consensual ideas. For example, the election and administration of New Right leaders, notably Margaret Thatcher in the UK (1979–90) and Ronald Reagan in the US (1981–9), were instrumental in disseminating policies of the deregulation of labour markets, the privatization of nationalized companies and the provision of welfare, move from Keynesian demand management to monetarist economic policies. Second, an obvious potential area for reflexivity is gender relations. All societies have culturally specific gender norms and localized patriarchal structures. When exposed to the differing gender norms from another society, it becomes apparent that gender norms in one's own society are contingent rather than 'natural'. The restructuring of social relations between Japan and Western countries has encouraged reflexivity about gender roles as well as attitudes towards work and leisure (see especially Chapters 4, 6 and 8).

Of course, the process of social change is more complex and contradictory than the adoption of new technologies. As Featherstone (1987) pointed out, people who watch the same television programmes and movies respond to and interpret them very differently according to their own social and cultural context. The diversity of flows can also lead to the establishment or strengthening of new identities, rather than convergence. Those involved in identity politics and new social movements use new technology to contact or exchange ideas and campaigning strategies with others sharing their identity or values. This contact with others who share one's values or identity can reinforce and increase the salience of such values or identities (Mann, 1997). The strengthening of non-territorial identities, the spread of ideas and ideologies and information technology, transport and communications have combined to augment the growth and effectiveness of transnational activism. Keck and Sikkink claim that transnational activism is particularly likely to be effective where it is centred around achieving the enforcement of issues around which there is an international consensus: these are likely to be issues involving bodily harm to vulnerable individuals and issues involving legal equality of opportunity (Keck and Sikkink, 1998). Chapters 7 and 8 examine how women's rights activists in Japan have attempted to use the growing international consensus around legal equality of opportunity to promote their cause domestically.

In summary, as well as being a political project and a transformative process, globalization is associated with attempts to establish a global standard of basic human rights, and of equality before the law. Thus, globalization can be viewed as a project by non-state actors to imagine and implement global rights (Sassen, 1996; Neysmith and Chen, 2002).

Hyperglobalizers and sceptics

There is considerable debate about the extent to which globalization is a real phenomenon that represents a significant discontinuity from that which has gone before. This debate is complicated by the fact the some of the analysts of globalization are also advocates of transnational production in a neo-liberal environment. Kenichi Ohmae has been described as a 'hyperglobalizer' (Held *et al.*, 1999). He advances the thesis that, as the result of the forces of technology, transnational corporations, advances in information technology and competition, we now live in a borderless world, where the actions of states are, in effect, irrelevant (Ohmae, 1995). Hirst and Thompson (1996), on the other hand, argue that globalization is a 'myth' (albeit a 'necessary myth') employed by policy-makers to justify the implementation of unpopular neo-liberal policies. Most theorists of globalization, though, fall into the third category, 'transformationalists' (Held *at al.*, 1999). The transformationalist literature, represented by the works of Scholte (2000), Held *at al.* (1999), Goldblatt *et al.* (1997), Appadurai (1990) and others, offers a more nuanced analysis. The transformationalist literature describes globalization as stemming from increasing frequency of economic, cultural, political and social interactions across borders. Although globalization is gaining momentum, it has not (yet) rendered territories irrelevant, according to this school of thought. While transborder flows have an impact upon all nations, the precise nature of that impact will depend upon the structures, institutions and actors relevant to those nations.

The 'hyperglobalization' thesis

Ohmae argues that we are now moving towards a 'borderless economy', where 'nationalityless' global corporations will serve consumers by targeting products towards different regions and that this task will become increasingly simple as consumer tastes converge. He further recommends that developing countries open their doors to foreign investment, and he implicitly rejects the criticisms of the disadvantages experienced by Third World countries that encourage inward FDI (Lim, 1997). According to Ohmae, 'nationalityless' global corporations are qualitatively different to colonial institutions, such as the East India Company, that sought to repatriate profits. He argues that the fixed costs of manufacturing, in particular, mean that multinational corporations are not so 'footloose' as has been assumed (Ohmae, 1995). This is a very contentious argument. The East Asian financial crisis demonstrates how very quickly investment can be withdrawn from a country, and the impact that this has upon manufacturing there.

Ohmae is also optimistic that there is an alternative to the 'hollowing out' of corporations in the First World. He envisages First World firms maintaining their profit levels by stimulating demand through innovation and 'branding' and by forming alliances with firms in other countries to create mutually beneficial supply networks. He relegates the role of government to that of producing adequate infrastructure to make their countries attractive to FDI and of educating its citizens to be wise consumers and good employees.

It should not, however, be assumed that the hyperglobalization standpoint is only associated with a neo-liberal viewpoint. Indeed, hyperglobalization does seem to be the logical conclusion of the Marxian thesis that firms will go ever further in the search for new markets to solve crises of overproduction and to cut production costs by finding sources of cheaper labour and raw materials. Amin (1997), writing in the Marxist tradition, also takes globalization as read, while Wallerstein (2000), though maintaining that an alliance of progressive social forces could produce different outcomes, also argues that globalization is merely a continuation of the logic of capitalism. The difference between neo-liberal hyperglobalizers and those on the political left is that the latter tend to view globalization as the triumph of oppressive global capitalism (Held *et al.*, 1999), while neo-liberals tend to view it as the triumph of individual autonomy over state power, a development which is rational, positive and efficient, benefiting all through comparative advantage.

Several criticisms can be levelled at the hyperglobalization thesis. Ohmae's analysis can be challenged on empirical grounds. Most trade is not 'global' but, at most, regional (Goldblatt *et al.*, 1997). Furthermore, at least formally, the nation state remains the locus of political legitimacy and power (Fukuyama, 1992; Goldblatt *et al.*, 1997; Weiss, 1998). Ohmae's prescriptions can be challenged on normative grounds. Ohmae does not differentiate between different groups of citizens in the new 'borderless economy'. He envisages consumers around the world benefiting, jobs being created in developing countries and employment levels being maintained in First World economies. His vision of a constantly innovating core of permanent employees is one of the characteristics of the shift from Fordist production, characterized by large plants employing semi-skilled workers, to a post-Fordist situation, where a small number of highly skilled expert workers conduct research and development. However, the move from the economies of scale to economies of scope also depends upon the existence of a 'peripheral' workforce: more work is outsourced to developing countries, and there is an increasing reliance on part-time, temporary and casual workers, who, in many countries have fewer employment rights than full timers. Migrant workers who come to First World states are also unlikely to enjoy the conditions envisaged by Ohmae. As even the most economically liberal states generally do not support a free market in terms of labour, many migrant workers are undocumented and therefore unable to claim labour rights. Groups in the peripheral workforce tend to be segregated by gender (as well as by ethnicity, nationality and/or geographical location), as Chapters 3, 6 and 7 will demonstrate.

The shortcomings and exaggerations of the hyperglobalization thesis have led some associated with the sceptical thesis to dismiss the whole concept of globalization as merely a discourse employed by political and economic actors in order to legitimate neo-liberal policies which are unpopular as they are seen to boost levels of exploitation for the vast majority to secure greater returns for an increasingly small global elite. Not only is hyperglobalization exaggerated but its prescriptions are unwelcome.

The 'sceptical' thesis

Hirst and Thompson argue that globalization is a 'myth', although internationalization is not. They argue that the observation of a growth of international trade and connection is not sufficient evidence that something fundamental has changed in the global economy. The authors claim there was more openness in international trade during the 50 years before the start of the First World War than there is today (Hirst and Thompson, 1996), and that the concept of the global economy, as currently described, is not significantly different from previous descriptions of the international economy. They criticize the tendency of globalization theorists to cite examples of internationalization of sectors and processes as evidence that global market forces increasingly dominate the economy. In a truly globalized economy national economies would be first subsumed by and subsequently reintegrated into a global system through international processes and transactions. The domestic policies of governments and private corporations would reflect the fact that the sphere where they operated was primarily determined internationally. As a consequence, the state would find it difficult to regulate an economy and provide social protection to casualties of market failure; faced with hypermobile transnational corporations (TNCs), states would ensure that their corporate tax rates were not 'too high', their welfare programmes not too costly, their environmental policy not 'too punitive' and their economic policies not too restrictive (Gertler, 1997).

Hirst and Thompson dispute that the world economy is now beyond regulation and control, but accept that global regulation is currently unlikely as the states which have the strongest economic power have divergent interests and the elites in the G3 countries (Germany, Japan and the US) have an ideological preference for laissez-faire economic policies. That is not to say that the system is rudderless or unguided: it is to say that it is guided to some extent by nationally based elites who wish to progress policies which lead to a deterioration in wage levels and conditions and the security of employment for many First World employees as part of a process of restructuring between the global North and South. Policies seen to be 'regrettable but inevitable' or 'hard choices' are often easier to force through. It is for this reason that globalization is described as a 'necessary myth' (Hirst and Thompson, 1996: 1). This argument is perhaps most clearly articulated in Japan, by Saeki Keishi, who claims that: 'The process of globalization currently underway is not the natural working of worldwide economic forces but rather a US-led undertaking.' (Saeki, 2000). However, translations of popular works critical of globalization such as *False Dawn: The Delusions of Global Capitalism* by John Gray (1998) and *Illusion économique* by French author Emmanuel Todd (1988) have also won a wide readership in Japan (Kojima, 2000).

There is some truth in several of Hirst and Thompson's main arguments. We are not yet in the era of the 'postnational' enterprise. Multinational companies are still headquartered somewhere, embedded in national and local chains of suppliers and producers, and benefiting from government-supported technical institutes and links with the scientific community, as well as managers having shared social norms of behaviour with workers (Harrison, 1997). For the hyperglobalization thesis to hold water they would have to become genuinely footloose, transnational companies, which would source the factors of production and carry out marketing at a global level with no commitment to place. However, even if TNCs have headquarters firmly based in one country, they have sufficient economic power to negotiate very favourable conditions with host nations. TNCs are often larger in economic terms than 'sovereign' nations. The top 200 companies control half of the global trade in goods (Went, 2000: 21). TNCs have the capacity to negotiate national boundaries to gain dominance in a global market (Sklair, 1997). Even if they form only a small part of the market, they can still intensify competition and force domestic firms to re-evaluate their deployment of labour. Yashiro writes of the copycat effect of even small-scale foreign entry on service industries in Japan (Yashiro, 1998). TNCs can also extend their influence through forming networks and alliances with each other, with all levels of government, and with the subcontractors and smaller firms which supply them, arguably producing a new paradigm of 'concentration without centralization' (Harrison, 1997: 9). There has been a massive increase in international mergers and takeovers. Since 1990, mergers and acquisitions have accounted for a third to a half of all FDI flows (Held *et al.*, 1999: 243). International ownership of assets is facilitated by lower transaction costs, financial liberalization and deregulation. Between 1991 and 1996, 95 per cent of the 599 changes to national FDI regulations worldwide facilitated FDI in some way (Held *et al.*, 1999: 243). Furthermore, even if firms continue to be domestically based, they may still be considerably affected by other firms' strategies of transnational production. There are many examples of companies which have remained domestically based but which have invested heavily in capital equipment to replace labour and so reduce production costs to compete with firms using cheaper labour overseas (Ohmae, 1995). These replaced workers are therefore heavily, if indirectly, affected by the globalization of production.

While levels of world trade might have been high before 1914, the world economy was less *integrated*: there were fewer *connections* between countries. Before 1913, integration, though extensive, was shallow and consisted of trade in goods and services and international movements of capital. There were high volumes of trade in a small number of goods and services, and most people would have been unaffected by this. Today's world is charac-terized by deep integration, where the production of goods and services is organized on an international basis. And there are many strong connections between countries on a very wide range of fronts from international travel to trade flows to call centres. In other words, there has been a functional integration of internationally dispersed activities (Dicken, 1998; Went 2000).

Hirst and Thompson's arguments that the deregulation of capital and the subsequent capital mobility have not led to a transfer of resources from advanced economies to developing countries, and that most FDI is highly concentrated in the First World and the NICs, are also not in conflict with the emergence of a globalized economy. Giddens accepts that the development of globalization is uneven and 'fragments as it co-ordinates' (Giddens, 1990: 175). Much of the African continent is excluded from the worldwide division of labour and the Asian NICs continue to have business systems which are distinct from those prevalent in the West. In addition, three-quarters of world merchandise exports come from the world's core economies, and 60 per cent of this trade is conducted within these same countries. However, this economic imbalance does not reduce the effect of increasing integration on the affected nations. The fact that the vast majority of trade takes place in the North rather than the South merely demonstrates the relative wealth of the two regions (Mann, 1997).

Hirst and Thompson claim that the world economy is regionalizing not globalizing, and that the existence of regional trading blocs such as the North American Free Trade Agreement (NAFTA), the European Union (EU) and the Association of Southeast Asian Nations (ASEAN) proves that sub-global regions can control footloose capital. Although regionalism entails a recon-stitution of political borders, regionalism still implies territorially based political projects. Globalization, on the other hand, implies the increasing irrelevance of geography. However, the distinction between regionalization and globalization is, in fact, a false dichotomy. Scholte lists five ways in which regionalization has facilitated the process of globalization:

- Standardization and harmonization of technologies, procedures and documentation facilitates supraterritorial connections.
- Regional common markets provide convenience and economies of scale for distribution and sale of global products.

- Regional customs unions facilitate transborder production.
- Governance at the regional level is effective in administering global norms of, for example, human rights or technical standardization.
- The growth of transborder consciousness prepares people for the construction of suprastate frameworks.

(Scholte, 2000)

In fact, the economic crisis in East Asia brought into question the extent to which regional powers other than the US can influence financial markets. Although Japan, the obvious regional leader, at first refused to help stricken East Asian economies by opening its markets, it did propose providing money to redeem the debts of the other nations through a new multinational financial institution. The realization of this proposal would have led to money being redirected away from loans to the US, and consequently to a large rise in US interest rates (Johnson, 1998: 658). Japan also proposed the following measures: keeping economic and trade links in place until the East Asian economies had had time to recover; transferring technology to enable the affected countries to move up the production chain and out of direct competition with China; guaranteeing sovereign bonds from East Asian states and banks, without imposing conditions similar to those of the International Monetary Fund (IMF) (Hughes, 1999). At a meeting on 19 November 1997 in Manila, the embryonic Japanese institution was abandoned and the IMF was entrusted with finding a rescue package. It made sizeable loans to Thailand, Indonesia and South Korea, on condition that budgets were austere, interest rates high and local businesses sold to foreign companies. It also challenged the distinctive model of economic organization in those countries. The influx of untaxable funds undercut women's savings investment co-ops in South Korea, and food and fuel subsidies in Indonesia came to an end. These measures were completely in keeping with the laissez-faire ideology of the IMF[1] and the Washington consensus,[2] despite criticism that they were ideologically driven remedies which had no regard for East Asia's particular circumstances (see Johnson, 1998).

The 'triad' (the idea of a tripder political and economic world order) thesis has been further undermined since the mid-1990s, given Japan's economic decline and the consequent limitation of its ability to be a regional power, the teething troubles of the Euro zone and a newly resurgent US following the events of 11 September 2001. The US is easily the most powerful single political and economic power in the world and the assumptions of US policy-makers are embodied in the strategies of international institutions such as the World Bank and the IMF. These hegemonic institutions have the power to impose their 'solutions' on East Asia, even when these measures prove inappropriate. It seems, therefore, that even the powerful East Asian part of the triad has proved politically incapable of bucking the trend of neo-liberal economic globalization while the US and the international financial institutions are opposed to it doing so.

In summary, there is something in the existence of 'globalization' as an observable phenomenon that has been gathering momentum in recent decades. Even though it has roots in earlier economic and political processes, there is something different about the world in the early twenty-first century when contrasted with the age of high empire in the late nineteenth century. The internationalization of production and trade has led to a rapid increase in transborder relations with respect to both extensiveness and intensity. Regionalization, rather than being an obstacle to globalization, has become a means of facilitating globalization. Although economic and cultural differences and inequalities persist between different regions and different countries within regions, these phenomena can be explained by viewing globalization as a continuing process rather than a state that has been reached. This is the position taken by advocates of the transformationalist book.

The transformationalist thesis

Transformationalists, such as Held *et al.* (1999), Went (2000), Mann (1997), Dicken (1998), Scholte (2000) and Appadurai (1990) deny that there is any *state* of 'globalization', the existence of which can be advocated or denounced. Rather they point to the existence of both globalizing and countervailing processes. They argue: 'We inhabit a globa*lizing* rather than fully globa*lized* world' (Scholte, 2000: 59, italics in original).

Goldblatt *et al.* (1997) define globalization as involving:

> a *stretching* of social relations across time and space such that day-to-day activities are *increasingly* influenced by events happening on the other side of the globe and the practices of highly localized groups and institutions can have significant global reverberations . . . it is best thought of as a multidimensional phenomenon applicable to a variety of forms of social action – economic, political, cultural or sites of social activity.
>
> (Goldblatt *et al.*, 1997: 271, my italics)

Globalization is seen as an uneven rather than simple and linear process. The different forms of globalization, including cultural, economic or social processes, will have different geographical extensiveness, intensities, impacts and degrees of institutionalization. This definition encompasses the differential integration of different nations into the world economy (Goldblatt *et al.*, 1997). As Appadurai states, individual state policy can play a role in regulating and determining the nature and extent of the flows of people, images and information, ideas and ideologies and technology and capital (Appadurai, 1990). Japan, for example, has proved very receptive to ideas and new technology and has been a pro-active player in economic globalization, while being less receptive to immigration. For comparison, the opposite might be true of Saudi Arabia. Therefore, rather than promoting convergence among different parts of the world, globalization can lead, at least initially, to divergence. Mann notes that there are varied patterns in the extent to which aspects of globalization touch different areas of the world (Mann, 1997). He observes that states differ in size, power, geography, degree of centralization, degree of democracy, level of development, infrastructural power, geopolitical power and national indebtedness. As the state is still the main legal and political entity through which the forces of globalization are mediated, it is likely that the changes it brings will also be differently embodied. Chapters 6 to 8 will show how the institutions of the Japanese national model of capitalism and the gender order in Japan combine with the pressures of economic and cultural globalization to produce a new gendered division of labour in Japan.

Neo-liberal hyperglobalizers view globalization as proceeding from microprocesses, particularly advances in information technology (Ohmae, 1995; Castells, 1996), which create reflexive global consumers and the technology to serve their needs. In contrast, Marxists tend to view globalization as the consequence of the logic of capital accumulation. However, transformationists, who do not believe that globalization is fully institutionalized, tend to see a role for the agency of states, networks, social groups and transnational organizations in promoting globalization or shaping the way it is realized.[3] Global economic change, for example, is partially attributable to the actions of states as they try to respond to domestic economic crisis (although it should be noted that these domestic economic crises often stem from external shocks over which states have little control (Weiss, 1998)). Sklair summarizes the roles of transnational corporations, states and financial institutions and actors in driving globalization. These roles include introducing flexible production methods, integrating production into global commodity and production changes, integrating sourcing and location strategies and embarking upon strategic alliances with other firms (Sklair, 1997). However, Sklair also posits the existence of a 'transnational capitalist class', made up of TNC executives, globalizing bureaucrats, politicians and professionals, and consumer elites, particularly merchants and media. Members of this class tend to consider themselves citizens of the world, rather than of their country of birth, and have outward-oriented global perspectives. They have often attended the same business schools, where they have absorbed the same approaches to economic management. The people in this class, he argues, exercise a disproportionate influence over the rest of society through their occupation of interlocking positions on the boards of not only companies but also think tanks, charities, universities and sport, art and science bodies (Sklair, 1997). The authority exercised by Japanese executives returning from US business schools with the Master of Business Administration (MBA) qualification is an example of this influence (Dore, 2000). The 'hard' networks of international diplomacy are being bypassed by far more fluid and ongoing 'soft' networks of the officials of international bodies (Mann, 1997).

Went goes further. He argues that the *concept* of globalization is 'abused' by the transnational capital class to legitimate and encourage more globalization (Went, 2000). For example, he describes politicians justifying harsh policies as necessary responses to an internationalized economy, even though these politicians have created the very requirements for the response (for example, the Maastricht Treaty's convergence criteria). They point to growing economic interpenetration to justify taking part in more international organizations like the European Union (EU), the North American Free Trade Agreement (NAFTA) and the World Trade Organization (WTO). In other words, globalization is both a project and a discourse used to legitimize the adoption of laissez-faire economic policies.

However, the use of the discourse of globalization by advocates of neoliberal economic policies does *not* mean that the phenomenon of globalization does not exist. Even those opposed to 'globalization',[4] such as protestors at the 'Battle of Seattle', are taking advantage of global networks and ideas to battle against what they see as non-democratic and unaccountable global institutions.

Globalization and national capitalisms

The idea that we are witnessing global political, economic and social convergence implies the decline of distinct national models of capitalism, such as the Japanese model outlined in the previous chapter. This section will describe and assess the validity of the most important claims made about the impact of globalization upon the state. It will discuss the proposition that the state has less capacity to govern now than it did during most of the twentieth century and the reasons for this perspective. It will then look at the opposing contention that states can maintain their political centrality and economic position by adapting to changing economic and political circumstances. The final part of this section will show that state regulation of the economy and society continues to be entirely necessary, although the nature of that regulation has changed.

The rise and fall of state power

The modern state is characterized by a tightening of relations between the state and society (rather than just the state and elites), and the stretching of social relations over national (rather than merely local) terrain. This deepening and expanding of state power has been termed 'social caging' (Mann, 1997). The role and functions of the state or, to be more precise, the majority of states in the northern hemisphere increased exponentially during the twentieth century. (The same generalization cannot be made about states in the southern hemisphere, many of which lack the capacity to govern the economy or society.) From the time of the Great Depression of the 1930s onwards, First World states assumed responsibility for protection of their population's welfare and levels of employment *against* fluctuations in the international economy by employing various instruments such as economic protectionism externally and models of corporatism internally. The Bretton Woods institutions, developed after the Second World War, attempted to prevent states from returning to destabilizing economic nationalism. States became responsible to international financial institutions, such as the International Monetary Fund (IMF), the World Bank and the General Agreement on Tariffs and Trade (GATT), which were designed to enforce trade liberalization and maintain exchange rate stability. Domestically, however, states continued to employ different models of economic management (Cox, 2000; Gilpin, 2000). Different national models of capitalism emerged, based on the institutions extant in each country: this will be further explored later in this chapter.

Nonetheless, the stagflation of the 1970s showed the limits to state control over national economies. Furthermore, as Wallace argues, three recent 'divergencies' have contributed to individual sovereign states being unable to control the trajectory of change in the world economy (Wallace, 1990).

First, economic change has become decoupled from the demand for resources. The introduction of less resource-intensive production, overproduction in agriculture and the increase in the proportion of First World production accounted for by services rather than goods means that economic growth does not necessarily correspond to increased production of resources. This implies that nations can no longer secure their prosperity by increasing industrialization and export of those goods produced.

Second, production has become decoupled from employment. Manufacturing jobs are increasingly 'exported' to low-wage economies, while new jobs in First World countries are increasingly concentrated in the service sector. Since Wallace wrote, technological advance has permitted the outsourcing even of service-sector jobs: flight booking is often carried out by computer operators in the Caribbean, and, as is well known, significant numbers of companies in Anglophone countries outsource their customer contacts to Indian call centres.

Third, financial flows have superseded flows of goods. Transborder flows of capital and credit have exceeded flows of goods and services since the 1970s, encouraging governments to manipulate exchange rates to gain comparative advantage.

The declining control of the state over national capitalisms in these circumstances can be characterized as 'the retreat of the state' (Strange, 2000). There are at least two important caveats here. First, economic development in the poorest countries has the potential to increase the capacity of the state (Mann, 1997). Second, even the most overtly neoliberal states have failed to reduce the size of the public sector, cut their total budgets or trim the scope of their regulation (Scholte, 2000).

Not only do states appear to have a decreasing capacity for economic management but non-state-based identities are growing in importance among their citizens. The former satellite states of the Soviet Union, for example, have seen a huge growth in ethnonationalisms. Improvements in information technology have made it easier for religious adherents, political activists, ethnic and sexual minorities, women and others to share information and build solidarity with their counterparts in other countries. This development has not only grown organically out of technological change but is also a pragmatic political strategy. Such groups may achieve a more sympathetic hearing at the international rather than the national level, and can combine to lobby at venues where transnational policies are developed. For instance, business lobbyists and trade unions keep offices near the IMF and the EU institutions; and anti-capitalist protestors won massive publicity for their actions at the 'Battle of Seattle' in 1999 and in Prague in 2000, as so much of the world's media was present to record, respectively, the WTO meeting and the IMF and World Bank summit.

Again, though, it is important not to exaggerate the depth of these trans-border connections. The vast majority of connections between individuals and groups take place within the nation state and the overwhelming majority of civic organizations are based within the state. What is more, the international connections between most anti-capitalist protestors quickly faded after the Prague and Seattle protests. Differences in opinion between members who appear to have the same interests often become more apparent as communications between them improve. Feminists, for instance, tend to be supporters of different types of feminism – liberal, radical, socialist, Black, eco (Scholte, 2000) – and some groups formed to advance women's rights eschew the label feminist altogether.[5]

The 'myth of the powerless state'

In *The Myth of the Powerless State*, Linda Weiss (1998) challenges the notion that globalization has rendered the state powerless. She uses evidence from East Asia, Sweden and Germany to support her argument that the most economically successful states continue to be governed by state-embedded institutions. Furthermore, different state capacities will impact upon how states adjust to changes in the international economic environment. She disputes that the state is powerless in the face of globalization for three reasons.

First, Weiss shows that states have successfully adapted to changing circumstances, adopting different policies depending on the regime's historical priorities and its capacity for transformation. As a supporting example, she cites the Japanese government's success in protecting employment since the two oil crises of 1973 and the early 1980s. However, Chapter 4 will show that this success was at the cost of the female secondary labour force and large-scale underemployment of women. Chapter 3 will show that, in the late 1990s, achieving even full *male* employment proved rather more difficult for the Japanese state. It is very likely, though, that individual states' ways of adapting to the exigencies of globalization will take different path-dependent forms.

Second, the state is portrayed as the 'midwife' rather than the victim of globalization. Japan, Singapore, Taiwan and South Korea, in particular, are offered as examples of states that have encouraged the offshore relocation of production plants, promoting alliances between domestic and overseas firms and creating incentives for overseas investment. Chapter 4 will summarize the considerable evidence for this. Other phenomena that can be cited as examples include governments' attempts to encourage FDI by adopting measures such as non-discriminatory treatment of foreign firms, deregulation of certain sectors (telecommunications, for example), various financial and fiscal incentives and various types of employment and labour policy (Wade, 1996). In other words, the globalization can be seen as a political project, as well as a transformative process.

However, this paradox does not disprove the retreat of the state. A state choosing to constrain its freedom or give up control of some of its functions nonetheless ends up with less freedom and control, in the same way that a debtor agreeing to a tough repayments arrangement ends up with less disposable income (Strange, 2000). In fact, globalization can undermine state autonomy and political effectiveness, while at the same time leading to an extension of state intervention and regulation to promote competitiveness and marketization (Cerny, 2000).

Third, Weiss assumes the emergence of the catalytic state, which attempts to maximize control over its national economy through assuming a dominant position in alliances of states, private sector groups and transnational institutions. Examples would include Australia's efforts to build the Asia-Pacific Economic Cooperation (APEC), in a way that would encourage other states to adopt its own relatively liberal approach to trade and industry, and the US's attempts to do likewise through NAFTA. Even if this does not indicate a decline in the role of the state, it certainly seems to indicate a transformation in the level of governance from a national to a supranational level.

In sum, some states have been pro-active players in the furthering of globalization, although the impact of the strategies they have adopted produced different results domestically. It also limits their future freedom of action. Some states have attempted to maximize their economic power by participating in transnational alliances; however, this indicates a change in the shift in the level of governance of the nation state. Other transformations in modes of governance under globalization, all of which have implications for the state, are presented in the next section.

The transformation of the state

The first point that it is necessary to make is that the state and the market are not totally counterposed. In fact, states and other actors have a central role in producing the rules, regulations, customs and practices and norms which are necessary for markets to function. Polanyi made a compelling case that, rather than being an organically arising and self-regulating mechanism, '. . . the market has been the outcome of a conscious and often violent intervention on the part of the government which imposed the market organization on society for noneconomic ends' (Polanyi, 1944: 250).

Polanyi traced a 'double movement' of two organizing principles of modern society. The first is the principle of economic liberalism, aiming at the establishment of a self-regulating market, supported by the trading classes. These classes aim to achieve their goals by laissez-faire economics and free trade. The second organizing principle is that of social protection, aimed at protecting man (*sic*) and nature, relying on the support of those adversely affected by capitalism, using protective legislation, restrictive associations and other means of intervention. Polanyi further argued that the classification of labour as a commodity, is, and always has been, fictive, and that working conditions, hours of work, and the basic wage are determined outside the market. (The alternative would be a situation of constant strikes, where workers refused to work until the market wage was reached.) The different roles played by trade unions, the state and other public bodies in this process depended on the *character of these institutions* and the *organization of the management of production*. Polanyi added that without some state intervention in the form of central banking and the management of the monetary system, the capitalist system would be constantly under threat.

The state also continues to have a crucial 'ordering role' in conflict situations (Falk, 1997a), although even warfare seems to be less and less often a conflict between states but within states, where national identification has broken down or where outside forces intervene to protect important economic or strategic interests.

Furthermore, efficient production depends on workers being healthy and educated, with the state providing the public goods to ensure this. Even James Wolfensohn, President of the World Bank, has attributed steps taken to improve health and education, reduce poverty and promote gender equity in Vietnam, China, Brazil, India, Uganda and Bangladesh 'first and foremost to action by the developing countries themselves' (Wolfensohn, 2002). This latter role for the state, though, is threatened by neo-liberal globalization, which creates downward pressures on public-sector welfare guarantees (Scholte, 2000). The state sector is not contracting. In fact, there is a body of literature which positively correlates 'openness' – measured as share of trade in gross domestic product (GDP) – and the size of government and government expenditure. A high trade share makes states very vulnerable to outside shocks, and they therefore need a larger public sector to counterbalance the potential negative social effects (Evans, 1997).

In spite of the need for state regulation, state sovereignty is in decline (Held, 1995). Falk (1997a) has gone so far as to declare 'an end to sovereignty'.

Governance has become more multi-layered as policies are increasingly formulated at a sub-state or suprastate level (Strange, 1996). The devolution of power downwards is demanded politically, as sub-state nationalisms increase, or membership of a supranational organization, such as the EU, make devolved power more practicable. Regional governments, for example, lobby the EU directly rather than through their national governments. The most obvious example of the yielding of national economic power is the adoption of the euro in 11 European countries.[6] Multilateral regulatory arrangements do not only deal with economic questions though: challenges such as AIDS, global terrorism and environmental protection can only be countered through transborder agreements and policing.

In some cases the character of international organizations has changed in such a way that they have become global governance agencies: one of the most obvious examples is the WTO. In 1994 signatories of the GATT signed the Marrakesh agreement, which established the WTO. Articles XVI–4 and XIV–5 read as follows:

> 4. Each Member shall ensure the conformity of its laws, regulations and administrative procedures with its obligations as provided in the annexed Agreements.
> 5. No reservations may be made in respect of any provision of this Agreement . . .
>
> (World Trade Organization, 2001)

Similarly, the OECD operates a regime of 'policy surveillance', releasing authoritative assessment of the macroeconomic conditions for each of its 29 members, and recommending policy adjustments. Perhaps reflecting the continuing validity of the 'double movement' model, the International Labour Organization (ILO) monitors the observance of its 174 Conventions and 181 Recommendations (Scholte, 2000).

Not only are national states losing their power, as it is transferred to supra- and subnational tiers of governance, but increasingly unelected groups and individuals are being formally and informally incorporated into the decision-making process. Global firms and global civil society actors have become instrumental in the policy-making process (Helleiner, 1996; Marchand, 2000). Business executives have participated in WTO talks, representing their governments (Scholte, 2000). The International Confederation of Free Trade Unions (ICFTU) has agreed to work with the World Bank to monitor privatization programmes and to make suggestions about how to improve the protection of workers' rights (International Confederation of Free Trade Unions, 2001). There is still a democratic deficit in the management of the global economy, for the following reasons:

- The extent to which non-governmental organizations (NGOs) represent their constituencies is a matter of debate.

- Participation via electronic means is open to a tiny fraction of the world's population.
- The neo-liberal conception of people exercising real choice, through increased individual freedom in the making of contracts and in purchasing, favours the rich and the skilled disproportionately.

Held (1995) and Scholte (2000), among others, have proposed ways to democratize the supraterritorial bodies, but as Cerny (2000) points out, economic globalization has yet to produce political globalization.

Weiss, as stated above, introduced the conception of the state as a 'midwife' to globalization (Weiss, 1998). States have facilitated cross-border trade, as well as establishing free trade areas, customs unions, and a common market. It is one of the paradoxes of globalization that states attempt to cope with globalization by adopting strategies that promote it (Cerny, 2000).[7] Cerny argues that the state is transforming itself from a nation state to a 'competition' state, which tries to maintain or improve its position in the world economy by making itself attractive to foreign capital.

Cox takes the Gramscian conception of the state as a network of ideology and practices through which the elite wins support for its own agenda, and sees transnational organizations as based on the consent of such states. The logical conclusion of this argument is that states are increasingly serving a non-territorial constituency, as the state is converted into '. . . an agency for adjusting national economic practices and policies to the perceived exigencies of the global economy' (Cox, 2000: 28).

Generally, then, the state is continuing to exercise a vital regulatory role in an age of globalization, although some of its functions have shifted to the sub-state or superstate level, leading to an increased salience of multi-level governance. Most states, under the direction of international financial institutions and multilateral trade agreements, are tending to move towards more neo-liberal policies and are seeing downward pressure on their ability to regulate. This encourages further globalization, as demands for regulation must then be addressed to supranational level. Suprastate levels of governance may be the only ones capable of dealing with the internationalization of finance and production, as well as environmental and human rights issues. However, supranational institutions have not yet been democratized.

Although this section has dealt with changes in the nature of the state generally under globalization, the same process of globalization affects different regimes in different ways, depending on several factors, including their role in the global production process, the way in which the process is refracted through existing institutions and culture and the strength of resistance to the process in civil society (Wade, 2000). These observations are very pertinent to this book's argument that:

- The Japanese state has been instrumental in deregulating the Japanese economy.
- The liberalizing processes associated with globalization interact with specific local institutions: as will be shown later, these include the ideal of the three-generation family and the position of women in the Japanese national model of capitalism.
- International institutions and transnational activism have been of key importance in shaping Japanese domestic legislation.

Political activism in a globalizing political economy

Social scientists have long been divided over the relative contributions of the actions of agents and of structural forces to produce social and political phenomena. Methodological structuralism explains socio-political phenomena by looking at the structures that impact upon a society, including, for example, capitalist development or patriarchy. These structures shape the needs and desires of actors. Methodological individualism, in contrast, sees the decisions and actions of rational actors such as firms, groups or individuals as being paramount. Social or political institutions, according to this perspective, are the equilibrium outcome of decisions made by these actors. For example, actors form different political parties as the best way to achieve their political ends. Structure and agency have usually been presented as antinomies. However, there is a body of theory, sometimes described as the 'structuration postulate' (Giddens, 1979), which sees individuals and groups as making decisions and/or being formed within the context of existing structures of society but also as playing a role in reproducing or reforming structures, and choosing actions based on the structures within a society. Beliefs and practices will be locally situated but are not immutable. When a social or political structure changes, then so may actors' beliefs and strategies for bringing about change.

The previous sections in this chapter have described the growing importance of international institutions and the declining power of the state. This chapter has also noted the increasingly rapid flows of ideas and ideologies in association with the process of globalization. These changes offer new opportunities for activists to adapt their campaigning strategies. Working transnationally is a pragmatic strategy for activists in that it:

- multiplies the channels of access to the international system;
- makes international resources available to new actors in domestic political and social struggles;
- blurs the boundaries of the state, and therefore helps to helping to transform the practice of national sovereignty.[8]

(Keck and Sikkink, 1998)

Keck and Sikkink (1998) suggest that activism is most likely to be able to secure a transnational basis where it is concerned with preventing physical harm or securing legal equality of opportunity. This is not as straight-forward as it first appears. Definitions of 'harm' do vary considerably between cultures.[9] Legal equality of opportunity is also open to debate: for example it could certainly be argued that in order for *meaningful* equal-ity to be achieved, states should initiate affirmative action for traditionally disadvantaged groups. Some Japanese feminists have also argued that formal legal equality in the workforce between men and women has led to a worsening of women's working conditions as they are forced to adopt the 'male model' of working long hours (Ueno, interview with Whipple, 1996).

Conclusion

There has been considerable geographical reorganization of manufacturing production and consumption, resulting in global and regional reorganiza-tion of labour, as manufacturing employment is transferred from developed to developing economies. This has had reciprocal effects on the division of labour in developed countries. This reorganization is both the result of the logic of capital accumulation and of the political priorities of the world's core economies. The rewards of deregulation have been very unevenly distributed within and between societies.

The process of globalization, too, has not been uniform across the globe. The world economic system is not entirely 'globalized', but the integra-tion between the leading economic regions in the world is having significant implications for the people who live there. In fact, one of the most striking geographical changes resulting from 'globalization' is the way that East Asia has increased its relative power in the world economic system.

The state continues to be a vital territorial unit in which most laws are passed. Furthermore, nationality continues to be a core component of the identity of most people in First World countries. In fact, it is the activi-ties of states in acting to re-regulate the economy that have been vital in facilitating globalization. Indeed, regulation has been shown to be essen-tial for the continuance of any economic system. However, globalization has also produced changes in the nature of the state. States in general are losing power to supranational and subnational bodies, and policy choices are being constrained by the fear of losing foreign direct investment. Increasingly, non-elected actors, such as business people, NGOs and other pressure groups are being incorporated into the policy-making process at all levels. Despite a hegemonic discourse in favour of free trade and laissez-faire capitalism, the particular policy mix each state chooses varies according to its political, social and cultural complexion, as well as the demands made on it by non-state actors.

A state's institutions contribute to structuring the behaviour of actors within those institutions, and leading actors to continually reproduce those institutions. However, institutions can also be reformed by those actors within, or outside, the state. In times of flux, such as that occasioned by the dislocations of globalization, institutions may become dysfunctional, and at these times they are particularly likely to be reformed. The success these actors have in achieving reform will depend on their power and the strategies they employ. The power they can influence and the strategies they employ will also be locally specific.

For the reasons stated above, the insights of mainstream literature around globalization are valuable and pertinent to the situation of working women in a globalizing Japan. However, as has been noted throughout this chapter, this literature does not sufficiently take into account the importance of gender. Globalization, state policies, and social, political and economic institutions all impact differently upon men and women. The following chapter will therefore critically review the theoretical literature about gender and globalization.

3 Gender and globalization

A critical review

Introduction

The mainstream theories of globalization have paid little attention to gender. Globalization, however, has very different effects upon men and women, as this and subsequent chapters will show. Feminist[1] critiques of global restructuring therefore fill important gaps in the mainstream literature on globalization. Evidently, women are not a homogenous group. As many of the theorists cited in this chapter have pointed out, the impact of globalization on individual women is mediated by social and cultural factors, such as their 'race', class, education and/or national citizenship. This book is a case study of the gendered impact of the processes of globalization in one national context.

Japan provides a unique and interesting case study of the gendered impacts of globalization. One of the most notable transformations associated with globalization is the increasing integration of Asian, and particularly East and South-east Asian, countries into the global economy (Katz, 1998; Dicken, 1998; Arrifin, 1999; Japanese External Trade Organization (JETRO), 2001).[2] Consequently, many case studies of the relationship between globalization and gender have focused upon this region (Lim, 1997; International Labour Organization/South-East Asia and the Pacific Multidisciplinary Advisory Team (ILO/SEAPAT), 1998a, 1998b; Chang and Ling, 2000; Gills, 2001; Neysmith and Chen, 2002). Japan has been a pro-active player in the process of the globalization of production, which has had such profound effects upon the Asian continent. However, as Japan is an affluent, industrialized liberal democracy, the experiences of Japanese women differ markedly from those of women workers elsewhere in Asia (even given that the rest of Asia is extremely diverse). The Japanese case also differs markedly from that of other First World nations. The specific economic, political, social and cultural institutions of Japan mean that it is adjusting to globalization in a way that is nuanced by its history. For reasons discussed in Chapter 4, Japan differs from other First World states in that it has followed a model of capitalism which is markedly different from the Anglo-American model. In addition, such cultural phenomena as the persistence of the ideal of the three-generation family, and homosocial norms have a distinctive effect upon women's reproductive and productive work, and strategies of activism.

In order to discern whether the impact of globalization on women working in Japan differs from or resembles the impact on women elsewhere in the globe, it is necessary to establish the relationship between gender and globalization generally, and women in the labour market in particular. This chapter will therefore critically review attempts to 'gender' the analysis of globalization.

The chapter also shows how feminist analysis augments and enhances the analyses outlined in Chapter 2. The following two sections develop the idea of globalization. First, the chapter discusses the macro-level feminist critiques of globalization and the gendered discourse surrounding it. Second, it summarizes the claims made about the impact of globalization upon women, both generally and in terms of their participation in the labour force, as well as noting the role of the state in facilitating or controlling women's employment. The chapter goes on to examine the strategies of activism employed by women in the changing governance structures emerging in the context of globalization. The existence of this activism shows how globalization is associated with attempts to establish a global standard of basic human rights, and of equality before the law; the sites of resistance chosen by activists demonstrate the changing position of the nation state in an increasing globalized political economy. Feminist analyses have been particularly helpful in drawing out how global and local forces interact, and, therefore, help illuminate cases where the experience of Japanese women appears to contradict general trends. The conclusion to this chapter:

- lists general hypotheses about gender and globalization;
- discusses what gendered analyses of globalization add to the mainstream theories outlined in Chapter 2; and
- suggests areas where the study of Japan can contribute to the feminist debate about the impact of globalization.

The extent of the validity of these general hypotheses in the Japanese case is examined in later chapters.

Macro-level feminist analyses of globalization

Although some of the earliest examinations of the globalization of production were the work of feminist theorists,[3] there has until recently been a dearth of feminist work examining the phenomenon of globalization at the macro-level. This has been variously attributed to a feminist trend to examine more micro-level concerns (Chang and Ling, 2000; Freeman, 2001; Eschle, 2002) or the desire to maintain a marginal and critical position with regard to masculine 'grand theories of globalization that ignore gender as a critical tool' (Freeman, 2001: 1007). However, feminists have increasingly recognized the importance of transnational corporations and international financial institutions on the world stage (Bergeron, 2001), and argued that as the globalization of economic relations proceeds, there is an increasing need to examine women's issues from a global perspective (Waylen, 1999). Recent years have therefore seen substantial 'gendering' of the analysis of globalization (see, for example, *World Development*, special issue, 1999; Meyer and Prugl 1999; Marchand and Sisson Runyan, 2000; Kelly *et al.*, 2001; *Signs* special issue, 2001; Peterson, forthcoming).

These feminist macro-level critiques of globalization have focused on two areas:

- critiques of neo-liberal economic globalization;
- analyses of the gendered and disempowering nature of the discourse around globalization.

Neo-liberal economic globalization

Feminist theoretical critiques of neo-liberal economic globalization are an extension of more general methodological and normative critiques of orthodox economic theory. The promoters of globalization argue for the free flow of goods, services and finance (though not of labour) across national borders, and deregulation of markets, including labour markets, within national borders. Essentially this is a neo-liberal agenda, associated with the laissez-faire economic policies, which have become hegemonic since the collapse of the Soviet Union. Proponents of neo-liberalism typically subscribe to the assumptions of neo-classical economics (Peterson, forthcoming), and many of the criticisms made of the discourse surrounding globalization can be and have been applied to feminist critiques of neo-classical economic thought generally (Brodie, 1994). The rational economic actor (*homo economicus*) is conceived as an independent, atomistic, self-interested acquisitional unit (Brodie, 1994; Marchand, 1996a; Peterson, forthcoming). This actor is based upon, and conceived of by, 'a particular subset of humans (elite males) in a particular context (modern Europe) (Peterson, forthcoming). Where women are considered at all in classical economic theory they are seen as dependents (Pujol, 1995).[4] This assumption allows employers to rationalize paying women lower wages than men, as it is assumed that their wages are only supplemental to those of a male breadwinner.

Whereas, according to neo-classical economics, a less regulated labour market should more accurately reflect the human capital and/or productivity of individual workers, in fact more market-oriented economies tend to have a wider wage gap based on gender.[5] In the absence of government regulation, cultural factors will determine the level of gender inequality in wages. If cultural influences lead some employers to discriminate against potential female employees, then the laws of supply and demand dictate that a wage gap will appear (Meng, 1996). Some commentators have even presented evidence that women tend to have higher productivity *and* lower wages than their male counterparts (Lim, 1997; Elson and Pearson, 1997).

As neo-classical economics tends to be blind to the differential effects of laissez-faire policies on men and women, the dominant arguments in favour of neo-liberal global restructuring are made in gender-neutral terms, and speak of the aggregate benefits of an international free market. Marchand (1996a) in her analysis of NAFTA, argues that the *faux* objectivity of economics means that economic issues have often been decided on the basis of inconclusive econometric models which rely upon unrealistic assumptions, such as full employment. This is, however, rather an overstatement, as it is now generally accepted within neo-classical economics that there can be market equilibrium at less than full employment.

Furthermore pitching analyses at an aggregate level has meant that the differential impact of free trade on men and women and on ethnic groups has been hidden. Even where recent work has been carried out at the micro-level, in an attempt to analyse the relationship between income inequality and retarded economic growth, this has been measured at the household level. 'Household' measures pool male and female incomes, thus obscuring any relationship between economic change and rates of income inequality by sex (Seguino, 2000).

Another shortcoming of conventional economic analysis of the labour market is that it looks only at the 'productive' economy of paid work. It does not take into account the unpaid 'reproductive' labour, which is essential to the productive economy's efficient functioning. The reproductive economy includes all those tasks, largely performed by women, which are essential to the economy but nonetheless, are not formally included in national economic statistics. These include caring for and maintaining the labour force, bringing up and socializing the next generation of workers and improving the interpersonal skills of workers (Elson, 1999). The caring work Japanese women are expected to carry out for their own or their partners' parents can be added to this list. The time spent carrying out these tasks very much affects women's capacity to engage in formal employment. As a result of what critics see as the blindness of neo-classical theory to the importance of the reproductive work, the proponents of neo-liberal economic globalization do not take into account that it will be largely women's 'infinitely elastic' reproductive work, such as extra child and elder care, that will make up the shortfall in state-provided services. This will, of course, further limit their capability to participate in the paid labour market on the same terms as men. Chapter 7 will examine how norms about women's reproductive work in Japan shape women's career opportunities and legislation around labour and welfare, and how the forces of globalization are interacting with these existing institutions.

The discourse of globalization

The previous chapter presented the views of Went (2000), Hirst and Thompson (1996) and Sklair (1997) that globalization is used in elite discourse to legitimate the adoption of neo-liberal policies. Feminist theorists have added considerable depth to this insight in their analyses of how gendered discourse is used to 'naturalize' neo-liberal economic globalization.

This is an extension of an important insight from feminist poststructuralists who have observed that language is based on oppositions (male/female, presence/absence, mind/nature) (Cixous, 1992). These oppositions are not only binary, casting maleness as the opposite to femaleness, but also hierarchical, privileging masculinity. While (most) people are born as one sex or the other, gender is entirely learned, socially imposed and internalized, rather than given. Not only does gender describe the characteristics of individuals, but it also becomes embedded in social institutions. The conflation of sex and gender, and the ostensible 'naturalness' of dichotomized and hierarchical thinking is the key to naturalizing power relations between men and women, which are in fact the outcome of social processes. Furthermore, the presentation of a patriarchal order which places the feminine as subordinate to the masculine as 'natural': 'serves as the model for depoliticising exploitation more generally . . . The ostensible "naturalness" of sex difference and masculine dominance is then generalized to other forms of domination, which has the effect of legitimating them as equally "natural" hierarchies.' (Peterson, forthcoming).

Although the hegemonic discourse on the advantages of global restructuring obscures its gendered impact, in other ways the language of those who make policy can quite overtly associate globalization with 'aggressive masculinity' (Hooper, 2000) or 'technomuscular capitalism' (Chang and Ling, 2000). For example, David Mulford, US Under-Secretary of Treasury under the first Bush presidency, quite explicitly linked masculine/feminine and First World/Third World hierarchies when he commented: 'The countries that do not make themselves attractive will not get investors' attention . . . This is like a girl trying to get a boyfriend. She has to go out, have her hair done, wear make up' (cited in Runyan, 1996: 238).

A further example is the 1994 article in the *Economist* magazine which described Myanmar's natural beauty and undeveloped land as 'Ripe for Rape' (cited in Hooper, 2000). As not all states can compete in the process of globalization on equal terms, the use of such sexualized terms to present less powerful actors seeks to naturalize hierarchies (Hooper, 2000).

J. K. Gibson-Graham (1996) criticizes the view that capitalist penetration is inevitable and natural. She[6] compares the gendered language used in descriptions of globalization and capital penetration with those used in Sharon Marcuse's description of the discourse surrounding rape. Marcuse writes of the concept of a 'rape script', where victim and rapist are filling predefined roles, because they have been socialized to accept the idea of rape as inevitable and biologically based. The discourse of globalization shares with 'rape scripts' terms such as 'penetration', 'virgin' and 'invasion'. Gibson-Graham challenges the presentation of globalization as inevitable, and argues that feminists should deconstruct the concept of the global economy, showing the many ways in which it is contradictory. For instance, she cites the observation made by Dicken (1998) that, of the four major sources of multinational investment, the UK, the US, Germany and Japan, the first three are also major hosts.[7] The discourse of globalization is also presented as disempowering: just as women circumscribe their activities as they become more conscious of the possibility of rape, workers in TNCs curb their wage demands, for fear of capital abandonment. In fact, the power of capital to operate or locate anywhere on the globe is constrained by language, culture and law (Gibson-Graham, 1996). Implicitly, therefore, Gibson-Graham is accepting, and extending, the view of globalization as project, as discussed in Chapter 2. Chapter 4 will examine the way the discourse of globalization is used by key economic actors in Japan to legitimate economic restructuring. However, as the previous chapter has argued, globalization can be an incomplete process, stemming in part from intentional activity by key political and economic actors, yet nonetheless can be real (cf., inter alia, Appadurai, 1990; Goldblatt *et al.*, 1997; Scholte, 2000).

In summary, feminist macro-level critiques of globalization reveal some of the shortcomings of the arguments in favour of states adjusting to economic globalization by adopting neo-liberal policies. Such critiques argue not only that neo-liberal theory neglects to analyse much of women's contribution to the economy but also that neo-liberal policies of rolling back state provision of welfare tend to increase women's productive and reproductive work.

Proponents of neo-liberal economic globalization have presented global restructuring as a natural phenomenon, and have presented it as a powerful and 'masculine' phenomenon. Acceptance of this analysis is disempowering to those who wish to challenge globalization or influence the shape it is taking. Writers on gender and globalization have therefore attempted to show that globalization is a mutable phenomenon, which can interact with local processes and be shaped by the agency of individual actors. The complex and contradictory impacts of globalization upon women will be examined in the next section of this chapter.

The impact of globalization

This section will examine how the trends associated with globalization impact on the productive and reproductive work carried out by women. Where integration into the global economy is leading to a state's economic growth, as appears to have been the case in East Asia,[8] the impact upon women can be significant. As the impact of capital penetration upon women is of marginal relevance to the case of Japanese women, debates about the extent to which 'development' increases the income and raises the living standards of women in Third World countries will not be dealt with in any depth here. This section will however explain how:

- processes associated with globalization result in a feminization of waged labour in both North and South;
- marketization and other neo-liberal prescriptions increase women's reproductive labour;
- increased migration impacts upon both women who migrate and women in host countries;
- women of different ages, classes and ethnic groups experience the effects of globalization differently;
- local and global forces interact, so that the *way* in which the processes associated with globalization impact upon women in different countries depends upon cultural or institutional factors.

The feminization of waged work

One of the most remarkable effects of the globalization of the economy is the feminization of work in many (though not all) areas of the world. In both North and South, an increasing number of women are being drawn into the waged labour force for the first time, and for longer periods of time than in the past (UN, 1999; Sircar and Kelly, 2001; Bayes and Kelly, 2001). Furthermore, work itself has been feminized, in that flexible production and the global shift in manufacturing has meant that many men in First World economies are finding that their experience in the labour market is increasingly coming to resemble the typical pattern of 'women's work'. In other words, they can no longer assume lifetime employment and are experiencing lower paying employment, less job security, frequent job changes, and part-time, temporary or home-based work (Standing, 1989, 1999; Bayes and Kelly, 2001). This section will discuss the reasons for the feminization of work, the likely reasons for this and the impact of this feminization upon gender relations.

As more countries are drawn into industrial capitalist production, more women are drawn into waged labour.[9] It is noteworthy that no country has successfully industrialized without harnessing the labour of large numbers of female workers (Standing, 1999). Industrializing South Korea, for example, saw a massive growth in women's employment. The overwhelmingly female composition of the labour force of export industries led to women being called the 'industrial backbone' or 'industrial soldiers' of South Korea's economic miracle (Yoon, 2001). Women's employment was certainly central to Japan's state-led development strategy of the late nineteenth and early twentieth century, as Chapter 5 will discuss.

This is partly the result of stereotypical views held about women's work by government elites and corporate managers. The newly industrializing countries have been harnessing women's labour as a development strategy. The Malaysian government purposefully attempted to harness sexual and racial stereotypes to encourage foreign investment with the following advertisement:

> The manual dexterity of the Oriental female is famous the world over. Her hands are small and she works fast with extreme care. Who, therefore, could be better qualified by nature and inheritance to contribute to the efficiency of a bench-assembly production line than the Oriental girl.
>
> (Cited in Mies, 1986: 117)

TNCs have also preferred to employ women workers because of a belief that they have nimble fingers and are more docile, and hence are less likely to challenge management and organize workers than men (Bergeron, 2001). Women's reproductive work and the work they have carried out in the informal economy may also have permitted them to develop capacities of value in the manufacturing process. Women working in the electronics industry in *maquiladora* in Latin American and export processing zones in Asia have to pass aptitude tests; and women working in the textile industry have often already learned sewing skills at home (Elson and Pearson, 1997). In spite of this, women's work in manufacturing is frequently classified as 'unskilled'. This can be attributed to pre-existing gender norms. The labour market both reflects and influences what happens in other spheres; therefore: 'To a large extent women do not do "unskilled" jobs because they are bearers of inferior labour; rather the jobs they do are "unskilled" because women enter them already determined as inferior bearers of labour' (Elson and Pearson, 1997: 194).

Apart from their fabled 'nimble fingers' and presumed docility, there are other reasons why transnational corporations prefer female employees. Women appear more ready to tolerate low wages and poor conditions. (Meng, 1996). In fact, Gills (2001) argues that in countries where women are also carrying out subsistence production, it is possible for them to experience super-exploitation, that is, because they are carrying out subsistence production, when this is combined with waged work it is possible for them to be paid less than the wages of reproduction. This articulation of subsistence production and capitalist production makes Asian women's work extremely competitive, as the supplementary work they are doing makes it possible for them to accept wages which do not even cover their basic living costs. Even if aggregate national income increases as a country adopts neo-liberal policies, and becomes increasingly integrated into the world economy, this does not necessarily mean that women's income relative to that of men will increase. Seguino's (2000) positivist cross-country analysis of economic growth demonstrates a positive correlation between economic growth and gender inequality in wages, thus reinforcing the hypothesis that globalization has different impacts on men and women. However, globalization does not mean continued disadvantage in the workplace for all women. All of the Asian countries examined by Meng (1996) have seen an increase in women's representation in management. Similarly, Suarez Aguila (1999 in conversation with Scholte, cited 2000: 251) pointed out that in the 1990s some women rose to traditionally 'male' management positions in the *maquiladora*. This implies that, for some women at least, globalization offers new opportunities for career progression.

In First World economies too there has been an increase in female labour market participation. In OECD countries women accounted for, on average, 43.9 per cent of the labour force in 2000 (OECD Employment Outlook, 2002a: 74). The traditional masculine attribute of physical strength is less valuable, as blue-collar jobs are shifted overseas or replaced with new technology. Traditionally 'female' skills, such as communication, team-building and networking, are the focus of much management training. The overall effect of these changes is that 'masculinity' comes to be associated with power rather than individual men (Hooper, 2000). This does not mean that all women are likely to have access to this power, or that the jobs women are doing have equivalent rewards to those men have lost. States in the North have generally attempted to remain competitive by deregulating and 'flexibilizing' the workplace, and women are disproportionately likely to be 'non-regular', 'casual' or 'flexible' workers (see Chapter 2; for the case of Japan see Chapters 5 and 7). Even states that have been attempting a policy of equal opportunities in the workplace can find that as their labour markets are increasingly flexibilized and casualized, it is difficult to ensure that labour regulations are enforced. Research shows that countries with centralized wage bargaining tend to have a smaller gender wage gap and that gender discrimination is less pronounced in countries where the government can exercise influence over enterprise wages (Meng, 1996). This positive association may be correlative as well as causal, but the implication of this is that with liberalization of the labour market the gender wage gap will widen.

In both First and Third World economies, women have also been propelled into the labour market by the decline of men's family wage[10] (Fernandez-Kelly, 2001). This has been associated with the erosion of union power and neo-corporatist wage bargaining and job protection agreements (Standing, 1999). The extent to which the relative strength of these institutions has been maintained in Japan, therefore, has implications for the extent of the feminization of labour there.

The degree to which feminization proceeds is somewhat path-dependent. All countries show a high degree of labour market segmentation by gender (United Nations Department of Economic and Social Affairs, 1999). If women are employed primarily in sectors where their country has a comparative advantage, then they are likely to benefit in terms of increased job opportunities, at least initially. In South-east Asia and the Pacific, the sectors of manufacturing, services, trade, tourism and entertainment have all seen a growth of women's employment (ILO/SEAPAT, 1998b). Increased international demand for Jordan's textiles and handicrafts has stimulated employment in these traditionally female sectors. A reduction in agricultural protectionism has stimulated the production of cash crops and led to an increase in the employment of rural women in the Third World (Beneria and Lind, 1995). There is an important caveat to this aspect of the feminization of labour thesis though. As countries develop and new technologies are introduced, then the gender composition of flourishing sectors can change. The introduction of Japanese just-in-time technology in Latin America has been accompanied by a 'defeminization' of manufacturing. Changing technology and work practices have necessitated worker retraining, which management and male workers viewed as unsuitable for women, whom they regard as secondary workers. Similarly, restructuring in the Catalonian textile industry, particularly the introduction of night and weekend shifts, led to a decline in the number of women working in the industry (Beneria and Lind, 1995).

Chapter 2 noted that globalization makes countries increasingly subject to *cyclical* forces (Dicken, 1998: 429). When there is recession and where states maintain male preference in employment, women who have experienced waged work may be the first to lose their jobs. This was certainly true of married women in South Korea, when that country was forced to undergo massive economic restructuring to meet IMF conditions after the IMF bailout in 1997 (Yoon, 2001). This male preference can change though. The recession caused by the 1970s oil shock in Japan resulted in a downturn in female employment. However, such a downturn has not happened in the recession of the late 1990s and early 2000s (see Chapter 5).

State action can also impact upon the extent to which feminization takes place. The previous chapter discussed how different state capacities impact upon how states adjust to changes in the international socio-economic environment. Dominant ideologies can lead states to negotiate a compromise between encouraging a neo-liberal form of globalization and maintaining the current gender order. For example, the Irish government negotiated with, and selectively funded, firms to encourage the employment of men rather then women to maintain a traditional nuclear family structure during the 1961–81 period of export-led development (Pyle, 1990). Later chapters will show how the deregulation of employment in Japan and the incorporation into law of the ideal of equal opportunities – both effects, I shall argue, of political, cultural and social trends associated with globalization – are profoundly shaped by the Japanese state and social institutions.

Women's reproductive labour

When states are faced with economic difficulty, the impact upon women is often particularly harsh. This is exemplified by the hardships wrought by 'the retreat of the state' (see Chapter 2). While some sectors of the state are actively engaging with the global economy, others, such as the ministries of health or welfare, are increasingly 'feminized' and having the scope of their powers reduced (Marchand and Sisson Runyan, 2000). This may be either through the demands of structural adjustment policies in the South, or, in the North, through the desire to reduce state expenditure in order to maintain international competitiveness, or because of a normative preference for neo-liberal policies. IMF and World Bank conditionality agreements mandate Structural Adjustment Programmes (SAPs), which have led to cuts in social services in Third World countries at a time when many women are increasing their participation in paid labour force to supplement the falling incomes of their partners. Diane Elson (1999) shows how World Bank SAPs assume that women's reproductive labour is infinitely elastic. The importance of the private sphere to the facilitation of restructuring calls into question the exclusive focus on governments, corporations and international institutions in mainstream works on globalization. A reduction in social protection is particularly important for women for the following reasons: women are more likely to be doing non-regular work, so are less likely to have work-related entitlements; usually they bear responsibility for caring for family members in ill-health; as women live longer they are more likely to need care in later life; social change has resulted in an increase in female-headed households; in the North, women are disproportionately employed in public services (ILO/SEAPAT, 1998b). Needless to say, any shortfall in the state provision of welfare is compensated for by the unpaid labour of women. Japan is an exceptional case in this respect. The model of state provision of welfare in Japan is distinctive, in that it is predicated on the assumption that women will provide the bulk of reproductive work in three-generation families. This means that the restructuring of welfare provision, which is taking place in Japan as elsewhere, is taking place in a different context, and an analysis of its impact on working women will add special insights to these debates.

Globalization and female migrant workers

The previous chapter mentioned globalization as characterized by growing transborder 'flows' of people (Appadurai, 1990). As globalization proceeds, migratory flows have become more diverse and more feminized (Kofman, 2000). The case of migration shows very clearly how globalization has profoundly different consequences for women of different national, ethnic and class backgrounds.

Within the context of globalization, some educated, cosmopolitan women have undoubtedly been successful in taking on the 'masculinized' traits of 'high tech mobility, autonomy and challenging opportunities' (Chang and Ling, 2000). Unlike the Czech women who have seen their job opportunities diminish in the context of global restructuring, foreign women working in the Czech Republic have reported that being seen as 'foreign experts' means that they receive more advantageous career opportunities than would have been the case in their home countries (True, 2000). Even where women migrate as part of a family group, they may find themselves in a new context in which they are more likely to work. The shortage of skilled workers in some professions, such as the computer industry, has brought well-educated elite groups from the Indian subcontinent to the US. Indian women who have come to the US to support their partners have claimed that migration was empowering, particularly the opportunities it gives them for participation in the workforce (Sircar and Kelly, 2001). It seems logical to extrapolate from this that these women's experience in working in different cultures has encouraged reflexivity about gender roles in their own. There are more Japanese women than men living overseas; one especially noteworthy trend is that the overwhelming majority of Japanese studying overseas are female. The next chapter will discuss the impact of this upon their later careers in Japan.

Female migration facilitates the entry into the workforce not only of (some) migrant women, but also of middle-class women in host countries. One consequence of female employment among the middle classes of the First World has been that these women have had less time to carry out unpaid reproductive work. Consequently, middle-class couples in the West and in several of the NICs have been more inclined to spend their dual incomes on domestic labour. A counterpart to this 'cosmopolitan, postmodern, freeing' masculine form of global restructuring, described by Chang and Ling (2000) as 'Global Restructuring 1' (GI), has been the emergence of a class of female overseas contract workers carrying out personal services, such as domestic labour for a cosmopolitan elite, a process which has been described as 'Global Restructuring 2' (GII) (Chang and Ling, 2000). State policy can encourage or discourage such migration. While states' ability to provide welfare for their citizens declines, the state continues to influence and benefit from women's labour. According to Chang and Ling, the state '. . . enjoys a renewed vigour in the regime of labour intimacy, e.g. the Philippines government supervizes, regulates, transports and taxes overseas contract workers' (Chang and Ling, 2000: 35).

The 'regime of labour intimacy' implicit in GII reinforces the stereotypes of, for example, Filipina women as naturally subservient. As Chapter 5 will discuss, Japan, unlike other relatively prosperous nations, does not have a culture of importing domestic labour, and it will be argued that this is due to cultural expectations of women's reproductive work.

Nonetheless, globalization has impacted upon female migration flows to Japan. Sex workers have come to Japan, having been recruited in countries where Japanese companies have established overseas production sites. Furthermore municipal governments in rural areas have sponsored the recruitment of women, mainly from the Philippines and Thailand, to marry farmers and provide farm labour. The reasons for this can be directly attributed to the globalization of production and the spread of neo-liberal economic globalization, and the reciprocal effects of these phenomena upon Japan. This will be discussed at greater length in Chapter 4, but, it is appropriate to note here that, while other developed countries have witnessed the phenomenon of migrant women providing domestic labour for middle-class and elite women, in Japan migrant women tend to be providing services for men. To discuss this in any detail would require the analysis of issues of 'race'/ethnicity, colonialism and sexuality which are outside the scope of this book, so migration in Japan will be discussed only in so far as it is relevant or irrelevant to women working in the Japanese formal economy.

Globalization and difference

Although globalization generally results in aggregate economic growth for newly integrated economies, women – even those in the same country – do not benefit equally from global restructuring. The first analyses in the gender and development community tended to present the young women employed in TNCs as a particularly vulnerable and exploited group. However, it has since become apparent that in reality TNCs tend to recruit from among the more educated sections of the population in Third World host nations (Marchand, 1996b). Older married women, and women with children in the host countries, are more likely to work in the informal sector, where they can more easily combine their productive and reproductive roles. The nature of the informal economy means that it is far more difficult to research conditions of work for these women.

Class, as well as age, affects women's experience of global restructuring. India's New Economic Policy of 1991 removed import quantity restrictions, allowed foreign capital into the domestic market and permitted the free flow of raw materials and intermediate and capital goods. The ensuing import of capital-intensive technology destroyed many of the low-skilled and semi-skilled jobs traditionally carried out by women and led to increased competition with men for those low-skilled jobs which survived. Furthermore, as deregulation and liberalization have progressed, large manufacturers have turned to outsourcing and subcontracting to reduce costs. This segmentation means that it is difficult to enforce labour legislation (Dewan, 1999). Development efforts aimed at encouraging women's micro-enterprises may also be futile if these ventures cannot survive new competitive trade pressures (Beneria and Lind, 1995).

Global restructuring also has different effects on women from different ethnic groups. As restructuring in the North leads to job losses, then women of minority ethnic groups, as well as refugees and asylum seekers, are increasingly scapegoated, face racist attacks and are subject to stricter immigration controls.

The interaction of global and local forces

Globalization can help to weaken local patriarchal structures, although this can also weaken some of the protection from, for example, abuse that these structures provide (Young, 2001). The opening of export-oriented garment factories in Bangladesh led to the employment outside the home of women who eighteen months previously had been in purdah. This was resisted by some Islamic fundamentalist groups, who issued fatwas against women's involvement in the export sector. However, women have been able to strategically employ social norms to maintain their employment by adopting familial terms of address with male co-workers, thereby desexualizing male-female interactions in the workplace (Feldman, 2001). In India, entering waged labour means women can negotiate more control over household economic resources and some sharing of household tasks by men (though in many cases social norms are such that men continue to control income and do not share household tasks) (Soni-Sinha, 2001). In the case of one migrant community, gender norms have changed to the extent that the age-old tradition of patrilocality has been abandoned. Female factory workers from rural Chinese families in Malaysia and Hong Kong have abandoned the patriarchal custom of living with their partners' families and have instead established conjugal households or moved back with their partners and children to their own childhood villages (Gibson-Graham, 1996).

The increased demand for women's labour though, does not *automatically* lead to enhanced status within the home. This depends to a large extent on the pre-existing social institutions,[11] including family structure and gender norms. While women in Asia seem to be given a greater say in family decision-making if they go out to work (Meng, 1996), for some women, ironically, earning an independent income can make them more subject to private patriarchy, as their family exercise more physical control over a valuable wage earner (Elson and Pearson, 1997; Sen and Correa, 2000). Women's ability to earn wages does not necessarily equate to social status either, where the cultural consensus is such that women's earnings are seen as secondary, whether or not this is truly the case (Steans, 1999). Wage earning can also be just one more burden to be added to the already considerable demands of domestic and family work.

In cases where foreign firms produce directly in a host country, new norms around working practices can be introduced. Even though working conditions in TNCs in developing countries are generally less favourable than the conditions for doing the same work in the TNCs' home countries (Beneria and Lind, 1995), employment in a TNC may be experienced by employees as more beneficial than the work they would previously have carried out in agriculture or family businesses. Although work in export-orientated industries is characterized by long hours, cramped dormitory-style living conditions, extremely strict supervision of work, and, for many younger women, sexual harassment from male supervisors (United Nations Department of Economic and Social Affairs, 1999; Bayes and Kelly, 2001), women themselves often consider the working practices of TNCs to be more enlightened than those of indigenous firms. One study of the *maquiladoras* found that two-thirds of domestic and electronics workers and more than half of all garment workers said they would keep working even if they did not need the money (Bayes and Kelly, 2001). The demand from foreign companies for female workers can also sometimes produce labour shortages in the local economy and lead to local firms, too, improving pay and conditions to entice female employees (Lim, 1997).

Certainly, working for a foreign firm is a common ambition among Japanese women, who feel that these offer greater career opportunities for women than Japanese firms, and there has been some evidence of the indigenous firms showing an interest in examples of good practice to attract promising female recruits. These changes are discussed in Chapters 5 and 6.

To summarize, globalization impacts upon women in a variety of ways. In so far as a country is benefiting from insertion in the world economy, the opportunities available to women are likely to expand. However, in so far as globalization produces a decline in state-provided welfare, the burden of reproductive work on women will increase, and limit their ability to participate in waged work. Generally, globalization is associated with an increase in female labour force participation, and a convergence of male and female ways of working, although some states and institutions have the ability to influence the extent to which this is so. Depending upon the resilience of social norms, women may use their economic power to achieve increased autonomy in the private sphere.

Globalization tends to increase inequality between women, as some women's traditional work is threatened by insertion into the world economy while others benefit from new opportunities. The participation of elite women in professional occupations is facilitated by the service work of other women, particularly migrant women from poorer countries. Cleavages between women tend to fall around nationality, 'race', class and age.

Women, though, are not just helplessly subject to the forces of economic globalization and the forces within the social and cultural structures in which they live; they are also actors in the global economy, who make choices about how to balance home and work, which work to do and how to negotiate with their employers, families, polity and wider society. They are also agents who resist or transform the process of globalization, working within the new political spaces that the process has opened up. Women's activism in the context of globalization is examined in the next section.

Women's activism

This section considers the extent to which globalization has facilitated the development of a global women's movement. It then explores the political spaces in which activists for women's rights can press their case. Finally it describes the responses of women to some of the effects of globalization, and their potential for success.

Globalization and the women's movement

Chapter 2 documented the potential for non-state-based identities to increase in salience in a globalizing world. In fact, feminists have long aspired to a notion of gender-based solidarity. Virginia Woolf famously claimed that, as a woman, 'I have no country' (Woolf, 1993: 234). There has been an international feminist movement since at least the nineteenth century. International networks supported claims for female suffrage in Europe, and against foot-binding in China (Sperling *et al.*, 2001). Feminist campaigning at the Versailles conference secured women's representation in the International Labour Organization.

Although other countries, such as Japan, had indigenous feminist movements, the three main international organizations, the Women's International League for Peace and Freedom, the International Council of Women and the International Alliance of Women, were dominated by European women. First wave Western feminism also arose alongside a virulent phase of imperialism, and sometimes replicated imperialist attitudes towards non-European women. Shohat (2001), however, makes the point that Eurocentric versions of feminism often present Third World women as victims, lacking any form of agency, and ignore the action that these women have taken, such as anti-colonial activism, because it is not overtly 'feminist'. Mindry also reveals that the ideologies used to enlist the 'help' of First World women for these 'victims' rely upon an essentialist discourse of women as naturally caring and concerned about others simply because they are women. She further implies that this discourse patronizes the Third World recipients of 'sisterhood' (Mindry, 2001).

Little attention was paid to differences between women, at least in Western feminism, until later writing, such as Robin Morgan's *Sisterhood is Global*, brought the voices of non-Western women to the attention of mainstream international feminism (Flew *et al.*, 1999). While there is still concern among non-Western activists about the domination of Western feminists, aspects of foreign feminism have been adopted if they are useful in a local context:

> Women around the world are actively engaged in deciding and organising around their own local, national and global priorities and considering for themselves which feminisms are appropriate to their own context. Women's activisms take many different forms, derived from different temporalities of struggle.
>
> (Flew *et al.*, 1999: 395)

While globalization of communications may have facilitated development of transnational identities, these communities house considerable diversity. There are multiple feminisms and in some parts of the world women's movements have eschewed the label of 'feminist' altogether (China Rights Forum 1995; Eschle, 2000). This does not mean that there has been a lack of women's activism under globalization.

Although women are disproportionately likely to be employed in non-organized sectors and non-unionized part-time, informal or home-based work, the incorporation of women into the workforce has coincided with an increase in female activism for labour rights. Fernandez-Kelly (2001: 1248) writes: 'Exploitation at least, entails a connection with the world of employment and, therefore, possible mobilization, resistance, and negotiation. Redundancy does not offer such possibilities.'

As women are increasingly concentrated in sex-segregated workplaces, so groups have organized themselves around issues specific to women, even if they reject the label feminist. This can be either because feminism is associated with co-option into the former state apparatus, such as in Hungary (Acsady, 1999) or because it is seen as a Western import. In South Korea, the rapid growth of women's employment, previously described, was paralleled by a growth in women's labour activism. In defiance of Confucian expectations about the role of women, female workers were at the forefront of labour activism, demanding better conditions in general, but also reforms to improve the position of women in particular by calling for the abolition of sex-based job classifications. The clerical women's labour movement in South Korea was particularly successfully in winning reforms.[12] Furthermore, having entered the workforce, some South Korean women showed a distinct reluctance to leave (Yoon, 2001). The custom of requiring married women to be the first to lose their jobs in times of recession led to the emergence of the *IMF chonyo* (IMF maidens), who delayed marriage or lied about their marital status in order to continue in paid employment. Another case of women organizing around gender interests is the case of Exportadora de Mano de Obra S. A. (EMOSA), a Tijuana-based satellite of US-based American United Global. Female employees of EMOSA mounted an international campaign against sexual harassment after they were allegedly filmed during a bathing suit contest on a company trip (Bayes and Kelly, 2001). In many countries the growth in women's formal political representation has paralleled the rise in women's employment (Walby, 2000). Even where it is the men who have become integrated into the world economy, this can have a politicizing effect upon women: in areas of Mexico from which men have migrated to find work, women have also assumed economic and political responsibility, including holding political office (Gonzalez, 2001).

The increased incorporation of women into the workplace associated with the processes of economic globalization has had a stimulating impact upon women's activism. However, women have also had a new impetus to activism. The decline in state services associated with marketization has given them reason to protest or organize. For example, the structural adjustment programmes imposed upon Mexico in 1982 mandated cutbacks in government welfare, privatization and increase in exports, in stark contrast to the post-revolutionary Mexican state's priorities. By the following year, the women in CONAMUP (Coordinadora Nacional de Movimiento Urbano Popular – National Council of the Urban Popular Movement) had formed women's regional councils to obtain services, including health centres, running water, schools, cooking gas, school lunches, co-operatives and other economic amenities to help women fulfil household duties (Bayes and Kelly, 2001). In Russia a vast number of self-help groups and employment training organizations have grown up, trying to fill the gap left by the collapse of the welfare state (Sperling *et al.*, 2001). Although a high profile way of continuing to show support for communal provision of services, this nonetheless meant that it was still women who were bearing the cost of restructuring. As will be seen in Chapter 8, women in Japan, too, have protested about shortfalls in state welfare provision.

New possibilities for networking have arisen as national boundaries become more fluid. As women meet and network, this puts new issues on the global feminist agenda. Following the United Nations Fourth World Conference on Women in Beijing in 1995 (hereafter referred to as 'the Beijing Conference'), for example, female MPs in Malaysia raised the issues of unmarried mothers and the status of foreign partners, and government women's officers held seminars to try to improve the relationship between the government and women's NGOs (Ariffin, 1999). The Beijing conference was catalytic for women groups in Japan too, as Chapter 8 will show. It also had an impact on the consciousness of individuals. Bayes and Kelly (2001) cite the case of a young woman from a highland village in Thailand who returned from the Beijing conference, and with her newly acquired status of international traveller, informed a village elder that it was not acceptable for him to beat his wife and that he should stop. Keck and Sikkink (1998) examine the way transnational activism has been instrumental in spreading concepts, and thereby permitting activists to articulate, problematize and campaign around issues: the case study they have chosen is domestic violence. However, the entry into the Japanese vocabulary of *seku hara*, from the English 'sexual harassment' is another pertinent example.

Furthermore, new forms of technology have facilitated international networking among women's groups, increasing women's ability to share information and campaigning techniques. Delegates from India, the Philippines, Sri Lanka, Nepal, Japan, Cambodia, Korea, Kyrgyzstan, Laos, Burma and Thailand attended the Asia-Pacific Forum on Women, Law and Development in 1999. The Conference Report noted:

In an ironic twist, globalization here was used to positive effect in expanding and strengthening the women's movement and the fight against transnational exploitative processes. This can be seen through the exchange of business cards, addresses, phone and fax numbers, and e-mail addresses. This interchange, in part facilitated by the global- ization of communication technologies, travel, and information will contribute no doubt, to a stronger network of women's organizations across the globe.

(Costa, 1999: 69)

Of course, the ability to travel internationally and network in cyberspace is open only to comparatively few women.

In summary, feminists have always aspired to a global women's move- ment, but the nascent international movement of first-wave feminism was strongly dominated by the concerns of European women. Globalization has drawn more women into the workplace and, with this, into activism for labour rights. Furthermore, the exigencies of globalization have pro- pelled women to defend the gains of state feminism. The fluidity of national boundaries has also allowed for women to share concerns and to network to build alliances with women in other countries.

Sites of activism

If globalization is impacting upon women's activism, it is also impacting upon the institutions and political structures which women attempt to influ- ence. This section will describe how the geography of political activism is changing. It will first examine the state, as, even though its role is changing (Chapter 2), the state continues to be a major player in its own right or as part of regional trading blocks (Bergeron, 2001). It will then go on to look at the local, transnational and global political spaces which have opened up or assumed greater importance under the process of globalization.

Feminists have tended to have a somewhat ambiguous attitude towards the national state, and of course, states take different forms in different his- torical contexts.[13] The German feminist movement, for example, tended to present the state as an instrument of patriarchal control; in the UK some feminists tended to see it as an arm of the capitalist class, mediating patriarchy and capitalism (Rai, 1996). Feminist activists in Japan, too, have until recently tended to eschew parliamentary politics (Mikanagi, 2001). Scandinavian feminists, in contrast, have chosen the path of 'state feminism' (Young, 2001). The post-revolutionary Chinese state promised, and largely delivered, equal pay for equal work, educational parity between the sexes, public health and childcare provision. The marketization of the Chinese economy has resulted in high unemployment and poor labour conditions for women, lack of protection for rural migrants and the commercialization of femininity. However, the formal state ideology of gender equality is still a tool for legitimating struggles for women's rights (Chun, 2001).

Globalization is often presented as accountable democratic bodies being superseded by the unelected forces of transnational capital. However, at the level of formal democracy, at least, globalization has seen a 'third wave' of democratization. Women can now exercise effective electoral choice in the new post-Cold War multi-party democracies, and women's representation in existing parliaments has increased. Furthermore, a higher proportion of countries have democratically elected assemblies today than 20 years ago, which itself increases the number of elected women representatives (Walby, 2001). This in itself implies an impact upon policy. A 1991 study by the Centre for American Women and Politics at Rutgers University found that, regardless of party or ideology, female politicians tend to have a different agenda to men (Fujimura-Fanselow and Kameda, 1995: 373). However, the gains of state feminism, such as the Danish welfare state model, with its emphasis on gender equality and redistributive politics, are now under threat from the exigencies of globalization (Siim, 2003).

The power of globalized capital has called into question the nation as a site of collective identity and the state as a force that can serve the collective interests of those who reside within the nation. It is one of the paradoxes of globalization that national legislatures are becoming more representative, just as those legislatures are losing effective power (Held, 1995; Falk, 1997b; Gilpin, 2000). However, the decline in state sovereignty is by no means unanimously viewed as detrimental to women: feminist scholarship has noted that the principle of non-intervention in sovereign states leaves women vulnerable to abuse and injustice (Sassen, 2001).

Globalization presents new opportunities for feminist politics as well as new difficulties. In times of change social movements can identify potential allies and note where elites are vulnerable to challenge. The 'global imperative' view says targets should be global and that there is a 'new geography of power' composed of TNCs, financial markets, insurance and information networks (Bergeron, 2001). Women are reacting by establishing a strategy that is simultaneously localized, regionalized and globalized (Chin and Mittelman, 1997).

The previous chapter explored the notion that one of the trends associated with globalization was the increasing trend towards multi-level governance, with more formulation of policy at sub-state levels. Many women activists have therefore chosen to work at local levels. Yoon (2001) describes how, in the early 1990s, women's organizations in South Korea began to seek women's representation in formal politics, particularly at the local level, where they have continued to work for legal and institutional change. Women in Africa have also formed local women's groups, including rotating saving societies, co-operatives and day-care associations in response to austerity measures and the reduction in male employment (Tripp, 1997).

The establishment, and increased profile, of global institutions of governance such as the United Nations (UN) has been strongly associated with a raised international profile of women's rights, particularly through the series of international UN women's conferences from Mexico City in 1975 to Beijing in 1995 (Flew *et al.*, 1999; Ariffin, 1999; Marcos, 1999;

Mbire-Barungi, 1999) and the development of a nascent set of international norms as embodied in UN and ILO resolutions and agreements such as the United Nations Convention on the Elimination of All Forms of Discrimination against Women (CEDAW). Transnational networks composed of non-state actors, notably the UN and women's non-governmental organizations, have been instrumental in the diffusion of 'gender mainstreaming' (True and Mintrom, 2001), that is, state policy to take into account the differential impacts of all policies according to gender. It is important to note that the institutional characteristics of some states are sufficiently strong that the states refuse to accept these global norms. Arat (2002) has noted the tendency of some Muslim states to express reservations about global norms, or to seek exemptions to parts of international conventions, based on their interpretations of religious law (despite modernist or feminist interpretations of Shar'ia, which stipulate sexual equality).

Women use international law and transnational organizing to negotiate with national states and individual TNCs for recognition and reinforcement of women's human rights. For example, some export-oriented firms in Mexico have tried to avoid hiring pregnant women, to whom they would have certain legal obligations. They have adopted such practices as giving women 28-day contracts (to coincide with their menstrual cycle), or requiring women to show proof of menstruation. If a woman becomes pregnant, she is not rehired. As ILO and UN agreements to which Mexico is a signatory forbid discrimination in hiring on grounds of sex, some NGOs representing these women's interests have filed a complaint about this kind of pregnancy testing against Mexico with the National Administrative Office (NAO) of the US Department of Labor. The subsequent publicity led two US firms which operated in Mexico, General Motors and ITT Industries, to voluntarily agree to discontinue the process of pregnancy testing (Bayes and Kelly, 2001).

As well as facilitating the application of transnational pressure, the prestige of the UN has lent credibility to national attempts to improve women's situation. The Russian women's movement, for example, purposefully adopts the language of international documents, such as ILO and UN resolutions in its struggle against sexist discrimination (Sperling *et al.*, 2001). Japanese campaigners, too, have deliberately adopted a boomerang strategy (see Chapter 1, note 7) to pressurize the Japanese government to enforce equal opportunities legislation.

This section has noted that globalization is resulting in women working for, and achieving, greater representation at the national level. However, this is of limited utility as the power of the national state retreats. As more power is devolved to the local level, some feminists have focused their efforts there. However, of perhaps more significance is the emergence of a global standard of sexual equality, although the extent to which this can be used to put pressure on individual states varies according to their history and political culture.

Modes of response

Having noted the different levels of governance that can be targeted by campaigners, I shall now explore the different strategies campaigners employ.

The strategies adopted by women in responding to some of the processes associated with globalization will be partially determined by the structures in which they are operating. Tripp (1994) notes that in Tanzania, which has a history of local women's organizations, women's reaction to austerity measures was to start collective economic strategies, for example, a sewing project that used the money they made to start a co-operative flour mill. Bergeron discusses research on women in Sri Lankan, Malaysian and Philippine free trade zones who have used their wages to build women's centres that provide legal and medical assistance, library services, training, co-operative housing facilities and food co-operatives. By doing so, they use multinational capital to provide alternatives to capitalism (Bergeron, 2001). Women have also effectively made use of culture-specific shaming strategies. In the case of women's campaigns for Y. H. Trading Company and Dong-il Textile in the Republic of Korea, protestors took off all their clothes to block riot police and corrupt male union leaders (Yoon, 2001).

The internationalization of production means that some women are able to enlist help in their struggles from more powerful groups in foreign countries. The EMOSA women described earlier in this chapter, who complained of sexual harassment, were all laid off, and the plant where they worked was closed, without compensation. The Support Committee for Maquiladora Workers based in Tijuana and San Diego contacted the United Auto Workers, whose employers has subcontracted work to the *maquiladora* where the women worked. United Auto Workers has an agreement with Ford, GM and Chrysler which says that these companies will not use parts made under unfair labour practices, and, after eight months of legal action and campaigning, 118 workers received acceptable severance pay (Bayes and Kelly, 2001).

The women who can afford to travel to the UN, or who work in professionalized NGOs, are an elite and not representative of the majority of the world's women. Some feminists have criticized the Beijing conference for excluding the poorest women (Bergeron, 2001). Other theorists have warned that those who engage with states and corporate interests risk being co-opted and encouraged towards conformity (Cox, 1999). Nonetheless, feminist activism has become 'more NGO-ized' (Sperling *et al.*, 2001). Those who have engaged with international bodies have '. . . countered the prevailing view that state commitments in the United Nations involve mostly lofty talk or mere lip service' (Suriyamongkol, 2002: 3).

Campaigners at this level have typically mixed scholarship and activism. Diane Orentlicher (cited in Bayes and Kelly, 2001: 156) argues that human rights methodology 'promot[es] change by reporting facts'. To hold governments accountable 'requires NGOs to: a) carefully document alleged abuses; b) clearly demonstrate state accountability for those abuses under international law and c) develop a mechanism for effectively exposing documented abuse nationally and internationally'.

Campaigners have therefore attempted to find facts, build consensus internationally and locally and create mechanisms to explore abuse and bring international, national and local pressure to bear (Bayes and Kelly, 2001). The Women in Development movement is a global advocacy network, engaging with international bodies and national parliaments (Walby, 2001). As a result of the work of Schools of Women in Development and Gender and Development:

- International agencies now pursue as a matter of course, research upon the gendered impact of policies.
- Nation states 'mainstream' women's policy agendas through official programs promoted by advocacy administrators and 'femocrats'.
- Feminist organizations engage regularly with the state, particularly through elected female representatives.

(Staudt, Rai and Parpart, 2001)

The strategy of collecting information to bring international pressure to bear on a national government has been adopted by an increasing number of national women's groups who provide alternative reports to the UN on the extent to which their state has implemented CEDAW's provisions.

A type of resistance at the opposite end of the spectrum to this highly organized and academic strategy is what James C. Scott (1990, cited in Chin and Mittelman, 1997) has named 'infrapolitics'. This refers to everyday forms of resistance exercised by individuals or groups which fall short of openly declared contestations. Infrapolitical activities range from foot dragging, squatting and gossiping to the development of dissident subcultures (Chin and Mittelman, 1997). In keeping with the dictum that the personal is political, feminists have not just limited their descriptions of responses to global patriarchy to the actions of formal groups but have examined the actions of individuals and informal social groups. Filipina maids in Hong Kong, for example, confined to the house for most of the week, gather in public spaces to socialize and share information, some-times to the concern of the local media (Youngs, 2000). Women go to work, sometimes in the face of opposition from men or local cultural tradi-tions. They may also use gender stereotypes to passively resist managers, for example, by demanding unique rest periods (Ward, 1990). Minority women in Silicon Valley have turned managers' stereotypes against them, by, for example, refusing to work with solvents on the grounds that it would ruin manicures for a special occasion or bringing a child to work on the grounds that the child's mother would be too tired to play with him after work (Hossfeld, 1990). Chapter 6 describes the infrapolitical resistance of Japanese 'office ladies' (OLs).

Women then employ a variety of protest strategies. These range from engaging with international and state bodies in a highly professionalized way and using their own modes of discourse to campaign for better conditions to linking with other women and other workers in transnational campaigns, through to using traditional feminized methods of protest, and employing 'infrapolitical resistance'.

Conclusion

Several general hypotheses about the relationship between gender and globalization can be extrapolated from the accounts described in this chapter:

• Globalization is presented as a gendered and natural phenomenon in political discourse, in a way that suggests nation states are powerless to resist its exigencies.
• States respond to the challenges of globalization by marketization and the adoption of neo-liberal policies. These policies have impacts which increase the reproductive work of women.
• Globalization can weaken local patriarchal structures by exposing culturally specific practices to global scrutiny, while flows of information and ideas increase reflexivity within cultures.
• Dominant ideologies can lead a state and existing institutions to negotiate a compromise between encouraging change and maintaining current gender orders.
• There has been a 'feminization' of waged work, as an increasing proportion of jobs are taken by women, and an increasing proportion of jobs are irregular, part-time and/or service-sector jobs which have typically been filled by women.
• The entry into the workforce of many First World women into professional positions is facilitated by the domestic work of poorer migrant women.

Whether these hypotheses are valid in the case of Japan, and how the case of Japan can contribute to the feminist debate about the impact of globalization upon women will be examined in the following chapters.

Feminist accounts of the multi-faceted nature of globalization significantly enhance our understanding of this phenomenon, as well as the way states and institutions nuance its effects. They show that globalization is a deeply gendered phenomenon. It impacts differently upon men and women. Macro-level analyses, which view the phenomenon through the lens of gender, show that attempts by states to respond to the challenges of economic globalization by marketization and the adoption of neo-liberal policies increase the reproductive work of women. They have also shown how the gendered discourse surrounding neo-liberal economic globalization (wrongly) constructs it as natural and irresistible, adding support to the hypothesis that globalization is not only a process but also a project.

Generally, in both North and South, processes associated with globalization, such as foreign direct investment and the desire to employ more non-regular workers, draw more women into waged labour, although in some cases this changes as development proceeds. Although women experience the changes brought about by global processes very differently according to their age, class, ethnic background and national culture, most women usually work under different conditions to those enjoyed by most men. The work that women do is usually relatively poorly paid and has less security than the work their male fellow workers have traditionally enjoyed. This can be partially attributed to institutional factors, such as a country's gender norms. However, the increase in women working also has the potential to alter gender norms. For this reason, most women seem to prefer waged work and employ strategies to keep their jobs when threatened with removal through restructuring or societal and familial opposition. Women may benefit in terms of health and education if capital penetration results in successful development. However, the marketization occasioned by globalization increases women's work in the home and reduces their availability in the labour market. A minority of elite women have found that globalization offers them opportunities for travel and a professional career comparable to that of elite men, but only if other women provide domestic labour for them.

An increase in women in the workforce and the adoption of a global norm around the idea of gender equality has led to an intensification of women workers' struggles for labour rights. Women have succeeded in gaining a more equitable representation at state level, but as the state has lost some of its capacity, women have focused their attention upon new institutions of global governance.

At the firm, local, national, regional and global level women have pursued a number of strategies of resistance, ranging from combining scholarship and activism to campaign upon an international stage to using the wages from global companies to build community services and jointly campaigning with women and workers from other countries and employing the passive resistance known as infrapolitics.

In some instances a study of the case of Japan exemplifies and enriches points made by feminist theorists about the relationship between gender and globalization. Claims made by representatives of the Japanese state do present neo-liberal economic globalization as natural and inevitable, and thereby justify the proposed restructuring of the labour market to respond to its exigencies. Japanese women are entering the labour force in greater numbers than previously, although the work they are carrying out is less secure than those jobs held by the majority of men in the post-war period. Through their exposures to nascent norms around sexual equality and experience of migration, some Japanese women are becoming increasingly reflexive about work and gender roles in Japan. Japanese women have long been involved in transnational feminist movements. The strategies of resistance they employ draw on the ideas and methods of actors in other countries, but are also shaped by Japanese social and political institutions.

In other instances though, analyses of gender and globalization do not fit the Japanese case so well. Expectations about women's role in the reproductive economy, and particularly in the three-generation family, have implications for female migration, for the impact of the retreat of the state in Japan, and for women's capacity to undertake full-time work. Furthermore, men and women's expectation of women's role in the labour force is influenced by the changing, but still distinctive, features of the Japanese national model of capitalism.

Part II

Background to the analysis

4 The Japanese model of capitalism and the globalization of Japanese production

Introduction

This chapter explains the development of the Japanese model of capitalism, in order to provide an essential background to understanding women's role in that model, which will be explored in more depth in Chapter 5. The chapter goes on to show how the globalization of Japanese production has facilitated the changing division of labour firstly in the East Asian region,[1] and then globally, and how this is having reciprocal effects upon that model.

Chapter 2 has argued that the state and national institutions play important roles in both facilitating the processes associated with globalization and determining the manifestation of globalization in different national contexts. This chapter discusses the role the Japanese state and Japanese companies have played in facilitating the global organization of production and the reciprocal effects this has had on the Japanese national model of capitalism generally. In order to contextualize changes in the Japanese model of capitalism, it is first necessary to gain an understanding of this model, and the way that it was forged. The chapter therefore describes how the conditions of international political economy led to a rebuilding of the Japanese economy after the Second World War, and a reshaping of its institutions. It goes on to deal with the security concerns, economic dependence and political considerations which prompted Japan to direct aid and investment to the rest of East Asia, and how this interacted with the economic development policies of other countries in the region thereby facilitating the globalization of Japanese production.

Rapid advances in information technology, transport and communications made it possible to organize production on an international basis. Economic and political expediency has produced the incentive for Japanese companies to undertake this reorganization. However, there have been four key discontinuities in the post-war international political economy, which have added a great deal of momentum to the process. These were the collapse of the Bretton Woods system in 1971, the Plaza Accord in 1985, the collapse of the Soviet Union in 1989 and the East Asian financial crisis of 1997. The chapter will deal with these events and their historical context, before summarizing the reciprocal effects of the globalization of Japanese production.

The emergence of the Japanese national model of capitalism

In the aftermath of the Second World War, US foreign policy strongly supported the idea of Japan as a 'bulwark against communism'.[2] US policy, as outlined in National Security Council Reports of the 1950s, encouraged the rebuilding of the Japanese economy, the re-arming of Japan, and also the intensification of Japan's links with the other East and South-east Asian countries. This would buttress Asian anti-communist regimes (Suehiro, 1999) and integrate these nations into the capitalist world.

The Supreme Commander for the Allied Powers (SCAP) had planned to break up the large family-owned conglomerates known as *zaibatsu*, as these commercial empires had, during the 1930s, joined the military in supporting overseas expansion. However, priorities changed with the inception of the Cold War so plans to radically restructure and democratize Japan's economy, particularly by dismantling the *zaibatsu*, were quickly shelved in the interests of rebuilding an economically robust anti-communist ally. Mitsui, Mitsubishi and Sumitomo therefore survived, reorganized themselves into industrial and financial corporate groupings known as *keiretsu*, which are a key feature of Japanese capitalism.

Gerlach identifies five characteristic features of *keiretsu*: transactions are conducted through alliances of affiliated companies; relationships between such companies are based upon longevity, stability and mutual obligation; relationships are characterized by cross-shareholding and personal relationships; relationships have symbolic significance which maintains links even in the absence of formal contacts; bilateral relationships take place within a wider 'family' of firms (Gerlach, 1992: 4, cited in Dicken, 1998: 224). The large companies at the 'top' of *keiretsu* were able to externalize through these intricate vertical relationships with small and medium-sized subcontractors. The subcontractors, which are almost entirely dependent on the larger company, provide flexible pricing and production and even absorb surplus employees of the company in times of economic difficulty. This system was instrumental in producing a dual labour market. In firms at the 'top' of the *keiretsu*, the (male) worker was virtually guaranteed employment for the rest of his working life, with even temporary discharge happening in only the most extreme circumstances (Abegglen, 1958: 11).[3] However, the stability of employment in large firms (see Chapter 1) was guaranteed by the flexibility of smaller ones.[4]

To encourage the rebuilding of civil society in Japan, under SCAP's influence, trade unions were legalized in 1945 (Lehmann, 2000).[5] These post-war unions had certain distinguishing characteristics. The unions were notable for their enterprise base and their cross-class membership, both legacies of workers' experience of the Industrial Patriotic Society (*Sangyou Houkoku Kai*). Enterprises branches of the Industrial Patriotic Society, which comprised both white-collar and blue-collar workers, had been formed to raise the spirits and provide mutual aid for the families of drafted employees.

As well as being based in enterprises and uniting blue- and white-collar workers, Japanese trade unions were characterized by the way they played a role in co-determining company policy. Co-operative labour-management relations had numerous benefits for male regular workers. Both blue-collar and white-collar workers received employment security, high-quality training and payment according to salary. Company welfare benefits, such as grants on marriage, childbirth, illness, death, provision of company housing and subsidized shopping facilities added to the cost of lifetime employment for companies (Matsushima, 1966). These high fixed costs prompted firms to seek numerical flexibility by using a secondary (and disproportionately female) workforce, who did not have the same job security or fringe benefits of male regular workers.[6]

After Truman's election in 1948, Detroit banker Joseph Dodge was appointed to Tokyo as 'economic czar'; his brief was to build a strong Japanese economy, thus ensuring that Japan would be a robust ally against communism in Asia. Dodge adopted a strategy of central planning ('The Dodge Plan'), which was aimed at maximizing production for export, while minimizing production for domestic consumption. One of the immediate effects of the Dodge Plan was large-scale layoffs. Between 1949 and 1950 around 700,000 workers lost their jobs (Halliday, 1995: 350). This severely weakened the union movement, as union membership fell by 880,000 between 1949 and 1950. As jobs became more scarce and union membership fell, union leaders acceded to the demands of management that, rather than representing all workers in a plant, unions would represent only the 'labour aristocracy' of those regular workers that the management would want to retain even in a period of maximum retrenchment (Halliday, 1995). Further strikes in the 1950s and 1960s following proposed lay-offs resulted not only in huge financial costs for the companies concerned but also in bad labour/management relations, low morale among workers and a public relations disaster for the affected companies. The consequence of this period of industrial relations was that a tacit understanding developed between labour and management that lay-offs of regular workers should be avoided as far as possible (Inoue, 1999). However, 'lifetime employment' would be the prerogative of only those full-time regular workers that had union representation, and this became recognized in law. Although Japanese company law is very similar to that of the UK and the US in its view of the supremacy of shareholders rather than other stakeholders in a company, actual practice has meant that 'lifetime' employment for regular male workers has become institutionalized. Case law has come to support the institution of lifetime employment. Employees can claim unfair dismissal if a firm cannot demonstrate that it has, for example, explored all reasonable market opportunities for diversification before resorting to layoffs (Dore, 2000).

Dodge strongly supported the creation of the Ministry of International Trade and Industry (MITI), which was to encourage export-oriented production by large, integrated firms. As well as providing aid to rebuild the Japanese economy, the US pegged the yen at a rate of 360 yen to the dollar, a low rate which made it easier for Japan to export to the non-communist East Asian countries. Special procurements from the US in 1950–3 during the Korean War were a further stimulus to Japan's economic development.

In April 1949 the Ministry of International Trade and Industry (MITI) was granted complete control over Japanese industrial policy. MITI not only controlled imports of goods but chose to license foreign technology rather than permit foreign direct investment. As Cerny (2001) has observed, late industrializing states do not typically wish to see capital flowing freely out of their borders; they wish to keep it at home. Early infant industry protectionism strengthened Japanese capitalism and proved highly successful at transforming Japan from a low-skilled, labour-intensive economy to a highly skilled, high-value added one. In its rejection of free flows of capital and technology and its restrictions on imports, the Japanese model of capitalism differed greatly from the current Anglo-American model of capitalism, and resembled more its East Asian neighbours at the time.

SCAP had expected the Japanese economy to adopt a strategy of specializing in low-value-added production at competitively low wage rates. Instead Japanese companies adopted a mode of production based upon the '3Ks': *keiretsu, kanban* and *kaizen. Keiretsu* have been defined in the previous section; *kanban* refers to the just-in-time system aimed at the elimination of 'waste' within companies, that is, the minimum level of equipment, materials, parts, space and worker's time that are absolutely essential to add value to the product. By reducing costs, inventories and fixed assets, the argument goes, the return to capital employed will be increased. The establishment of lifetime employment for male company employees gave companies every incentive to ensure that workers were multi-skilled and flexible. These multi-skilled workers were created through the practice of continuous improvement (*kaizen*), and the ability to carry out high-value-added production ensured Japanese companies captured a higher share of the profits to be made in the production process than would have been the case if Japan had specialized in low-skilled, labour intensive work. Japanese manufacturing productivity rose annually by an average of 9.7 per cent during the period from 1955 to 1970, and real wages rose by an annual average of 5.7 per cent in the same period (Itoh, 2000: 4). Exports grew 17 per cent annually in the 1960s (PBS online, 2002a).

The reconstruction of the Japanese economy was a top political priority for the Japanese government, as it was for the US. Development policy concentrated on heavy industries and chemical production, and between 1955 and 1970 there was no increase in social welfare spending. In 1951 the Social Security Advisory Council recommended that the Japanese government introduce a comprehensive social security system which would provide social insurance, social welfare and public hygiene. However, the government failed to implement this. The 1949 Second Plan for Economic Reconstruction maintained 'there was a vital need to consider accumulating as much capital as possible by slowing down the rise in living standards, which was vital for a while even though it was expected to cause hardships in people's everyday life' (cited in Takeda, 2002: 163). This policy of prioritizing economic over social development has been instrumental in shaping expectations of women's productive and reproductive labour, as women tend to 'fill the gaps' in state-provided welfare. As Takeda (2002: 164) observes:

> in this sense, ideas from the previous family system were utilized through remodelling in appropriate ways for the period of high economic growth, and functioned as a substitute for a public social security system, which was given only secondary importance after the economic policy.
>
> (Takeda, 2002: 164)

Even in 1996 Japan paid only 67.5 trillion yen, or 17.2 per cent of the national income, in social security benefits, compared to national income proportions of 18.7 per cent in the United States (1992), 33.3 per cent in Germany (1993), 37.7 per cent in France (1993), and 53.4 per cent in Sweden (1993) (Japan Access, 2002) This formal assumption of reproductive work being the responsibility of family members continues to be embodied in Japanese policy pronouncements, as Chapter 7 will show.

The early post-war period, then, established a dual model of employment in Japan. A division was made between security and conditions of work in larger and smaller firms. A division was also established between those full-time workers who were enterprise union members and received a virtual guarantee of lifetime security, combined with payment by seniority and a raft of company provided welfare benefits, and those in non-regular employment, who were not union members and did not have such guarantees. In large firms, innovative production systems, such as *kanban*, led to impressive growth in production. The Japanese national model of capitalism was initially characterized by administrative guidance and control of capital flows. This proved to be successful in effecting the take-off of many of Japan's successful export industries. While the state was given responsibility for economic development, the provision of welfare was formally considered to be the role of the family. As noted in the previous chapter, reproductive work carried out within the family is overwhelmingly carried out by women.

The globalization of Japanese capital

Although MITI controlled imports and outward foreign direct investment, there was tension between the desire to keep capital 'at home' and pragmatic political concerns about rebuilding relationships between Japan and the rest of Asia. Bilateral, as well as global, politics and traditional geopolitical security concerns were also instrumental in encouraging a flow of funds from Japan to the rest of Asia.

Akaha (1999) suggests that the ideological divisions of the Cold War and the US's prioritization of the nurturing of Japan as its principal ally in the region meant that, unlike Germany in its relations with Europe, Japan did not need to reach full reconciliation with its neighbours. However, while the military security need may not have been urgent, the economic rationale for rebuilding first trade, then investment, then production links with Asia certainly was. Colonized China, Manchuria and Korea had provided the Japanese empire with raw materials and markets for its manufactured products. Japan was keen to rebuild its manufacturing industry, and so in the post-war period Japan had every incentive to rebuild economic partnerships.

From 1950, under the premiership of Yoshida Shigeru, Japan adopted a policy of co-operating with the US to develop South-east Asia. Reparations to the region were paid in kind – first by services and then by capital goods, which made it relatively easy for Japanese companies to establish cross-national production. Japan supplied nearly 946 billion yen to various Asian countries, including the Philippines, Indonesia, Malaysia, Singapore and the Republic of Korea, in reparations and other payment (Umezu, 2000). Reparations payments were always made in combination with loans for economic co-operation and development (Suehiro, 1999). Japan also cultivated links with countries to which it did not have a duty of reparation, including India, Pakistan and Sri Lanka (which was then known as Ceylon) (Suehiro, 1999). In 1954, it signed up to the Colombo Plan, to help with socio-economic development in Asia.

From the 1960s onwards, corporations put pressure on MITI to permit more FDI (Cowling and Tomlinson, 2000). Post-war austerity plans were replaced by income doubling plans, when, in 1960, Prime Minister Ikeda was sufficiently confident of the strength of the Japanese economy that he announced a National Income-Doubling Plan. Industrial policy would be used to funnel investment finance into high-growth export industries. Throughout the 1960s investment rates represented around 20 per cent of income and produced high real growth throughout the decade (Shea, 2001). Japanese firms began to locate some actual production overseas as a reaction to the increased salaries at home (Mackie, 1999).

Political change in 1965 was a watershed for Japanese relations with East Asia. That year saw the outbreak of the Vietnam War, a military coup in Indonesia and the signing of the Japan–South Korea Treaty, normalizing relations between the two countries. The political instability of Asia in the late 1960s and early 1970s led to the formulation of the Fukuda doctrine, an explicit articulation of the idea that aid and investment to the rest of Asia were essential to the defence of Japan's national interest. Prime Minister Takeo Fukuda, in 1977, recognized Japan's unique position as a developed industrialized economy in the region and spoke of the need for Japan, as an 'advanced country', to take responsibility for stabilizing the region, which was the source of so many of the raw materials needed by Japanese manufacturing. Most Japanese Overseas Development Assistance (ODA) was, like reparations, 'tied'. Japanese trading companies are involved from the project planning stage, and attach conditions aimed at maximizing their own business opportunities. Thus ODA, in effect, subsidized the multinationalization of Japanese firms (Itoh, 2000).

In summary, for reasons of political pragmatism, from the 1940s onwards capital from Japan entered the rest of East Asia. These funds strengthened links between Japan and the rest of the region, and when Japanese businesses were looking for ways to cut production costs, moving some production to East Asia was an obvious strategy.

As the rest of this section shows, East Asia was not the sole recipient of Japanese FDI. Political pragmatism, and economic rationalism encouraged Japanese FDI flows first to East Asia, then Western Europe, then Eastern Europe and the former Soviet Union, and also, to a certain extent, to the US. Japanese companies were increasingly persuaded to produce outside Japan as a result of four key discontinuities in the developing international political economy, and the international political climate in which they took place. The rest of this section will explore the impact of the collapse of the Bretton Woods system, the Plaza Accord, the end of the Cold War and the East Asian financial crisis upon the investment and production decision of key economic actors in Japan.

The collapse of the Bretton Woods system

Although Japanese companies had begun to locate some production overseas as far back as the 1960s, the 1970s acted as a spur to increase this trend. In 1971 the Bretton Woods system broke down (see Chapter 2) and between 1971 and 1974 the yen rocketed from 360 to 290 against the dollar. By October 1978, it had risen to 110 yen to the dollar. This made Japanese products increasingly expensive and wages in the rest of East Asia cheap relative to those in Japan. An extra incentive to produce overseas was that the Japanese economy was also suffering as a consequence of changing international political relations. US recognition of China in 1971 under the Nixon administration (1969–74) downgraded the importance of the US's relationship with Japan. The US administration had been worried for some time about the mushrooming costs of containment in Asia. The link with Japan became less and less strategically important with the opening to China, arms limitations treaties with the Soviet Union and the end of the Vietnam War. It was also under Nixon's presidency that Japanese imports to the US were restricted.

These factors combined to increase the pressure on Japanese firms to invest abroad, as it was becoming increasingly difficult to export to the US from Japan because the rising value of the yen, the phenomenon known in Japan as *endaka*, inevitably raised the cost of Japanese exports, and because, following *endaka*, the rest of the world's prices for land, labour and entire corporations had, for Japanese buyers, fallen dramatically (Pempel, 1999).

As new social movements reacted to several industrial pollution incidents, firms had an additional reason to locate overseas. Almost 100 female environmental activists, complaining of industry's contamination of Japan's waterways, were elected to local and municipal government (Arimura, 1996), the Japanese government increased state regulation of environmental matters (Mackie, 1999), and laws became more effective after the creation of the Environment Agency in 1971 (Kelly, 1998). Companies were also encouraged to invest overseas by Japan's relatively high corporate taxes. (Corporate taxes today account for around 24 per cent of Japan's tax revenues.)

Large corporations had long pressured the Ministry of International Trade and Industry (MITI)[7] to be able to invest directly abroad. Large-scale production had resulted in Japan's domestic markets becoming saturated with consumer durables and, given Japan's high saving ratio, led to firms turning to world markets. However, it was only in 1971, with the added spur of the collapse of Bretton Woods, that the Japanese government abandoned its previous policy of only allowing FDI which was in Japan's long-term interest, and allowed unlimited investments abroad.

The growing desire of Japanese firms from the 1970s onwards to produce overseas articulated with the desire of East Asian economies to attract foreign direct investment. Japan's rapid economic growth encouraged other East Asian states to copy the Japanese development model, a policy known as the 'Look East' or the 'flying geese' model. There was a spate of such programmes, including Singapore's 1978 'Learn from Japan' initiative; Malaysia's 1981 'Look East' policy and Philippines sources urging the country to become more like 'Japan Incorporated' (Katz, 1998). Post-war East Asian economies had hitherto generally attempted to develop economically by adopting import-substitution policies. A corollary of the abandonment of such strategies in favour of export-oriented development was that East Asian governments adopted export policies to encourage foreign capital. This led to the building of export zones (EZs), which, by the mid-1970s existed in Taiwan, South Korea, the Philippines and Malaysia. Later, China adopted the same policy. Typically workers in these export zones did not have the trade union rights and freedoms of their counterparts in Japan. This lack of union rights and the low wages of export zone workers made them an attractive labour force for foreign investors. Under Malaysia's Look East policy, for example, Mahathir Mohammed curbed workers' civil and political rights, banned the unionization of certain industries and imprisoned political and labour militants under the Internal Security Act (Ariffin, 1999).

The Plaza Accord

The model of capitalism which emerged in the late 1940s and 1950s proved to be a very successful foundation for Japan's export-oriented economic development. So successful was Japan's export strategy that by 1985 the US was suffering from record trade deficits with Japan. Consequently representatives from France, Germany, Japan, the United States and the United Kingdom came together at the Plaza Hotel in New York where they reached agreement to drive down the price of the dollar. The aim of the Plaza Accord was to make Japanese imports more expensive and US exports cheaper, hence reducing trade balances. The dollar consequently fell 30 per cent over the next two years. The corollary rise of the yen from 260.24 yen against the dollar just before the agreement to a high point of 80.3 yen in 1995 provided a further spur for Japanese companies to cut production costs by producing overseas, of course.

The export-oriented development strategy that Japan had pursued was severely undermined by the Plaza Accord, as the rising value of the yen made Japanese exports more expensive. Steven (1996) argues that domestic crisis is one of the main motors driving the globalization of Japanese production. He notes that in the Japanese mode of production, wages are downwardly flexible (that is, they can easily and legally be reduced by employers), as up to a third of the annual pay of core workers comes in the form of yearly bonuses, and higher paid workers can be replaced by irregular workers (see Chapter 5). Japanese producers, then, concentrated on manufacturing producer goods purchased by Japanese capital rather than consumer goods for consumption in the domestic market. Japanese consumer goods could not be absorbed by the domestic market and were exported. The rise in the exchange rate of the yen following the Plaza Accord severely damaged this strategy by leaving Japanese wages 'simultaneously both too high and too low': too high to produce cheap goods and too low for workers to buy all that they produced (Steven, 1996: 58). By the second half of 1993, Japanese prices were 1.72 times US prices, while real wages were less than 60 per cent of US real wages (Steven, 1996: 58). This made producers more likely to move overseas to cut production costs and make it more affordable for those outside Japan to buy goods produced by Japanese companies.

Further globalization of production was encouraged by bilateral relations with the US and the EU. Following trade friction with the US and the EU during the first half of the 1980s, Japan had agreed to voluntary export restrictions on steel, television and car exports and MITI even opened an import promotion office. However, these could be circumvented if the goods were produced elsewhere. For example, when limits were imposed on cotton from Japan, Japanese firms pragmatically shifted cotton production to other Asian countries, while diversifying into synthetics at home (Schwartz, 2000). Japanese firms had an incentive to invest in Europe to enjoy the intra-European trading advantages of EU firms. In the late 1980s particularly, there was a massive surge in Japanese investment in preparation for the end of 1992, when Europe became a unified free trade zone. In 1989 Japanese investment in the European Community reached a peak of US$752,000,000 (JETRO, 1997).

The end of the Cold War

As shown previously in this chapter, US political priorities during the Cold War led the US to assist in Japan's economic recovery and to enable Japan to integrate its production with that of its Asian neighbours. The end of the Cold War meant that US political priorities shifted sharply.

Although the Plaza Accord had the effect of changing Japanese production techniques and encouraging Japanese firms to produce overseas, it had not put an end to the US's persistent trade deficit with Japan. Although by the end of the 1980s Japan actually had lower formal barriers to imports than most of the US's other trade partners, the first Bush administration began the Structural Impediments Initiative: an attempt to bring about the restructuring of Japan's domestic institutions in the name of free trade (Upham, 1996: 264). Examples of the deregulation that has taken place include: the reform of the Large-scale Retail Stores Law, facilitating the entry of large discount foreign stores into Japan; Big Bang, the 1998 deregulation of Japan's financial markets, subjecting Japanese banks to increased competition from the likes of Merrill Lynch and Citibank; and the deregulation of the airline industry. The gendered impact of globalization upon the banking and airline industries in Japan will be explored in Chapter 7.

Although these changes ostensibly came about as a result of *gaiatsu* (pressure from outside), there was behind-the-scenes support for them from groups within Japan. For instance, discount stores supported the overturning of the Large-scale Retail Stores Law – and paid back the US for its support during the yen rise of the early 1990s when they increasingly stocked relatively cheap imports. Similarly, managers of corporate pension funds, which received comparatively low returns in Japan, were more than happy with the 1986 negotiations which opened the Japanese pension market to US securities firms (Katz, 1998). Japan's dependence on the US both for security and as a vitally important export market continued to make it particularly susceptible to US pressure for deregulation (Carlile and Tilton, 1998).

The end of the Cold War has also opened the possibilities for establishing overseas production and trade links with the former Communist bloc as well as expanding the global market. After President Clinton announced the end of the US boycott of Vietnam in February 1994, Japan began to invest heavily there (Preston, 2000). Japan has had limited transborder projects with Russia, since Japan set up a consular office in Khabarovsk. Generally, the expansion of the global consumer market following the adoption of market economies by formerly socialist countries, has expanded export opportunities for Japanese firms. However, this has not necessarily increased job opportunities within Japan. While the collapse of the Berlin Wall enabled an influx of cheap labour from East to West in Europe, Japan's restrictive immigration codes meant that Japanese companies had to go overseas in search of cheaper labour (Fukai, 1999). With the collapse of actually existing socialist regimes in Eastern Europe, Japanese firms are increasingly investing in the region. In Eastern Europe, they can enjoy the triple advantages of a highly skilled workforce, low wages and, since the mid-1990s association agreements with the EU, access to the EU markets. Certain countries in the East are particularly attractive because of 'sweetener' deals. For example, Poland exempts foreign firms from corporation tax for their first ten years in the country (JETRO, 2001). Although Japanese direct investment in Poland, the Czech Republic, Slovakia, and Hungary fell by two-thirds between FY1995 and 1996, it has again been climbing since 1997, and in 1999 FDI inflow into eight countries in Central and Eastern Europe rose 29.3 per cent from the previous year to a record US$16.9 billion (JETRO, 2001: 34).

The East Asian financial crisis

A third discontinuity which led to the increased globalization of Japanese production was the East Asian financial crisis of the late 1990s. The results of the changes in East Asia's policy towards foreign penetration, described above, have been striking. East Asia is host to more than 300,000 foreign companies (METI, 2001: 10) and has produced an increasing share of the world's manufactured goods. In 1963 East and South-east Asia produced 1.5 per cent of the world's manufactured goods, while in 1995 this had risen to 19.9 per cent (Dicken, 1998: 36). However the region's high dependence upon foreign investment made it particularly vulnerable to capital flight, and a speculative boom in the early 1990s was rapidly followed by speculator panic and capital flight. The depreciation of the Thai baht set off a contagion effect on the currencies of Malaysia, Indonesia, Philippines and then South Korea. In these five countries, net private inflows fell from US$93 billion in 1996 to an outflow of US$12.1 billion in 1997 (Radelet and Sachs, 1998: 65).

This had particularly important consequences for the Japanese economy. As East Asia's prosperity has grown, it has become advantageous for Japanese companies to be situated near their new major markets for consumer electronics. The Japanese government has developed a range of policy instruments to encourage firms to invest in the Asia-Pacific region, including low interest loans for overseas investors and foreign investment insurance (Hatch and Yamamura, 1996: 123). Before its collapse the Asian market accounted for nearly 45 per cent of Japan's exports (*Economist*, 1998, September 26: 17).

Japanese production became even more closely integrated with the region. In 1990, 42 per cent of machinery exports to Japan from the NICs (the Newly Industrialized Economies of South Korea, Hong Kong, Singapore and Taiwan) consisted of machine parts. This figure had increased to 57 per cent by 1998. The equivalent figures for exports from the ASEAN 4 the core members of the Association of Southeast Asian Nations: Malaysia, Thailand, Indonesia and the Philippines) went from 24 per cent to 58 per cent, while the share of machine parts in total Chinese machinery exports to Japan doubled from 32 per cent to 64 per cent.

As might be expected, the collapse of countries that were both major markets and major sites of investment for Japan had negative repercussions for the Japanese economy. Predicted growth for FY 1998 had been 1.9 per cent. There was actually negative growth in real GDP for five consecutve quarters, from the fourth quarter of 1997 onward, for the first time since the start of GDP statistics in 1955 (Mori, Shiratsuka and Taguchi, 2000). Initially, Japanese banks reacted by repatriating funds to pay for domestic debts. However, the damage to the Japanese economy gave Japanese companies extra stimulus to reduce production costs by locating overseas, and by FY 1999 overseas investment was higher than it had been before the crisis (see Table 4.1).

Investment in East Asia was facilitated by a raft of measures to further liberalize trade and inward investment. The Second Information APEC Economic Leaders' Meeting in Indonesia had ended with the production of the 1994 Bogor Declaration, which stated these countries' intention to reduce barriers to trade and investment. This was given extra impetus by the East Asian financial crisis of 1997, in reaction to which the countries

Table 4.1 FDI outflow from Japan by destination in US$ million (based on reports and notifications), 1997–9

	FY 1997	*FY 1998*	*FY 1999*
World	53,972	40,747	66,694
North America	21,389	10,943	24,770
US	20,769	10,316	22,296
Europe	11,204	14,010	25,804
EU	10,963	13,850	25,191
UK	4,118	9,780	11,718
Netherlands	3,295	2,118	10,361
Germany	732	553	649
France	1,736	521	1,127

Source: adapted from JETRO, 2001: 18.

of the region cut tariffs and reduced or removed a wide array of tariff and non-tariff barriers. Significantly, in the first three quarters of 1999, Japanese investment in China was 25 per cent more than in the same period the previous year, a much faster investment growth rate than its investment in other regions (*People's Daily* online, 1999).

The apparent benefits of overseas production have persuaded Western companies, too, of the benefits of investment in East Asia; and, particularly since the East Asian currency crisis, they have been quicker at undertaking mergers and acquisitions (M&As) than Japanese companies, who prefer to establish direct subsidiaries. Between 1990 and 1999 the proportion of direct investment in East Asia accounted for by Japanese capital fell from 26 per cent to 8 per cent. This means even more competition for Japanese companies, as competitors from other developed countries can also produce at lower costs.

The reciprocal effects of globalization on the Japanese national model of capitalism

As shown, Japan has played a significant role in stimulating the internationalization of manufacturing production. This has resulted in 'reciprocal dynamics' (Hasegawa and Hook, 1998): forces which have implications for the survival of the Japanese national model of capitalism. Three interrelated trends are particularly apparent: increased competition from other countries; the liberalization of the Japanese economy; and migration to and from Japan.

Increased competition for the Japanese model

Japan's economic engagement with the rest of Asia has been encouraged by economic rationalism and political pragmatism. Japanese desire to cut costs by producing overseas has been complemented by the desire of other Asian countries to encourage foreign direct investment and technology transfer. Through its engagement with the rest of Asia, Japan has been instrumental in creating industrial competitors.

Unlike Japan, East Asian governments chose to develop through taking steps to attract inward foreign investment, and they have been very successful in this goal (as Figure 4.1 shows). As the phrase 'flying geese' suggests, East Asian governments were keen that their countries should follow the development trajectory of the Japanese economy. Paradoxically, their copying of that model threatens to undermine the Japanese economy. In 1963 East and South-east Asia produced 1.5 per cent of the world's manufactured goods. In 1995 this had risen to 19.9 per cent (Dicken, 1998: 36). They also increased their share of total OECD exports from 5.7 per cent in 1979 to 8.8 per cent in 1993 (Dicken, 1998: 39), and, significantly, these exports were high-value-added manufacturing goods.

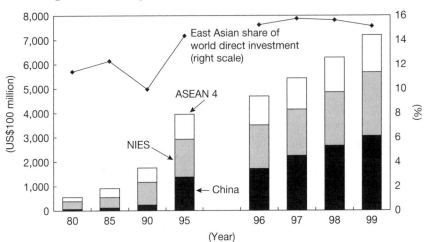

Figure 4.1 Trends in direct investment (stock) into East Asia and share of world
          direct investment: METI, 2001:10.

The technology transfer that results from the high-value-added FDI
needed to manufacture high-technology goods has enabled other Asian
countries to develop their own indigenous companies, so that Japanese companies come to face ever increasing global competition. For example, in the
1990s a number of Chinese companies which had originally been engaged
in technology transfer agreements with Japanese firms began to produce
colour televisions themselves. Their local production networks, price competitiveness and after-sales service meant that they quickly overtook the
Japanese companies. In the two years from 1996 to 1998 Japanese affiliate
companies went from being the top-ranking sellers of colour televisions to
not even being in the top four companies in terms of sales (METI, 2001).

As other industrialized countries have seen the benefits that result from
offshore production, they too have been attracted to investment in East
Asia, especially after the East Asian financial crisis reduced the cost of
undertaking mergers and acquisitions in the region, which sharply increased
between 1995 and 1999 (METI, 2001: 10).

Imports of manufactured goods from the emerging Asian economies
increased sharply in the first half of the 1990s and caused concern about
a possible 'hollowing out' of the entire Japanese manufacturing industry.
There were numerous closures of small businesses and cottage industries,
as well as a significant deterioration in the local industries in some areas.
This was because the distinctive character of *keiretsu* meant that, if the
'head' company in a vertical chain went overseas, the entire market of
the smaller supplier companies disappeared.

These developments in East Asia have had the effect of making Japanese
goods less and less competitive. The Global Competitiveness Report 1996
of the World Economic Forum ranked Japan as thirteenth in a comparison

of global competitiveness, shocking many in Japan, as for the previous ten years Japan had always been top-ranking (Kojima, 1996). This in turn provided further incentive for Japanese companies to produce at a lower cost overseas.

The international competitiveness of products manufactured in Japan has been further undermined by the marketization and growing dynamism of the Chinese economy. Japan's trade surplus with China of 700,000 million yen in 1986 changed to a negative trade balance of 2,223,200 yen in 1998 (Ministry of Finance, 1999). FDI-led investment in China has led to remarkable growth, both in absolute terms but also relative to the rest of East Asia. China's share of East Asian GDP rose from 25 to 37 per cent between 1980 and 1999, and it accounted for around 40 per cent of East Asian growth in the 1990s (METI, 2001: 11). By 1998 China's GDP was the seventh largest in the world, and over the last decade Chinese exports have quadrupled, so that by 1999 it was the world's ninth largest exporter (METI, 2001: 11). Japan supported China's early accession to the WTO (Ministry of Foreign Affairs, 2000), which took place on 10 November 2001.

Increasing production in China, with its lower wages and growing local markets, is also likely to prove irresistible, as communications technology continues to improve. In fact, in December 1999, Citizen watches, which has for some time been assembling the largest number of its watches in China but continuing to assemble high-value-added watches in Japan, announced that changes in the environment in China and better Internet and other communications made it possible to take advantage of lower costs and shift 100 per cent of production overseas. The economic liberalization and development policies of China pose a particular challenge. China is both far larger and rather more protectionist than other East Asian countries (though even here tariff rates have fallen sharply), and its rapidly developing manufacturing sector produces the same types of goods for export as the other countries in the region (see Figure 4.2).

The competitiveness of the Japanese national model of capitalism has been undermined not only by cheaper production in developing countries but also by more efficient production in developed economies. The distinctive mode of production which had assisted Japan's post-war production was gradually studied and adopted by some of Japan's industrial competitors. Schwartz writes: 'Just as production innovation in the US and Germany undercut the basis for British hegemony in the 1890s, innovation in Germany, and particularly Japan undercut US dominance in manufacturing and thus eroded US hegemony in the 1970s and 1980s' (Schwartz, 2000: 281). And the apparent success of Japanese management, as shown by high levels of productivity and apparently low levels of industrial strife resulted in much academic and popular interest in the possibilities of adopting key points from this model.

Ford Motor Company's alliance with Mazda enabled the former to increase its productivity to the levels of the latter. By 1992, General Motors

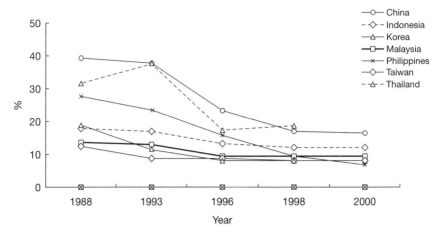

Figure 4.2 Trends in average tariff rates of East Asian countries as reported in APEC individual action plans, 1988–2000: METI, 2001: 19.

had established its 'Saturn' division, which used *kanban* and *kaizen* princi-ples (Schwartz, 2000). This process was not always unproblematic: Fucini and Fucini (1990) describe resistance to Japanese production techniques at the Mazda plant in Detroit, as does Graham's account of worker resis-tance at the Subaru-Isuzu Automotive plant in Indiana (Graham, 1994). Rinehart *et al.* (1994) also describe a level of resentment to *kaizen* in Canada. However, Mary Saso (1990) writes positively of the acceptance of Japanese management techniques among women in Ireland and Britain and Dedoussis and Littler (1994) write of the way techniques have been adapted in Australia. Hatch and Yamamura (1996) examine various case studies which suggest that it was somewhat easier to 'clone' Japanese practices in Asia, either because of cultural similarity or because East Asia and the US were at different stages of economic development. Nonetheless, Japan's competitive advantage was slowly disappearing, and by 1999, a heavily indebted Nissan was forced to seek financial assistance from Renault.

Liberalization of the Japanese economy

The Japanese state has attempted to regain its former competitiveness by introducing more liberal economic policies. It is important to set this in con-text. In recent decades the world has seen a massive expansion of free trade and deregulation, achieved through the General Agreement on Tariffs and Trade (GATT) and its successor, the World Trade Organization (WTO); regional trade agreements have been promoted in the form of the North American Free Trade Agreement (NAFTA), the European Union (EU) and the Asia-Pacific Economic Cooperation Forum (APEC), as well as bilateral negotiations on trade. Stephen Gill (2002) condemns the emergence of non-democratic and unaccountable global governance, and argues for the need to recognize the influence of neoliberal *ideology* in shaping state policy (see Chapter 2 for a fuller discussion of this). Ideology, Gill argues, is instrumental in states' decisions to adopt policies of deregulation, the liberalization of domestic markets and the privatization of state services and social services. All of these tendencies have been evident in Japan.

The Japanese state began to undertake neo-liberal administrative reform, beginning in the early 1980s. The second Blue Ribbon Commission of Administrative Reform submitted a series of recommendations in 1981, which were, according to Itoh (2000), overtly influenced by Thatcherism and Reaganomics. Following these recommendations, three nationalized industries, Japan National Railways (JNR), Nippon Telegraph and Telephone Public Corporation (NTT) and the Japan Tobacco and Salt Company were privatized in 1985. During the privatization process prominent trade unionists lost their jobs (Itoh, 2000).

The late 1980s saw a proliferation of the terms 'internationalization' (*kokusaika*) and 'globalization' (*gurobaruka*), which increasingly appeared in slogans of Japanese corporations, ministerial directives and governmental and quasi-governmental organizations (Sedgwick, 2001) and have now achieved popular currency in Japan (Menju, 1999).

Japanese companies and government policies have greatly facilitated the globalization of Japanese production and neo-liberal economic reform. Chapter 3 cited Gibson-Graham's (1996) analysis that globalization is presented as a gendered and natural phenomenon in political discourse, in a way that suggests nation states are powerless to resist its exigencies. In the discourse of political elites in Japan, globalization is often presented as an unstoppable outside force to which Japan has no option but to submit. Government Council Reports such as *Strategy for the Rebirth of the Japanese Economy* (26 February 1999) and *Plan for the Next Ten Years* (*Nikkei* 14 April 1999) argue in favour of domestic adjustment towards a neo-liberal economy to fit with changing global conditions (cited in Hook and Hasegawa, 2001).

Keidanren (Japan Federation of Economic Organizations) was established in 1946 as a nationwide business association, and its membership includes 1,007 leading corporations as well as 116 industry-wide groups representing, inter alia, manufacturing, trade, distribution, finance, and energy. Keidanren Chairman Takashi Imai and Vice Chairman Josei Itoh have written and campaigned extensively for neo-liberal reforms, presenting them as an inevitability in a globalized world. Imai wrote in January 2001:

> With globalization and network building accelerating ever faster, making an all-out effort jointly by the government, industry and the general population to implement economic structural reforms, and to build the foundations for sustainable growth are *the duty imposed upon us*.
>
> (Imai, 2001, my italics)

In 1995, the Japan Federation of Employers' Association (*Nikkeiren*) published an 'employment portfolio' recommending a shift towards new Japanese style of management. They argued that the workforce should be divided into three types of labour power: the core workforce, which would, as now, receive all the benefits of security of tenure and seniority wages but would be much reduced in size; specialists who would be hired for short-term contracts and paid according to merit rather than seniority; and a third group which should be used for numerical flexibility. This is in line with the current trends in economic globalization and its flexibilization of the workforce. As the next chapter shows, these changes have different implication for men and for women.

In 1997, in the wake of the East Asian financial crisis, the use of stock options as a form of payment was legalized. Dore (2000) attributes this measure to the desire to encourage directors of firms to identify with their shareholders, instead of prioritizing continued employment for all regular employees. Josei Itoh, Vice Chairman of Keidanren, wrote in a similar vein:

> Japan's prosperity, seen as a gloriously successful example of capitalism with socialist elements, was once the focus of international attention. Yet, as the rate of economic growth slowed, the nation's image began to lose its former splendour. . . . A firm commitment is also needed by Japanese corporations to undertake internal reforms. *With the globalization of the economy, management practices that place the priority solely on the expansion of one's own company are no longer in step with the times.* Companies must now earn the trust of their stockholders while creating new business operations, *increasing earnings by cutting costs and other means*'
>
> (Itoh, 1997, my italics)

The attempt to cut costs has included the downsizing of the regular workforce and an increase in the hiring of non-regular workers. The Japanese government has also passed a raft of legislation, including the liberalization of temporary employment agencies and the facilitating of part-time work, in an attempt to make the Japanese workforce more numerically flexible. While forced layoffs are still rare, even male regular workers can be strongly encouraged to accept redundancy, and, older male regular employees, because their seniority-related wages make them so expensive, are more vulnerable than younger regular workers. In December 2001 the unemployment rate in Japan peaked at 5.5 per cent, a 50-year record high (BBC, 26 April 2002).

In sum, in the context of a hegemonic neo-liberalism, Japan is moving away from its post-war model of capitalism which was characterized by support for banks and large firms, relative income equality and a guarantee of security for regular male workers.

Deregulation, though, has not so far had the effect of attracting much foreign business to Japan (although the exception of banking is discussed in Chapter 7). Wages in Japan are high. Furthermore, few Japanese, including business and political elites, are fluent in English (Lehmann, 2000), and Japanese is rarely taught as a second language overseas. Taken together, these factors mean that Japan is an unattractive environment for foreign direct investment. Japanese markets are unattractive to FDI, so if companies go abroad, it is unlikely that foreign firms will enter Japan to replace them. This supposition is amply borne out by the experience of the deregulation of the Tokyo Stock Exchange, which was followed by an actual drop in trading. Foreign firms and traders were discouraged by the high cost of doing business in Japan, including wages, rents, fees and corporate taxes, differences in accounting systems and other drawbacks such as lower living standards and the complexity of the Japanese language (Takenaka and Chida, 1998).

Japan has the lowest transnationality index[8] of any developed economy (UNCTAD World Investment Report, 2000). This lack of transnationality means that the leakage of jobs and investment from Japan has not been compensated for by an increase in jobs and investment from foreign companies in Japan. However, as Yashiro (1998) points out, even the minor presence of a foreign firm in a market can introduce new ways of working. The implications of this for women will be examined in Chapter 5.

Globalization and Japanese migration

A third impact of the globalization of Japanese production is the increase in inward and outward migration. Japanese immigration laws are strict and Japan still has the lowest proportion of foreign residents of any major industrialized country (Sellek, 2001). However, during the Bubble economy[9] boom, there was a surge of foreign, unskilled (and largely undocumented) workers entering Japan to solve Japan's labour shortage. To cope with this influx, the Japanese government amended the existing Immigration Control Act, and new regulations came into effect on 1 June 1990. Although the general prohibition of unskilled foreign workers remained, the government attempted to solve the problem of labour shortage by allowing *Nikkeijin* (South Americans of Japanese descent) and an increased number of foreign trainees to enter Japan. Despite the Japanese recession, the number of foreign residents with alien registration permits increased by 60.7 per cent between 1988 and 1998, in which year the numbers reached 1,512,116 (Sellek, 2001: 9).

The globalization of Japanese production has encouraged emigration as well as immigration. The export of Japanese production has necessitated the growth of Japanese business communities in cities as diverse as Beijing, Taipei, Seoul, Hong Kong, Bangkok, Singapore, Los Angeles, San Francisco, New York, London, Paris and Düsseldorf. These are often serviced by a community of more long-term residents who provide services such as the provision of Japanese food, schools and hairdressers. Of course, this makes life more comfortable for Japanese executives, students and other Japanese living outside Japan. When these short-term overseas residents return to Japan, they bring with them the ideas that they have encountered overseas: many young economists return to Japan with PhDs in economics and diffuse the neo-liberalism that they have learned in the US through their teaching; while the greatly increased number of business executives who go the States to study for MBAs cannot fail to be exposed to US conceptions of the firm and the economy (Itoh, 2000; Dore, 2000). However, the contacts between Japanese expatriates and short-stay residents can also prove a conduit for the transfer and sharing of deeper cultural values and a way of organizing cross-nationally. For example, the US Pan Asian American Chamber of Commerce presented a seminar on workplace diversity, inviting executives at Mitsubishi, Sony, Honda, Marubeni, Toyota and other companies (Pan Asian Chamber of Commerce, 1999). The well-publicized case of a culture of sexual harassment at Mitsubishi in the US also received much publicity in Japan and was used by feminist campaigners to some effect (see Nakayama, 1996).

While Japan is host to far fewer migrants than other advanced industrial economies, Japanese people are increasingly going overseas for educational or business purposes. The relative economic equality in Japan means these opportunities are not restricted to a small elite. This results in the development of a more cosmopolitan and reflexive Japanese population, who have been exposed to different models of work and gender relations.

Conclusion

Japanese post-war economic recovery was heavily aided by the US in the context of post-war politics. This resulted in the development of a very successful model of production, characterized by a dual labour market, where lifetime employment, yearly negotiated pay rises and continuous training was guaranteed to regular workers in large export-oriented firms. The same guarantees were not available to non-regular workers, nor were they available to the same extent, to workers in small and medium-sized enterprises. Initially, the state gave guidance to and facilitated the growth of enterprises in targeted sectors producing for export. The government pursued a policy of licensing foreign technology and controlling inward and outward flows of capital in order to protect infant industries and convert Japan into high-skilled, high-value-added economy.

Despite government attempts to control the flow of capital inside and outside Japan, trade with and aid to the rest of Asia have gradually escalated. Security considerations in the 1970s provided further encouragement to Japan to invest in the region, helping to stabilize it and ensure a continued supply of raw materials to Japanese industry. Furthermore,

Japan's economic success made FDI host countries receptive to the idea of learning from Japan. Japanese policy-makers have come under pressure from both inside and outside Japan to allow firms to produce overseas and to allow entry of foreign companies into the Japanese domestic market, and, as the yen has become stronger relative to the currency of other East Asian countries, it has become economically rational for Japanese firms to produce overseas. The collapse of Bretton Woods, the Plaza Accord and the East Asian financial crisis were key breaks which increased the momentum of this process. The end of the Cold War has also increased the possibilities of overseas production.

The strategy of overseas production undermined the success and stability of the Japanese model, however, by 'hollowing out' Japanese production. Goods came to be produced more cheaply elsewhere and undercut the prices of Japanese exports; at the same time, wages in Japan were not sufficiently high for workers to consume Japan's surplus in manufactured goods. Innovations in production, such as the 3Ks, have to some extent been copied by Japan's competitors.

The success of newly industrializing countries in developing high-value-added manufacturing industries and Japan's increased acceptance of the principles of free trade mean that there has been a flow of imports into Japan, and there has been very little inflow of FDI. New flows of jobs and finance, therefore, appear to be leaving Japan. Japanese industry has tried to counter this challenge by attempting to cut the costs of domestic production, by reducing labour costs and making the workforce more numerically flexible. In Japan, as elsewhere (see Chapter 3) elite discourse around globalization presents the phenomenon as an irresistible outside force, to which Japan has no choice but to submit, in order to continue to be competitive with the Anglo-American model of capitalism. Typically globalization is presented as requiring the Japanese model to adopt neo-liberal prescriptions of deregulation and a diversification of the labour force.

The effects of this for women will be examined in later chapters. As well as the apparent economic effects of the globalization of production, there has been some incremental socio-cultural change: Japanese managers and students today have more diverse experiences through work overseas, this leading to an exposure to different models of capitalism and different models of workplace social relations, including relations between men and women.

5 Women workers in the post-war model of capitalism in Japan

Continuity and change

Introduction

In order to show how the various facets of globalization are changing the position of working women in Japan, it is first necessary to understand what role women have played in the Japanese model of capitalism. This chapter therefore discusses the position of women in the Japanese labour force from the end of the Second World War, showing the patterns of continuity and change. This provides vital background for examining the impact of restructuring upon women's work in Japan. As Chapter 4 has demonstrated, many of the distinctive aspects of the Japanese national model of employment arose in the unique circumstances prevailing in the immediate post-war period. It was the specific context of the Cold War, the changes made to Japanese institutions by the Occupation forces, the development priorities of the Japanese state and the actions of the Japanese trade union movement that led to the emergence of the distinctive Japanese model of capitalism.

The position of women within that model has variously been attributed to the late impact of capitalist relations and the persistence of Confucian ideas in Japanese society, through the influence of the household, or *ie*, as the fundamental unit of domestic and economic organization (Clark, 1979; Stockman *et al.*, 1995; Tsukaguchi-Le Grand, 1999) or of continuity from rural patterns (Abegglen, 1958; Dore, 1973). This chapter will argue that the position of women in the Japanese model of national capitalism, far from being the continuation of consensual patterns of social organization with deep roots in ancient Japanese culture, was in fact a break with pre-war patterns, shaped by the interaction of Japanese post-war institutional arrangements and state regulation. To show that this is so, this chapter outlines the role that women played in Japanese industrialization before the Second World War. It then shows how the specific institutions of the Japanese national model of capitalism which arose in the post-war period, most notably lifetime employment enterprise unions and payment by seniority, interacted with political priorities, legal change and social expectations about women's reproductive work to create demand for a female secondary labour force. Institutions, though, do evolve. Social and demographic change, an increase in educational provision for Japanese girls and women,

women's activism and, in the context of globalization, the increased accep-tance of the ideology of equal labour rights have meant that the situation of women in the Japanese workforce has gradually altered. The chapter goes on to examine patterns of continuity and change in women's employment in post-war Japan, thus providing background information to examine the impact of restructuring upon women's employment in Japan.

The final section in this chapter introduces the changes globalization is causing to women's position in the labour force generally, thereby con-tributing to the feminist debate about the impact of globalization upon women by bringing insights from the case of Japan into the wider academic discourse.

Chapters 6 and 7 explore in more depth the particular implications that globalization is having for women in the regular and non-regular workforces in Japan.

Women's role in Japanese industrial development

It was observed in Chapter 3 that no country has successfully industrial-ized without a large-scale incorporation of women into the labour force. Japan is no exception. Japanese women have long been active in the labour force, albeit in subordinate positions, whether in domestic service, agri-culture or industry. The first phase of Japan's industrial development began towards the end of the nineteenth century. In this period, even in non-manufacturing sectors, it is apparent that there was nothing unusual about women entering the workforce.

The *ie*, or household, was the fundamental unit of economic organiza-tion of pre-industrial Japan. The household rather than the individual was the legal unit; everyone had to register as a member of a household; and all were subordinate to the male head of that household. Merchant houses recruited extra staff through the adoption of young men, and the master of the house assumed parental responsibility towards them. Although women in the merchant class followed different routes, they too might enter the household of another (Bacon, 1902, cited in Stockman *et al.*, 1995) to learn feminine skills, such as flower arranging and tea ceremony (which they could later teach), or as servants. However, whether they were servants or blood relatives of the head of household, in accordance with Confucian teachings, their position was formally and actually subordinate. Among the peasantry, it was the norm for women of all ages to work. In fact, since the 1930s more women than men have worked in the agricultural sector (Hunter, 1993). At the end of World War Two, the proportion of working women in the total population was arguably the highest of all developed nations, because of Japan's still heavily agricultural labour force (Iwao, 1993: 154).

The paid and unpaid labour of women was vital to Japan's successful industrialization. Samurai and government officials patriotically sent their own daughters to work in the first state-run silk factory at Tomioka, which opened in 1892, after rumours that the French specialists working there would suck the blood of employees deterred farming women from applying (Matsumoto, 1976). In pre-war Japan, women frequently worked in sales, domestic service, factory work and cottage industries. Uno (1993) has probed the lives of female pieceworkers, entrepreneurs, workers in family businesses and employers in the early twentieth century. In 1939, women over 25 were ordered to work in coal mines (Paulson, 1976) and from the early 1940s unmarried girls were drafted to work in factories. However, while industrialization accounted for a growing proportion of the female workforce, in 1950 more than 60 per cent of working women were still engaged in agriculture (Japan Institute for Workers' Evolution, 2001a: 1).

It is true that there were some state attempts to restrict and redefine the role of women. The definition of the ideal role of woman as *ryosai kenbo* (good wife, wise mother) emerged in Japan at the end of the nineteenth century, in tandem with the rise of modern Japanese nationalism, which sought to modernize the state and strengthen it against Western imperialism. The *kazoku kokka* (family-state) exalted the family as the foundation of the nation, and filial piety was seen as analogous to loyalty to the emperor. A woman's role was essentially home-based. She was to provide her husband with comfort, care for the old, raise loyal and patriotic subjects and manage the household (Uno, 1993). The 1880s and 1890s saw laws passed stifling the emerging women's suffrage movement and excluding girls from advanced education, such as the college preparatory course in which female students had been enrolling since the 1870s. The 1898 Civil Code placed nearly all women under the authority of a male head of household. Though a central part of official discourse, *ryosai kenbo* did not achieve hegemonic status as it demonstrably did not reflect the reality of the lives of Japan's factory workers and farm workers. The term fell out of use after 1945 because of its associations with imperialism, but the assumption of women's *tokusei* (special character) has continued to influence official policy.

Despite the long traditions of women working in Japan, in the years following the Second World War Japan was unique in the developed world in seeing a decline in the number of women working outside the home. The proportion of women of working age holding a job was 57 per cent in 1955, 51 per cent in 1965 and 46 per cent in 1975 (Woronoff, 1982: 138). The next section will describe why this participation rate fell, and how the nature of women's employment changed after the Second World War.

Women's employment and the Japanese national model of capitalism

The fall in female participation in the workforce

Figure 5.1 shows the fall in women's overall participation rate between 1955 and 1995. The decline in women's full-time employment can be

attributed to a range of institutional and social factors, all of which combined to limit the choices of most women to providing a temporary assistant
workforce before retiring to provide reproductive labour within the home.
This section will explain how Japan's changing international position, legal
change and lack of union protection led to an immediate and dramatic
fall in women's employment in the years immediately following the end
of the Second World War.

From 1945 onwards, Japanese women came under pressure to leave
the jobs they had occupied during the war. Most of the seven million
demobilized servicemen were unemployed (Brown, 1998: 131). The end
of the war had also resulted in the end of Japanese colonization of other
Asian countries. Many Japanese expatriates had returned from former
colonies. The government tried to secure jobs for these men. The 1947
Employment Security Law set up a network of public employment offices
and prohibited 'worker-dispatching' activities[1] in order to ensure the
employment security of workers. Between February 1944 and December
1945 the number of women employed (excluding those employed in agriculture) fell from 5.25 million to 2.31 million (Brown, 1998: 58).

SCAP's plan to democratize Japanese society included raising the status
of women. Article 14 of the new 1947 Japanese Constitution, which was
largely drawn up by SCAP, guaranteed women equal legal rights and freedom from discrimination in political, economic or social relations. The
Constitution also sought to dismantle the *ie* and to secure equal treatment
between the sexes in the household. However, SCAP did little to counter the
mass replacement of working women with demobilized soldiers, possibly
because in the US, women were coming under the same pressure to leave

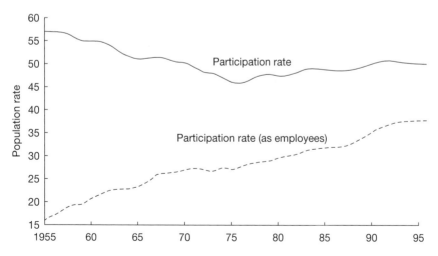

Figure 5.1 Women's participation in the labour force, 1955–95: Management and
Coordination Agency, 1999a.

their wartime occupations. Widows in particular complained that they were often rejected for jobs because they had children, and were therefore in receipt of family allowances (Ogawa, 1997). The assumption that women's earnings were of secondary importance to those of men led to more women than men being dismissed in the recessions of 1949–50 and 1952–3.

Another element of SCAP's 'democratization', the legalization of trade unions, did not advance, and sometimes retarded, the case of women wishing to remain in employment. After the deflation of the 1940s, and the Dodge Plan (see Chapter 4), union leaders agreed to the demands of management that unions should move from including all non-managerial employees to a membership limited to those whose job security was assured. The corollary of this is that as non-standard forms of employment have increased, the proportion of labour which is unionized has fallen: from around 33 per cent in the 1960s and 1970s to 22.4 per cent in 1998 (Rengo, 1999: 5). In some cases, trade unions even acted to reduce the level of women's employment. In 1966, Tokyu Kikan Kogyo (an engine manufacturer) changed its retirement age from 50 years for both men and women to 30 years of age for women only, a result of an agreement between management and an all-male delegation of labour representatives (Shiozawa and Hiroki, 1988).

Many women also lost their jobs because the legislation that was intended to protect them was either ineffective or counterproductive. The Labour Standards Law, imposed upon the Japanese government by the US Occupation Forces in 1947 (Roberts, 1994), institutionalized several provisions for the 'protection of motherhood', including: six weeks' maternity leave both before and after childbirth; the right to request leave for childcare, paid menstruation leave (*seiri kyuuka*, literally 'physiological leave'); restrictions on overtime; and a ban on night work. Carney and O'Kelly (1990) argue that this institutionalized the contingent and marginal character of women's work, noting that thousands of women workers in railway transport and similar occupations immediately lost their jobs when the Labour Standards Law came into effect. The rights were in effect difficult to exercise. Courts upheld a firm's right to refuse a bonus – which could be worth several months' salary – to employees who took menstrual leave.

Article Four of the Labour Standards Law also specified that men and women should receive equal pay for equal work. However, there was no obligation to treat women equally with regard to recruitment, hiring, promotion, fringe benefits and retirement (Asakura, 1998). Until 1966, the Ministry of Labour took the view that terminating a woman's employment upon marriage did not violate the Labour Standards Law.

State policy, lack of union protection, and legal change then led to a drastic fall in the proportion of women in the workforce. The next subsection describes how the emergence of a model of employment with high fixed costs and state development policy priorities, combined with social expectations about the role of mothers, gave women a position in the labour force which, though changing over time, remained largely marginal to that of men.

Women as peripheral labour force

Chapter 4 described the post-war capital-labour 'bargain', whereby union members in large firms, whether blue-collar or white-collar employees, would enjoy the benefits of lifetime employment and payments according to seniority, but that only 'regular' workers would qualify for union membership. These 'regular' workers included men and women, but as women customarily retired from their positions upon marriage or child-birth, the overwhelming majority of such workers were men. The 'classical Japanese model' of the firm as community, worker commitment and flex-ibility in exchange for employment security, the seniority-plus-merit (*nenko*) principle in pay and promotion and enterprise unionism (Kato and Steven, 1993) only ever pertained to a minority of workers, though. Large corpo-rations were able to afford these benefits for their workers, by externalizing risk, and requiring firms further down the *keiretsu* subcontracting chain to provide flexible pricing and production. A higher proportion of women than men were employed within these small and medium-sized companies. Women were and are also more likely to work in those other groups of non-regular workers excluded from the Japanese employment system, such as contract workers, temporary workers, family workers, part-timers, agro-industrial workers and homeworkers.

Women were not only more likely to find themselves in the peripheral labour force but to have a peripheral position in the core labour force. The whole system of payment by seniority, described earlier, was depen-dent upon the 'early retirement' of female employees. Even within large companies, supposedly permanent women workers would usually retire upon marriage or the birth of their first child. In fact without women's short tenure and confinement to lower level positions, it would not have been possible for men to rise upwards through the company and take on more responsibility as the *nenko* system required. Some firms even specified retirement upon marriage in female employees' job contracts (Kawashima, 1995). Rohlen (1988) shows how the number of women employed in manufacturing fell rapidly in the first two years following the 1973 oil crisis and how 'natural' wastage, as women left at the time of marriage, made possible the continuation of permanent employment poli-cies for company 'core' workers even in times of recession. Other strategies employed by companies in the 1970s included laying off (predominantly female) part-time workers and suggesting that because of the special economic circumstances, women give up work even before they married or had children. Approximately 700,000–800,000 women left the labour force between 1974 and 1975 (Fox, 1999: 2).

The reciprocal social effects of women's role in the Japanese national model of capitalism

Labour markets operate at the intersection of the productive and reproductive economies[2] (Elson, 1999). In the post-war period in Japan, the relationship between the productive and reproductive economies changed. Part of Japan's 'normative social order' (Ikenberry, 1988: 226) has long been the expectation that children will care for their elderly parents. In the 'ideal' *ie*, the eldest son would take his elderly parents into his home, where they would be cared for by his wife.[3] In a family which had no sons, the eldest daughter's husband would be formally adopted as a son (Martin and Tsuya, 1991). Urbanization and industrialization during Japan's economic miracle were accompanied by moves towards a nuclear family structure (although the proportion of three-generation households in Japan still exceeds the proportion in other First World countries). This meant that for many middle-class women there was less help with childcare and housekeeping from relatives.

Chapter 4 explained that although the US supported the rebuilding of Japanese manufacturing industry, between 1955 and 1970 there was no increase in social and welfare spending, therefore women's caring work in the family took the place of social welfare (Fujita, 1987). The rapid rise in men's incomes also meant that it became economically possible for a family to manage on the wages of a sole breadwinner. As the chances of finding outside childcare decreased, there was a concomitant social pressure for mothers not to work outside the home while their children were young. Working mothers became the focus of popular debate in the late 1950s, when the women's magazine *Fujin Koron* (*Women's Opinion*) launched a discussion on whether women had the right to pursue a career other than that of wife and mother: the magazine's readership generally sided with arguments for the priority of motherhood (Buckley, 1993). A 1963 White Paper on child welfare claimed that 'a deficiency in the level of nurturing is creating a risk for the children of this generation' and linked 'the decline in child welfare' and 'women's increased penetration of the workforce' (Buckley, 1994: 155). Cases of death due to improper care or staff shortages in public day care centres also made the headlines (Knipe Mouer, 1976).

This moral panic succeeded in stimulating guilt in at least two of the women who answered questionnaires in the author's 1996/1997 pilot survey. A 60-year-old woman answered a question about whether she had faced any problems on returning to work after having children by writing: 'My children became what is called "door key" children (*kaggiko*), because there was no-one who could take care of them after school.' A 39-year-old employee of a multinational corporation responded to a questionnaire about problems experienced when returning to work after having children:

> In the beginning it was only four hours a week, so there was no difficulty with the children. The only one difficulty was during the weekend,

there is no . . . it is not certain that I will be able to get days off in the weekend, so the children are here alone and I have to work outside, and the children get a little bit embarrassed about the situation.

Japanese society is often described as being characterized by 'educational credentialism' (*gakureki shugi*) (Choy, 1999). Exam success determines which schools, universities and later, companies, men, at least, can enter. This puts pressure on parents, and on mothers in particular, to devote much time and energy to providing assistance to their children. Mothers are considered to be almost wholly responsible for ensuring that their children succeed at school (Imamura, 1993). Mothers commonly help children with their schoolwork. They may spend time watching educational TV programmes; attend school or local government sponsored classes for educating mothers, or they may undergo instruction from their child's class teacher in the topics that the child is studying (Lebra, 1984). There is now rather widespread and high-quality childcare provision in Japan, with subsidized preschools serving 40 per cent of three-year-olds and 90 per cent of four- and five-year-olds. Evidence suggests though that the expectation, established in the few decades after the Second World War, that mothers of young children will have a full-time role in the reproductive economy means that the raison d'être of these institutions is more to socialize children than to relieve mothers. Nursery and primary schools place significant burdens on mothers' time. Working or not, mothers may be expected to attend regular parent-teacher meetings, provide highly elaborate *o-bento* (lunchboxes) according to school recommendations and arrange for children to follow specific timetables, even during the vacations (Allison, 1996).

As the organization of work and the demands made of workers become institutionalized, they affect what happens and:

> in a more general way, the attitudes and principles and patterns of social relations found in the workplace are likely to have a certain congruence with those shown in other social spheres, simply because of the tendency towards consistency in individual personalities and sets of values.
>
> (Dore, 1973: 280)

From 1969 to 1989 homemaking courses in schools were compulsory for girls. After this date, and after much vigorous campaigning from the Women's Action Group and the Association for the Promotion of the Study of Homemaking by Both Sexes, homemaking courses became a requirement for boys too. It has been noted by several commentators that Japanese parents' educational aspirations for their sons tend to be rather higher than for their daughters. Brinton (1993) attributes this to parents choosing to invest more in sons' education as, in keeping with the tradition

of the three-generation household, they may expect financial help from
sons in later life and are also aware of the discrimination women face in
the labour market, so they consider money spent on a four-year university
education to be wasted. As recently as 1994, only 40 per cent of women
in tertiary education were attending four-year universities, compared to 96
per cent of men entering tertiary education. Most of the remainder entered
two-year junior colleges. (Fujimura-Fanselow and Kameda, 1994: 46).
Women anxious to have a career might of course make a rational decision to curtail the length of time they spend in higher education. As the
expected tenure of women workers was so short, companies often did not
hire female four-year university graduates, who, they expected would stay
in the workforce for an even shorter period of time than their junior college
peers. Brinton cited the comments of a mother, in the 1980s, who was
keen for her daughter to go to a university:

> Now my daughter is debating whether to go to junior college or univer-
> sity education. She says that getting a university education will be a
> handicap [. . .] when she looks for a job; it's true that the situation
> for women university graduates is very bad and close to 100 per cent
> of junior college graduates can get jobs. But even so, I think she should
> go ahead and go to university. It's a hard situation and it's hard for
> me to give advice to my daughter.
>
> (Brinton, 1989: 552)

However, as graduation from a four-year university is the usual requirement
for a management position with a large company, the different educational
paths typically followed by young men and women in Japan has had an
impact of the effectiveness of equal opportunities legislation.[4]

The previous paragraphs describe how the social expectation that
women should carry out all reproductive work has been, and continues
to be, a factor in women's exit from the labour market. However, even
this may to some extent be institutionally determined. In the case of
Japan, it is evident that the long hours worked by Japanese company men
mean that they are unlikely to share housework or to service themselves
regarding the cleaning of clothes and provision of meals, nor to play a
major role in childrearing.

In summary, legal change and the political conditions at the end of the
Second World War led to an exodus of women from the workforce, and
state policy and the organization of work combined with expectations of
women's role in providing reproductive labour meant that most female
regular workers provided a temporary, peripheral labour force. These
expectations became institutionalized and reflected in the education system
and other social institutions. As a result of social expectations, their
husbands' long working hours, and the move to a nuclear family, most
Japanese women in most of the post-war period have had little alternative

but to leave work while their children are young. The next section will examine the nature of women's employment, and the extent to which it has changed or remained constant during the post-war period.

Women's work in post-war Japan: continuity and change

The gendered nature of work

The jobs that men and women do reflect the positions of men and women in society generally. Particularly, the work that women typically carry out in the reproductive economy has been reflected in the tasks assigned them in paid employment. In white-collar jobs in the years following the Second World War, it was common practice for male employees to expect female workers to serve tea, clean the offices and even polish their shoes. These menial tasks have, increasingly, become a focus of resentment among some female employees. Serving tea, in particular, seems to have attained a certain symbolic importance. In a 1984 article Susan Pharr describes the prolonged resistance to tea pouring among female employees of Kyoto city government as an example of 'status conflict' in Japan. Although it is highly unlikely that today a female office worker would be expected to clean her male co-workers' shoes, it appears that carrying out gendered tasks is still an integral part of the positions filled by women employees. Although no questions were specifically asked about this, many survey participants spontaneously mentioned such tasks among their dislikes. For example, a 25-year-old medical clerical worker wrote:

> My position as a medical clerical worker is lower than that of a pharmacist and I have to do chore work like cleaning the office. [My duties include] Calculation, computer operation, remuneration of medical charges, work in the office (including serving tea, cleaning the office, taking care of the office plants).

An employee of a non-profit making organization said: 'They treat me as a girl. They think serving tea is a woman's job.'

Female office workers were commonly referred to as 'office flowers' (*shokuba no hana*),[5] with the strong implication that their presence was decorative, and short term. This has been reflected in recruitment practice. For example, in February 1983, newspapers reported that the labour union at Kinokuniya bookstore was protesting against a memo sent to branches and sales offices throughout Japan, which advised against the employment of full-time women workers who were 'Ugly, short, unsophisticated, or wear glasses' (Shiozawa and Hiroki, 1988: 26).

Chapter 3 cited Feldman's observation that some women strategically employ social norms to maintain their employment (Feldman, 2001).

Women in Japan also, in certain circumstances, use the discourse of femininity and gendered work to justify their employment in certain high-status careers. Writing in the 1970s, Dilatush (1976) noted the relatively high proportion of female professionals, compared to women in management (see also Shinotsuka 1994). Saso (1990) also notes that some women have been successful in rising in the professions or the civil service. However, she convincingly attributes this to the relative gender-blindness of these areas of employment, which rely upon competitive examination for entry. Success in competitive examinations can be one way for women to establish a paid career: Shinotsuka (1994) notes that a greater proportion of women (13.8 per cent) than men (11.3 per cent) work as specialists (*senmonka*),[6] and anecdotal evidence suggests that this a route being purposefully chosen by an increasing number of women (see Chapter 6). Nonetheless, women's professional success in these areas has often been attributed, in public discourse, to stereotypically female qualities.[7] Even in the area of dentistry, which does not have immediate nurturing associations, a female dentist, close to retirement age, told me:

> If you're a woman you can talk to children more easily. I can say, 'There, there. It's okay.' I feel that the nature of women – to be gentle and caring. That sort of thing is very suitable for my job. So concerning the occupation I feel that I am happy because I am a woman and I feel happy in my job because I am a woman. In my ordinary life occasionally, well often actually, I have had the feeling that I would like to be a man, but as far as my occupation is concerned I have never had that feeling and I am happy to be a woman.

Women's tenure in the regular workforce

Although a series of court judgements from 1966 onwards formally outlawed the practice of companies requiring women to retire at marriage, social expectations and the culture of the workplace informally continued to lead women to leave work upon marriage or pregnancy. Women's jobs outside the home were referred to as an *koshikake* (temporary seat), where women could observe social life (*shakai kengaku*), before retiring upon marriage (*kekkon taishoku*) taking up lifetime employment (*eikyuu shuushoku*) in the home (Woronoff, 1982; Iwao, 1993). A trading company employee told me of the practice of one large firm that would only take on women who lived with their parents. Parents were expected to attend the firm's welcome ceremony for new employees and told it was their responsibility to ensure that their daughters retired at marriage.

As women were expected to retire, they did not receive the same high-quality on-the-job training as their male co-workers. Even now women's training is often limited to instruction in how to properly greet customers and speak to colleagues. A 27-year-old insurance clerk, who responded to the author's 1996–7 survey, when asked if there was any difference in the training she and her male co-workers received, answered: 'Yes, male staff [. . .] have training for two months at head office just after being taken on, but female staff [. . .] have no training and are posted to general clerk [work].'

Many companies took on board assumptions that women are essentially short-term workers, unlikely to have, or to be interested in acquiring, skills useful to the company. It is interesting to read the recruitment literature of some of the larger Japanese corporations that stress the opportunities for female employees to acquire what might be described as human capital for the marriage market. Brother, for example, in the late 1980s, emphasized the opportunity to learn tea ceremony at the company dormitory and claimed that learning bookkeeping at the company would be useful because it would help women learn how to do household accounts. The ideal path for a female employee was shown in cartoon form: at eighteen she enters the company; at nineteen she prepares for marriage by undergoing bridal training, taking company-provided classes in cooking, sewing, knitting and becoming *onnarrashii* (feminine or womanly); at twenty she dates, and by twenty-one is at the altar in a wedding dress, quitting the company and using her savings to set up home (Lo, 1990). This indicates something of a mismatch between the expectations of companies and those of their female employees: the average age of marriage for women today is 26.8 years. In 1990 at the time Lo was writing, it was around 25.8 years (Ministry of Public Management, Home Affairs, Posts and Telecommunications (2004)).

Despite the assumptions of companies, women's tenure in the regular workforce has lengthened. The average number of years women worked continuously in 1960 was four years while men worked, on average, for eight years. The average number of years women worked had come to exceed six years by 1980 Ministry of Public Management Home Affairs, Posts and Telecommunications (2004). As Table 5.1 shows, this has now increased to nearly nine years. This can be attributed to increased longevity, a declining fertility rate, an increase in housing and education costs, the return of 'baby boom' wives to the labour market and changing social attitudes about women's place in society (Whittaker, 1990).

Of course, doing monotonous work, with little chance of advancement, hardly encouraged women to stay on at work, but if they did, the system of payment by seniority could mean that long-serving female employees were paid more than the limited jobs they were given merited. Some companies had different formal retirement ages for men and women:

> [X company] had a rule for women to quit the job by 25, regardless of whether they were married or not. So I quit when I was 25. Well, you could continue to work for the company, but the working conditions and payment would not be the same level.
>
> (Home-based kimono-wearing teacher, in her
> fifties, describing her earlier career)

Table 5.1 The average age of male and female regular employees and average years of service, 1980–2001

Year	Men		Women	
	Average age	*Average years of service*	*Average age*	*Average years of service*
1980	37.8	10.8	34.8	6.1
1985	38.6	11.9	35.4	6.8
1990	39.5	12.5	35.7	7.3
1995	40.1	12.9	36.5	7.9
1999	40.6	13.2	37.6	8.5
2000	40.8	13.3	37.6	8.8
2001	40.9	13.6	37.7	8.9

Source: adapted from Ministry of Public Management, Home Affairs, Posts and Tele-communications, 2004.

Even when there was no official policy, tacit pressure meant many older questionnaire respondents had felt under psychological pressure to leave. A 49-year-old clerical worker commented:

> In my case, when I was pregnant, as I did not have a job-related skill, *I had no choice but to retire, because around me no women took maternity leave.* But later I often regretted that. I shouldn't have retired from a responsible job. So if my daughter-in-law hopes to work all her life, I'll help her.

Even in the 1980s and 1990s when women stayed in the workforce longer than their employers had envisaged, subtle and not-so-subtle pressure could be brought to bear.[9] Ms Shirafuji, whose sex discrimination lawsuit against her employer, Sumitomo Electric, continued from 1995 to 2004, described how at every year-end party her boss would ask the women what their plans were for the next year, implying that there was no expectation that they would stay with the firm. Another employee of a large trading company claimed that on returning to work after giving birth she was segregated from other office workers, placed at a desk by the window sitting alone behind her boss and given no work to do for six years (*sic*). This case also offered an interesting example of infrapolitical resistance. The woman continued to go to work, where she kept herself busy reading the company handbook and watering the plants. She received tacit support for her persistence from one male co-worker who gave her chocolates on Valentine's Day. This was not a romantic gesture: it is normal practice in Japanese offices for women to give *girichoko* (obligation chocolates) to male co-workers they respect.

Subtle pressure can be brought to bear even on single employees who continue to work. A 27-year-old employee of a multinational company, when asked whether her marital status affected the way she was viewed at work, answered, 'When they ask me "You aren't married yet. How old are you?", it feels unpleasant.'

As Table 5.1 indicates, women are willing to spend longer periods of time in the labour market. However it is very difficult to re-enter a large company after a career break, as the reactions of companies to women with longer than average tenure (described above) might suggest. Even women who were successful in finding a job in a new company would not be able to transfer any eligibility for seniority pay. One of the major changes in women's position in the Japanese labour market since the Second World War has been women's increasing participation in the type of non-regular work know as *paato* (*paato taimu*, from the English 'part-time'), which has grown in response to contradictions of the position of women in the Japanese national model of capitalism.

The rise in paato work

Part-time work has increased in many industrialized countries in recent decades (as Figure 5.2 shows). Furthermore part-time work cross-nationally tends to share the following characteristics: it is primarily performed by women; it is associated with marginal employment; its expansion has coincided with a period of economic restructuring; and its increase has coincided with an increase in the number of women in the labour market (Fagan and O'Reilly, 1998). This might suggest that the Japanese model has been converging with other economies at similar levels of development. However, the increase in part-time work varies between countries with even quite similar industrial structures. Wakisaka and Bae (1998) have observed that despite both being 'Asian cultures' and developmental states, the level of part-time employment, compared to full-time employment is far higher in Japan than in South Korea. This they attribute partly to the different tax regimes in the two countries, which give Japanese women, but not South Koreans, a reason to limit their working hours. This section will trace the development of the *paato* workforce in Japan, showing how state policy was instrumental in the development of a largely female part-time workforce.

Large firms in Japan began to make regular use of part-time workers in 1954, when Daimaru Department Store in Tokyo took on 250 part-time workers plus 600 high-school graduates, to enable the store to stay open until 8.00 pm. Suzuki Kensuke Daimaru's General Manager introduced the system after being impressed with its use in the United States, where it enabled businesses to cope with fluctuations in demand. This would of course be a very significant advantage to firms in Japan, with a numerically inflexible workforce.

Over the next several decades, the desire to cut wage costs and to increase the numerical flexibility of the workforce, combined with social change, promoted the growth of a female *paato* workforce. The number of female part-timers more than quadrupled between 1970 and 1984 (Hunter, 1993: 479). By 1965, nearly 70 per cent of women who completed

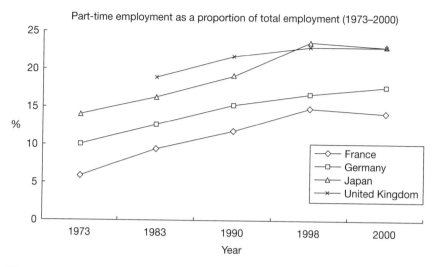

Figure 5.2 Part-time employment as a proportion of total employment, 1973–2000:
1973–1990 data adapted from Lemaitre *et al.*, 1997: 141 and 1998–2000
from OECD, 2002b: 319.

junior high went on to senior high school. This meant that there were far fewer young women available to carry out factory work, and firms were forced to turn to older married part-timers. By 1970, 51 per cent of married women were working (Iwao, 1993). One particular stimulus was the Japanese Archipelago Reformation Plan of 1970, under the auspices of which companies were given incentives to locate factories in rural areas. Most factories at the time were clustered around urban areas and the resulting pollution was a matter of public concern (McCormack, 1996). Around the same time, under the Rice Acreage Reduction Policy, rice production was being cut back, which meant that many farming women were looking for work to supplement the family income. The increasing mechanization of agriculture also freed rural women for part-time work (Shiozawa and Hiroki, 1988).

It is important to explain that regular and *paato* work are not necessarily distinguished by a difference in job content or hours worked but rather in the rewards that accrue to the workers. Indeed, the Ministry of Labour's 1990 Comprehensive Survey of the Condition of Part Time Workers actually defined the main criterion for inclusion in the survey as being 'treated as so-called part-timers' rather than as regular employees. The term *paato taimu* seems in practice to mean therefore that such employees do not receive the same fringe benefits as regular employees. Part-timers receive few seniority raises and are unlikely to receive bonuses. As the bonuses of full-time employees are usually equivalent to several months' salary, this is a very significant difference. Many part-timers work long hours: in 1993 there were 5.65 million workers who were defined by their workplaces as *paato*, but who worked more than 35 hours per week. (Wakisaka, 1997: 144). Employing *paato* workers is therefore a very efficient means for companies to defray the high fixed costs of the regular workforce.

As well as being economically beneficial to employers, *paato* work has also provided employment for women, who have been spending less time childrearing as birth rates have fallen (see Chapter 1, note 3), and who, as seen in the previous section, seem increasingly ready to spend more time in the labour force. Where it is genuinely part-time, *paato* work can fit in with the expectations of women's reproductive work described earlier in this chapter. Part-time work may act as a 'bridge to reconcile private care work and public waged work' (Fagan and O'Reilly, 1998: 23) and might in some cases help to further transform the 'gender contract', as maternal employment becomes normalized. However, Imada (1997) suggests that the increase in part-time work may have retarded change and to have institutionalized women's 'dual burden' of productive and reproductive work. If it is customary for wives to work part-time, this means there is less incentive for men to take equal responsibility for the care of children, the elderly and housework. A married part-time worker with adult children told me:

> When I returned to work I didn't like to see my husband's frowning face, but he has changed now. He is okay now, if I don't do too much – if I'm not excessive . . . [W]hen I'm very busy and I don't cook good food for him, he weeps. He acts. Usually he doesn't speak a lot. He is a quiet, very kind person, but one day, he made me a whiskey. He offered me a whiskey. He said, 'Why don't you drink a glass of whiskey?' I thought something had happened, something serious had happened. And he said, 'Do you have any complaints?' I said, 'No' and I asked why, and he said, 'You have been ignoring the house-work recently.' So he thought I had some complaint about him, or home. But it wasn't true: I didn't have any complaints.

State policy and consequent legislation has been instrumental in the growth of the female *paato* labour force. In 1963, the Economic Council of the Prime Minister's Office proposed 'extensive use of young, unmarried female workers in simple jobs', 'only a small number of educated women in supervisory positions', women returning to their families at 'a suitable age for marriage' and the rehiring of 'persons of middle age' (Lebra, 1976b: 110). However, in 1972, the Economic Deliberation Council argued that women's abilities had been insufficiently developed and recommended that women's labour be more effectively utilized by making part-time workers a permanent feature of the workforce, rather than regarding them as temporary workers (Shiozawa and Hiroki, 1988).

The tax and benefits system in Japan has offered married women few incentives to work full-time. The 1949 Sharp Report recommended that a new tax system should be devised centred on the individual rather than the *ie*. A new tax system based on the individual came into effect the following year. Tax was based upon the individual but deductions were permitted for dependants, with deductions of equal value for both spouses and dependants. In 1961, an effort was made to recognize the contribution of women's work within the home (*naiyo no ko*) and to distinguish spouses from children by the introduction of the 'Deduction for Spouses'. (State payments to mothers had in fact been a major demand of almost all leading feminists in the Taisho era, 1911–25, (Molony, 1999).) However, once a wife's income exceeded a certain amount this deduction was lost. (This was changed to the benefit being phased out gradually as income rose, following complaints from companies that their workforce were trying to cut back their hours, just at the busiest time of year, (Higuchi, 1997).)

The system was changed again in 1987. Since 1975 the difference between the allowance for spouses and the allowance for child dependants had been eliminated. In the wake of a backlash to a recently introduced and very unpopular consumption tax, the state introduced what was, in effect, a subsidy to male-breadwinner couples. From 1987, if a woman earned less than 700,000 yen, then her husband not only received the 350,000 yen Deduction for Spouses, but a further 350,000 yen in recognition of the woman's *naiyo no ko*: in effect, wages for housework, but paid to the husband. If a second earner in a couple earned more than 1.3 million yen annually, then valuable tax breaks were lost, and the primary earner might also lose their entitlement to company family allowances. (The average household income in 2000 was 6,731,448 yen (Ministry of Public Management, Home Affairs, Posts and Telecommunications, 2001).) These restrictions have a strong disincentive effect upon women seeking to further their careers: there is in fact a negative correlation among recipients of benefit between the wages of husband and wife. According to the Japan Institute for Workers' Evolution (2001: 2): 'More than 30 per cent of part-time housewife workers adjust their income to match what is allowable by Japanese law and not to exceed their husbands' monthly spouse allowance.'

This was reflected in responses from focus group and survey participants. One respondent made it clear that this had affected her work choices, stating:

> There is a tax regulation. If I earn top one million yen, my husband can get tax relief for his wife and children. If my income exceeds one million yen, the tax relief . . . he can't get tax relief, so I have to work less than 120 hours a month.
>
> (57-year-old employee of large corporation)

Sometimes this encouragement can be even more overt. According to one participant who took part in a discussion the author organized with the English Discussion Society:[10]

I am working as a part-timer. I pay tax, but [. . .] the clerk at the tax office said a few years ago, you should . . . you work too hard . . . too much. If you work this much, you have . . . you don't have to pay this tax, something like that. If I cared about such a small thing, quite small, I can't work, so I don't care [about] that kind of thing. But I pay. I mean the pension, I pay the health insurance by myself, so the city tax . . . so I know how much [. . .] disadvantage I have. And [. . .] I have no bonus.

(Comment made in group interview with
English Discussion Society, 1999)

In 1986 the Pension Fund Law was revised. Changes made it possible for non-working women to claim retirement benefits, although they had not paid towards a state retirement plan, even if their husbands had not paid a supplementary premium. Widows were also entitled to 75 per cent of their husbands' pensions. A working woman who paid social security benefits, on the other hand, would receive retirement benefits in her own right, but after her husband's death, she would have to choose between this benefit and her husband's. She would therefore either forsake Bereaved Family Benefit or the benefits for which she has made contributions.

Other benefits also strengthened preferential treatment for married couples where the woman did not work full-time (Higuchi, 1997). If a woman works less than 75 per cent of a normal working week or earns less than 1.3 million yen per annum, she does not have to pay health insurance or social security payments, and is treated as a dependent of her husband (or father).

This system is particularly likely to deter educated women from continuing full-time participation in the labour force. Disparity in educational attainment between a couple is rare in Japan, so a highly educated high-earning husband is likely to have a better paid job, which would give the couple sufficient resources to survive on only one full-time income. Among couples claiming spousal deductions there is, in fact, a negative correlation between the earnings of husbands and wives (Higuchi, 1997: 114). The system also disproportionately subsidizes higher income couples, as women in manual occupations are relatively keen to continue to work full-time after marriage or childbirth (Roberts, 1994).

There has then been change in the position of women in the Japanese national model of capitalism. Women's tenure in the regular workforce has lengthened, but it is still usual for women to leave regular employment upon pregnancy. Although women still tend to be assigned stereotypically 'feminine' roles in the workplace, reflecting their presumed reproductive work, an increasing proportion of women are finding work as 'specialists' or professionals. With the fall in Japan's birth rate, although assumptions of women's responsibility for almost all reproductive work persist, mothers spend a smaller proportion of their lives childrearing. Their availability for employment is articulated with employers' demands for a flexible and relatively inexpensive workforce, and state tax and pensions regulations to encourage the growth of a female non-regular workforce.

The reciprocal effects of globalization on women workers in Japan

The previous chapter listed some of the effects of globalization upon the Japanese national model of capitalism. As men and women have had very different roles in that national model, changes to that model, brought about by globalization, will impact upon them in different ways. This section will briefly outline some of the gendered impacts of globalization upon Japanese working women generally, before Chapters 6 and 7 go on to discuss in detail the way globalization impacts upon Japanese women in the regular and non-regular workforces respectively.[11]

Liberalization and deregulation

It was observed in Chapter 4 that leading business organizations have recommended a shift towards the increased employment of non-regular workers. This shift has been facilitated by legal change, including the liberalization of temporary employment agencies, and the facilitating of part-time work in an attempt to make the Japanese workforce more numerically flexible. As much of the increased employment of women has been in non-regular employment, this suggests employment opportunities for women will increase. However, as has been discussed above, non-regular workers tend to have different conditions of work to those traditionally experienced by male regular workers. The cutting of tax rates and the reduction in welfare spending, referred to in the previous chapter, are also likely to have implications for women's reproductive work, and consequently their capacity to enter paid employment. These changes will be discussed in more detail in Chapter 6.

Another effect of deregulation and liberalization is that it has eased the entry of foreign firms into the Japanese marketplace. The entry of foreign firms into the Japanese market appears to provide more attractive opportunities for high-achieving women who intend to continue working than is generally the case with Japanese firms. About 60 per cent of third-year university students of both sexes express an interest in working for foreign companies and their affiliates in Japan, commonly believing that they offer chances for employees to improve their skills and to reach their full potential (Economic Planning Agency, 1999). While the transnationality index in Japan is lower that that of any other developed economy (see Chapter 4), even the minor presence of a foreign firm in a market can be influential in introducing changes in the organization of work (Yashiro, 1998). There can, however, be a gap between the image and the reality of working for a foreign firm. This will be discussed in the next chapter.

Re-regulation

It has been observed (see Chapter 3) that globalization can weaken local patriarchal structures by exposing traditional practices to global scrutiny and increasing reflexivity. Japan's economic success had stimulated outside interest in the Japanese organization of production, and thereby raised awareness of the role of women within this (Kawashima, 1995). There is widespread agreement in academic circles that Japan's 1986 Equal Employment Opportunities Law was passed partly in response to foreign criticism of the position of Japanese working women (Gelb, 1998). The next chapter will examine in more detail the role of the processes of globalization in the promulgation of the Equal Employment Opportunities Law (EEOL) in 1986, and its revision in 1997 and its crucial role in reshaping women's employment.

Dominant ideologies can lead a state and existing institutions to negotiate a compromise between encouraging change and maintaining current gender orders (Pyle, 1990; Arat, 2002). The EEOL was vigorously opposed by important sections of the business community. While business elites have been keen for Japan to adopt some of the deregulatory measures characteristic of Anglo-American capitalism, they have not reacted with the same enthusiasm to attempts to bring Japanese laws surrounding sexual equality in the workforce into line with those elsewhere in the First World. The way the EEOL has been framed and interpreted have made it of limited practical applicability to most non-regular women workers and to regular women workers carrying out different roles from men, as Chapter 6 will show. In fact, equal employment legislation has actually contributed to the institutionalization of a gendered dual labour market.

Women and migration

One of the processes associated with globalization is increased transnational flows of people, and the previous chapters remarked upon the increased flow of people into and out of Japan. Two special features of the gendered nature of migration into Japan should be noted here. The location of production overseas had implications. As economic links between Japan and other East Asian states grew, and Japanese FDI in these areas increased, there was a corresponding upsurge in Japanese men's sex tours to South Korea, Taiwan, the Philippines and Thailand. These were usually offered by regular travel agents. Women's groups in these countries protested against these tours, castigating Japanese men as 'sex animals'. These Asian women's groups forged links with Japanese women's groups. The latter were successful in placing the issue on the agenda of the Diet, and tourist offices ceased offering such tours (Okura, 1996). However, their success in achieving their goal did not end the use of foreign prostitutes by Japanese men. In the mid-1980s the *yakuza*[12] became involved in the procurement of sex workers from overseas to work in Japan. Around 100,000 women come to Japan each year to work in the sex industry (Murata, 1996: 116), from countries where there are strong trade and investment links with Japan. Matsui (1996a: 56) observed: 'The number of Thai women being sent into Japan's sex industry skyrocketed at the same time that their country's economic growth rate went into double digits.'

The 1980s saw *japa-yuki-san*[13] from South-east Asia being trafficked to Japan. Recession in Latin America, then the economic decline and the increased possibility of travel following the end of Cold War saw Eastern European and Russian women being trafficked. There has also been a significant increase in the migratory flow of brides (Piper, 2001). Another unique feature of the interaction between globalization and migration in the case of Japan is the phenomenon of local government sponsored recruitment of foreign wives. Japanese agriculture has become increasingly unprofitable in the face of economic globalization (Hikita, 1996), which has hit the traditionally protected farming sector. Japanese women are increasingly unwilling to marry farmers and to accept the hardships of work in an agricultural industry. Municipal governments in rural areas, therefore, have sponsored the recruitment of women, mainly from the Philippines and Thailand, to marry farmers and provide farm labour. This policy had been adopted by around 100 rural governments by 1992. Although it is difficult to find records of exactly how many couples have married because of this system, in Yamagata prefecture alone, as of May 1992, there were 472 Filipino women married to Japanese men as the result of community projects to provide brides (Sellek, 2001: 183).

The nature of 'flows' of people out of Japan is also gendered. More Japanese women than men live overseas. By the early 1990s, almost 80 per cent of Japanese students studying abroad were female (Kelsky, 2001: 2). The emergence of the internationally active Japanese woman has been attributed to Japanese institutions. Such women argue that their 'adaptability' to the expectations of the Other is because, variously:

- Marriage in Japan is traditionally patrilocal.
- Daughters are not as indulged as sons and thus develop 'inner resources'.
- The academic success of young women is not as highly valorized as that of young men, and therefore they have more liberty to explore their own interests.
- They are excluded from 'avenues of advancement' in Japanese corporations (Kelsky, 2001).

Experiences of Japanese female migrants

Study or work experience overseas can sometimes allow Japanese women to gain career or educational experiences that would have been more difficult to obtain in Japan. This can prove the foundation for later careers in Japan. Renshaw (1999) found that 70 per cent of the Japanese women managers that she had interviewed had been educated or lived overseas at some point in their lives. It should be noted that Japan, unlike other relatively prosperous nations in the region, does not have a culture of importing domestic labour. This means that Japanese women's entry into paid employment has not been facilitated by the emergence of a class of female migrant domestic workers in Japan.

Conclusion

The Japanese national model of capitalism, though, emerged in the very specific conditions of the immediate post-war period. Although there was a long tradition of women working outside the home in Japan, legal change and political conditions led to an exodus of women from the labour force at the end of the Second World War. Firms' high fixed costs and traditions of pay and promotion by seniority meant that they relied on women's early retirement from regular jobs to maintain numerical flexibility in the workforce and to keep down wage costs. As firms expected women to leave the workforce upon marriage or childbirth, they gave them little training, and the vast majority of women worked in 'gendered' jobs. Married women, especially mothers, on the other hand, were expected to carry out almost all reproductive labour in the conjugal household, and thus could not carry out the 'double shift' of full-time paid work and childcare and domestic work.

Societal and demographic change, educational advance and the increased acceptance of the ideology of equal labour rights have meant that Japanese women's determination to continue to work has gradually increased, with a number remaining at work in the face of pressure to leave. A minority of determined women have succeeded in establishing themselves as professionals. Many more women have re-entered the workforce as non-regular employees. This position both fits in with and reinforces the Japanese gender order.

Both as short-term regular employees and as non-regular workers, Japanese women have enabled Japanese companies to maintain secure and well-rewarded employment for most male company employees. Japan is becoming ever more integrated into a very different international economy to that prevailing in the 1940s and 1950s when the Japanese model took shape. Consequently, there has been deregulation and liberalization of the economy, regulation of, and changing attitudes to women's labour rights and patterns of migrations into and out of Japan. These changes will both impact upon and be affected by the actions and choices of men and women within it. These changes will be examined in Chapters 6 and 7.

Part III

The impact of globalization and restructuring on women working in Japan

6 'Re-regulation', restructuring and women in the regular workforce

Introduction

The previous chapter introduced the idea that the complex trends associated with globalization are producing pressures for two kinds of, ostensibly contradictory, employment reforms. There are pressures for labour market deregulation, in order that the Japanese model might regain its former competitiveness in an increasingly globalized economy. There are also pressures for the re-regulation of labour to establish a principle of sexual equality at work. The latter pressures are exemplified by the passing of the EEOL, which has been instrumental in the restructuring of the Japanese workforce. Chapters 6 and 7 examine the impact of restructuring upon women in the Japanese workforce and contribute to the debate about the impact of globalization upon women by bringing in insights from the case of Japan.

The first section in this chapter records how, in according with the hypothesis that localized patriarchal structures can be weakened through exposure to global scrutiny, global processes were instrumental in the promulgation of equal opportunities legislation, in the form of the 1986 EEOL and its 1999 revision. It shows how the Law, and its revisions, have played a part in changing social attitudes to women's paid employment, and to sexual harassment in the workplace.

The next section demonstrates how the EEOL illustrates the premise that dominant ideologies can lead a state and existing institutions to negotiate a compromise between encouraging change and maintaining current gender orders. The section argues that although the Law has proved relatively weak in correcting discrimination and ensuring equality of opportunity, it has been instrumental in formalizing the secondary status of many women in the regular workforce, by encouraging companies to introduce a gendered dual track employment system and to shift an increasing proportion of their female employees into the non-regular workforce. As the rewards and conditions of the regular and non-regular workforces are so different, the two workforces will be analysed separately. The way in which the restructured workforce is evolving, and how this is affecting the educational and career choices of Japanese women, will be described first, with the growing and increasingly diverse non-regular workforce then described in Chapter 7. It will also be shown how social expectations about women's reproductive labour in Japan continue to distinguish the experience of working women in Japan from those in other First World countries, particularly with regard to the use of childcare and the hiring of domestic workers.

The promulgation and immediate effects of the EEOL

The transformationalist thesis of globalization (see Chapter 2) sees globalization as a process where the flow of ideologies, images and information across the globe leads to reflexivity about, and consequent change in, national institutional practices (Appadurai, 1990; Giddens, 1990; Goldblatt *et al.*, 1997; Scholte, 2000). Japanese society is particularly susceptible to reflexivity about national institutions: Takenaka and Chida note the phenomenon apparent among Japanese people of intense interest in foreign countries and concern about how Japan is seen by people from other countries (Takenaka and Chida, 1998). This has been attributed, by Nakatani (1987) among others, to the legacy of Japan's years of isolation from the West during the Edo period, and has the consequence that *gaiatsu* (foreign pressure) from the international community has proved to be effective in promoting reforms. One of the ideologies spread with globalization is that of equal rights for men and women (albeit that countries' formal or constitutional acceptance of this standard has not resulted in equal outcomes for men and women in any country). This section will examine the impacts of legal change, in the shape of the EEOL, its revisions and the revision of the Labour Standards Law and the impact of exposure to 'foreign' legal or social concepts, exemplified by the introduction of sexual harassment as a legal and social concept.

The role of global processes in the promulgation and revision of the EEOL

International Women's Year (1975) and the United Nations Decade for Women (1976–85) stimulated much popular and media debate in Japan, and impacted upon public opinion (National Institute of Employment and Vocational Research, 1988). In response to the Decade for Women, the Prime Minister became the Director of the Headquarters for the Promotion of Women's Issues, which in turn initiated an action programme with the goal of improving women's status at home and in the workplace (Tamura, 1999). According to Yamashita Yasuko, law professor and managing director of the Japanese Association of International Women's Rights, 'The progress in women's issues [in Japan] cannot be discussed without taking internationalization into consideration' (Yamashita, 1993: 83).

As Chapter 3 made clear, the same point could be made about many countries.[1] In 1979, the UN General Assembly adopted the Convention on the Elimination of All Forms of Discrimination Against Women (CEDAW), a document consisting of a preamble and 30 articles defining discrimination and setting an agenda for national actions to rectify such discrimination. States which sign the Convention commit themselves:

- to incorporate the principle of equality of men and women in their legal system, abolish all discriminatory laws and adopt appropriate ones prohibiting discrimination against women;
- to establish tribunals and other public institutions to ensure the effective protection of women against discrimination; and
- to ensure elimination of all acts of discrimination against women by persons, organizations or enterprises.

(United Nations, 2001)

After pressure from female members of the National Diet, women's groups and journalists raising the issue in the media (Hayashi, 1996), the Japanese government became the 72nd signatory to CEDAW in 1980. In order to comply with CEDAW, the Japanese government needed to urgently enact legislation against employment discrimination (as most other industrialized countries had done by the mid-1970s) as well as revising the Nationality Act so that mixed heritage children of Japanese mothers (instead of just fathers) could inherit Japanese citizenship, and changing the school curriculum to make home economics compulsory for boys as well as girls. Although Japan could not ratify CEDAW without introducing new laws on employment equality, the Equal Employment Opportunities Law did not reach the Diet until 1984, and then only after intense discussion. In May 1982 a committee of academics and representatives of management and labour was formed to work on a report. The outcome of their deliberations was that Law No. 113, 'Respecting the Improvement of the Welfare of Women Workers Including the Guarantee of Equal Opportunity and Treatment Between Men and Women in Employment', generally known as the Equal Employment Opportunities Law (EEOL), was passed on 17 May 1985 and came into effect on 1 April 1986. The Law had the stated aim of eliminating sexual discrimination in opportunity and treatment in all forms of employment. The main points of the EEOL were as follows:

- Companies were to make voluntary 'endeavours' to treat women equally in recruitment, hiring, assignment and promotions.
- Prohibitions were attached to treating women differently from men with regard to vocational training, fringe benefits, retirement age and dismissals.

There is widespread agreement in academic circles that the EEOL was also passed partly in response to foreign criticism of the position of Japanese working women (Gelb, 1998). Previous legislation that touched upon the rights of women in the workplace was limited to the 1947 Japanese Constitution – which stated: 'All of the people are equal under the law and there shall be no discrimination in political, economic or social relations because of race, creed, sex, social status or family origin' (Art. 14, Constitution of Japan, 1947, cited in Hook and McCormack, 2001) – and, as referred to in Chapter 5, the 1947 Labour Standards Law (LSL). Both the Constitution and the LSL were imposed by the Occupation Forces (although they were largely supported by Japanese women). However, the Labour Standards Law's protective legislation for women was not supported by employers' organizations.

Although pressure to sign CEDAW had come from women's activists in Japan, some opponents of the EEOL played on the idea that it was imposed on Japan from outside, and portrayed the law as a form of Western cultural imperialism in order to discredit it. Most notably, the academic Michiko Hasegawa in an article in the intellectual journal *Chou Koron*, lambasted the EEOL as un-Japanese and a threat to the 'cultural ecology' of Japanese society. Its passage would, she said, destroy traditional sex roles, demoralize housewives and encourage the kind of selfish individualism characteristic of Western society (Brinton, 1993). Opposition from employers' representatives took two main forms. Some argued that men and women were different and should therefore be treated differently, while others argued that it was Japan's protective legislation that was the cause of women's disadvantageous position in the workplace, and the key to sexual equality was less, rather than more, regulation. The Japan Federation of Employers' Associations (*Nikkeiren*) opposed the introduction of the new EEOL on the following grounds: women had no 'work consciousness'; women were uninterested in long-term work; and if the female workforce were enlarged, then granting 'protections', such as maternity leave and limited overtime, to a larger proportion of the workforce would prove costly to business (Kawashima, 1989 cited in Molony, 1995). These arguments were rather contradictory. For instance, if women were disinclined to stay in the workforce, then they would be unlikely to take advantage of maternity leave to stay in the workforce. However, as a result of these discussions, when the EEOL was promulgated, the Labour Standards Law was simultaneously revised. Restrictions on overtime were declared not to apply to women in managerial positions and in 14 jobs defined as requiring specialized knowledge or skill. In other words, women who were doing 'men's jobs' were expected to suffer the disadvantages of male 'core' workers.

The EEOL was revised and strengthened in 1997 (with revisions becoming effective from June 1999). The new law:

- banned discrimination in recruitment, hiring, placement and promotion;

- granted the government authority to arbitrate a dispute based on just one party's complaint;
- required that the Ministry of Labour publish the names of companies that fail to comply with its administrative warnings;
- required companies to take steps to prevent sexual harassment.

However, when the law was passed, all remaining sex-specific protective legislation, with the exception of maternity leave, was deemed 'special treatment' and removed from the statute books.

The impact of the EEOL on attitudes to women's work and sexual harassment

Feminists have, on the whole, been unimpressed with Japan's equal opportunities laws, deriding them as *honenuki* (spineless). Campaigners on the left felt that the EEOL's emphasis on training and promotions meant that it was directed towards middle class or elite educated women. As far as blue-collar women were concerned, the removal of night work and overtime protection could, labour representatives and social reformers argued, force them out of their positions as regular workers (Roberts, 1994).

However, there is also some evidence that the discussions and publicity around the Law may have had a consciousness-raising effect on the general population. The proportion of people believing it was acceptable for a woman to continue working after giving birth rose from 16.1 per cent in 1987 to 32.5 per cent in 1995 (Araki, 1998). Though indirect and informal discrimination continued, only 17 per cent of companies excluded female job applicants in 1987 compared to 41 per cent in 1986; and 78.9 per cent of companies offered equal starting salaries to men and women in 1987 compared to 31.7 per cent in 1975 (Watabe-Dawson, 1997: 48). It also seems likely that the EEOL contributed to a climate of more pro-women legal judgements. The Nihon Tekko Renmei case was decided just after the EEOL came into effect in 1986. Nihon Tekko Renmei and its union had decided a scale of pay rates and bonuses, differentiated according to gender. The court judged that this was null and void according to the Labour Standards Law (Art. 4 and Art. 13) and the Civil Code (Art. 90). Although these laws had been in existence since the 1940s, it seems (judging from the way custom and practice had differed from the letter of the law until that point) that the EEOL was instrumental in making the courts enforce existing legislation.

The immediate revision of the EEOL also had immediate consciousness-raising effects. Like the signing of CEDAW, the revision of the EEOL, which stipulated that firms take steps to protect against sexual harassment, was an interesting example of the impact of transnational activism in effecting change. The profile of sexual harassment (*seku hara*)[2] in Japan had been raised, partly because of cases concerning Japanese companies abroad. This is a prime illustration of the way transnational networks can produce discursive change, i.e. it *labelled* an already existing practice and thereby facilitated discussion about, and resistance to, that practice. When the EEOL was revised, therefore, this provided the opportunity to introduce legislation on the matter, and its inclusion in the Law appears to have been the direct result of joint action organized by Japanese and American women working together to organize a high profile campaign.[3] The subsequent publicity and the fact that women now could use the changing legal institutions raised the profile of the issue. The profile of sexual harassment was further raised shortly after the law came into effect when, in March 2000, 'Knock' Yokoyama, the former governor of Osaka, admitted a sexual harassment charge brought against him under the new law by a young campaign worker. The number of enquires about sexual harassment received by the Ministry of Labour has risen sharply, especially after it seemed there might be legal redress. In FY 1995 there were 968 enquires about sexual harassment to the Ministry of Labour's Prefectural Women's and Young Workers' Offices in 1995; 1,615 in FY 1996, 2,534 in FY 1997, 7,019 in FY 1998 (*Japan Labour Bulletin*, 1999). In 1999, the Ministry of Labour received 9,000 enquires regarding sexual harassment (International Reform Monitor, 2001).[4]

According to a survey of 2,254 enterprises in June and July 1997 (response rate of 34.8 per cent), only 5.5 per cent of enterprises were implementing measures against sexual harassment while another 14.3 per cent were planning or considering the implementation of such measures. The EEOL was revised on 18 June 1997, and by October 1998, a Tokyo Metropolitan government survey of 3,000 enterprises (effective response rate of 46.8 per cent) found that 20.5 per cent of enterprises with 300 or more regular employees had measures in place to prevent sexual harassment and 19.5 per cent were considering such steps (*Japan Labour Bulletin*, 1999).

The persistence and impact of existing institutions

Previous work on the impact of globalization upon women has shown that existing institutions can interact with changes resulting from globalization to produce path-dependent changes (Pyle 1990; Beneria and Lind, 1995). This has certainly been the case in Japan, where:

- The EEOL has been insufficiently strong to prevent or correct indirect and even quite overt sex discrimination.
- The repeal of sex-specific protective legislation, combined with the expectations about women's reproductive labour, has made it more difficult for women to hold regular jobs.
- The EEOL has, ironically, facilitated a formal division on labour according to sex, in the context of a remodelled tripartite division of labour in the regular workforce.

Failure to correct for discrimination

The 1986 EEOL set out a procedure for the resolution of disputes. In the first instance, according to the law, employers shall 'endeavour to find an amicable settlement, by such means as referring the said complaint to a grievance machinery', composed of representatives of the employer and the employee body (Art. 13). If this fails, then the Director of the Prefectural Women's and Young Workers' Office, if approached by either the woman or the employer, is empowered to give necessary advice and mediation (Art.14). The Director in question is empowered to refer the dispute to the Equal Opportunity Mediation Commission (EOMC) but 'where only one of the parties concerned applies for mediation, the Director may make such a referral *only if the other party concerned agrees to the mediation*' (Art. 15, my italics).

In practice, the mediation mechanism has proved to be less than effective. Between 1986 and 1996, 103 people brought cases against 11 companies. Of these Sumitomo Metal was the only one to be successfully mediated, as in the other cases either the Director of the Prefectural Women's and Young Workers' Office decided not to pursue the case or the employers concerned did not agree to mediation (Working Women's Network, 1996). In 1991, for example, female employees of Tokai Radio Company asked the local Director of the Prefectural Women's and Young Workers' Office for referral to the EOMC, but the case did not progress because the company withheld consent for mediation. This particular problem for complainants should be overcome with the 1997 changes to the EEOL. The mediation procedure can now be initiated by just one party, without the consent of the other (International Reform Monitor, 2001).

The EEOL has generally been interpreted as having no retrospective applicability. Not only can it not be used to compensate for discrimination that occurred before the Law was passed (although this discrimination would have been unconstitutional) but women in subordinate positions today, because of sexist treatment in the past, have not been entitled to any correction of this. This is demonstrated in a court case filed in 1995 by two female employees of Sumitomo Electric. Ms Nishimura was hired by the company as a clerical worker in 1966, and Ms Shirafuji was hired by a local branch of Sumitomo Electric in 1969 also to do clerical work. At the same time the headquarters of Sumitomo Electric hired 'special office workers', who were nearly all men, on a national basis. 'Special office workers' were given more training than clerical workers, higher wage raises and were groomed for management responsibility. Although the vast majority of clerical workers were women, between 1969 and 1977 male high-school graduates were occasionally assigned to the same clerical work as women. However, these men were eventually all transferred to the special office work track, following their taking of a transfer test, which was not open to their female co-workers. The test was abolished after all the eligible male workers had passed it. The five male high-school graduates who began work in the same year as Ms Shirafuji had all been promoted to the level of chief inspector in managerial work by 1991. Consequently, Ms Shirafuji was paid 180,000 yen per month less than her former co-workers and received 2.7 million yen less annually (Working Women's International Network, 2000). The company argued in court that the male high-school graduates were hired on a national basis, so they were eligible for promotion, while their female co-workers were not.

The plaintiffs requested that the system should have been changed at the time that, following a high-profile court case, Sumitomo Electric reviewed its retirement system to establish a common retirement age for men and women. They argued that if the wage difference had been reviewed at this time, they would have received an extra 9.5 million yen, and thus they claimed this sum in compensation. However, they also argued that if the court did not accept this position, then the company should have reviewed its employment practices at the time the EEOL came into effect – in 1987 the company established a formal dual track system where 'general office work' replaced 'clerical work' and 'professional work' replaced 'special office work'. In the latter case, if the plaintiffs had been treated in the same way as their former male co-workers, they should, it was argued, have received back pay in compensation to the value of 5.5 million yen (Working Women's International Network, 2000). On 31 August 2000, Osaka District Court judged that a recruiting system that did not allow women to be recruited from headquarters was in breach of Article 14 of the Constitution, which bans discrimination based on gender. However, it judged that 'in the late 1960s, when there was a strong division of labour by gender in society and many enterprises used such a dual employment system, Sumitomo management did not violate social order and did not act illegally' (*Japan Times*, 2000).

There are numerous reports of persistent discrimination against women, particularly new graduates and particularly during the recession of the mid-1990s, during which 'female university graduates face[d] an employment environment so hostile it is commonly described as the "Ice Age"' (Sasaki, 1995: 33). Among the complaints listed by new women graduates are: not receiving responses to requests for company brochures; not being allowed to take some entrance examinations; being excluded by such conditions as only accepting students who lived with their parents or who were unmarried (Nakano, 1996). In 1996, 61.7 per cent of companies recruiting four-year university graduates for the technological field hired only male graduates, compared to 37 per cent who hired both men and women. This compares to figures of 49.6 per cent and 48.2 per cent respectively in 1992 (Imada, 1996: 6). In fact, more than half of companies responding to research carried out by a private think tank in 1995 said that it was economic performance, rather than the law, which determined the number of women they employed (Nakajima, 1997).

One much-reported phenomenon that some young women have faced while looking for work is the discriminatory interview (*appaku mensetsu*). One interviewee mentioned the assumptions of the recruiter who interviewed her and asked about her future plans:

> And then, actually, the funny thing is when [I had an] interview, I think it was with [B company] he asked me, 'You're a woman. Why do you actually, you know, want to go to graduate school? What about if you get married?' And then I said, 'Well, I can still do my graduate work, if I . . . even though I'm married.' . . . And he said, 'Yeah, but what about if you have kids?' And I said, 'There are a lot of women doing graduate work and they all have kids, and they're still doing fine.' And he said, 'Oh, well, okay.' (Laughs) So they actually, I guess, sometimes have stereotypes of women.

She went on to relate the story of her friend, who was also a job-seeker:

> She was having interview with . . . I forgot what company, but they asked her, like, what she thought a woman's happiness was during the interview. Like, 'Well, what do you think a . . . what do you think is woman's happiness?' And then she's like, 'Well, is it related for the job?' And then they said, 'No, but, well, what do you think it is, I mean,' and she said, 'Well, I want to get married, and I want to have children, but it's not necessary for a woman's happiness, because it can be man's happiness too?' And, I don't know, that was just one question that she told me. She thought it was weird, that they actually, you know, they asked her in an interview . . .'

This practice has not gone unchallenged. In 1994 and 1995 approximately half of the complaints to the EEOL mediation bodies have concerned recruitment and hiring (Gelb, 1998: 50). Young women have been resisting this form of discrimination by forming bodies such as the Association of Female Students Against Job Discrimination and by recording instances of and swapping information about company job discrimination in the *minikomi* (informal photocopied bulletin) *Girls Be Ambitious* and on websites. Furthermore, young female graduates who took jobs for which they were overqualified during the 'Ice Age' are not content to stay with an unchallenging job as a stopgap before marriage or childbirth: 'According to one survey conducted this spring by a job information journal for women, one in three women who desire to change their jobs belongs to the "ice-age" generation of recruits' (Trends in Japan, 1997).

Since it was revised, the law has stipulated that the names of firms which constantly violate its provisions will be publicized. Nonetheless, Tadashi Hanami, Research Director General, The Japan Institute of Labour, argues 'the 1997 Amendment – providing for publication of names of companies violating its provisions, along with disclosure of the nature of their offences – might be better than nothing, but it is still far from what is really needed, namely, effective enforcement measures' (Hanami, 2000: 2).

The repeal of protective legislation

According to Chizuko Ueno, perhaps the best known of Japan's feminists:

> the government forced us to have either an equality law or a production law [*sic*]. I called it the masculinization of female work. It was of no interest at all. Actually the workman's law for Japanese men at the time was already destructive to family life. So we never supported it. Instead we demanded both equality and protection. We didn't want an equal opportunity law, we wanted an equal employment law.
>
> (Ueno, interview with Whipple, 1996: 2)

Chapter 5 details the reasons, including long working hours combined with expectations about women's reproductive labour, that would have made it difficult for women to adopt the male work model, and indeed most women have not been able to do so. Nonetheless, they have lost some of the protections offered, at least formally, by the previous 'female model'.

The passage of the EEOL gave opponents of protective legislation the opportunity to revise the Labour Standards Law. Not only were legal protections for 'career women' immediately withdrawn but many companies who had their own guidelines on the treatment of women workers revised such guidelines 'downwards', so that they met only the minimum requirement of the Labour Standards Law. At 'T' company maternity leave was changed from a paid to an unpaid leave of absence and bonuses were considerably reduced. Another example is the case of 'K' company. Prior to 1986 the company's maternal protection agreement was somewhat more generous than that strictly required by law. After the EEOL was passed, the company revised its regulations as follows:

- Menstrual protection: Before 1987 any person could take time off when necessary, but after the revisions only a person who 'has trouble working, and if she requests, can take time off' (LSL Art. 38).
- During pregnancy: Overtime and weekend work were both prohibited before 1987, but after this time this was changed to 'if a woman asks not to work overtime and/or weekends, then the company cannot force her to do so' (LSL Art. 66.2).
- Reassignments during pregnancy: The company's former Maternal Standards Agreement had previously stated that, in general reassignments should not occur during pregnancy. Its post-1987

regulations merely stated that, if reassignment occurs, the company had to take the pregnancy into consideration by not assigning work more difficult than before (LSL Art. 65.3).

(Shosha ni hataraku josei nokai: 1989: 19)

The pressure group Shosha ni hataraku josei (Women Working in Trading Companies) argued further that reassignment of pregnant women was used as a way to force them to leave.

The removal of overtime restrictions was no doubt of some use to some female managers and specialists: a journalist told me that she was hampered by her employers' refusal to let her work at night (albeit that this was during an interview some years after the EEOL came into effect). However, it seems unlikely that a person could combine the expectations of 'career track' work with, say, childcare responsibilities.[5] A *sogoshoku* pensions analyst described her work schedule as follows:

> Respondent: I work from 7.30 to 21.00–22.00 a day. How many hours I work per month, I wonder.
> Interviewer: Do you work five days a week?
> Respondent: Yes.
> Interviewer: Do you do overtime for free?
> Respondent: Most of them, yes.

It was of dubious benefit to the great majority of working women, though, when remaining protective legislation was abolished. *Nikkeiren* had put great premium on the abolition of remaining protective legislation during the 1997 revision (*Japan Labour Bulletin*, 1997), although there was considerable debate in Japan between those campaigners who felt that legal restrictions gave employers an excuse to exclude women from certain jobs and those who felt that the working hours of Japanese men were inhumane and that protective legislation should be extended to cover men (Gordon, 1998). Evidence is mixed. On the one hand, employment of women increased immediately at Mazda Motors, Toyota Motor Corporations and Nissan Motors when LSL restrictions on overtime were lifted. Furthermore, the companies improved dormitories for single people, women's bathrooms and locker rooms (*Japan Labour Bulletin*, 1 May 1999). On the other hand, Working Women's Helpline run by Tokyo Josei Union reported that after night work was deregulated in April 1999 the number of telephone calls about overwork increased. Their records cited the following:

> Her boss gave work to her and asked her to work overtime. She had to work every day until 11 and work even consecutive holidays. She worked over 100 hours a month and became ill.

> After April she had to work until 11 and 12 and work on holidays. She became ill.

> Workers are not enough and lunch break is only 15 minutes. No paid leave. She worked more than 9 hours a day.

Working-class women were particularly vulnerable. Through the post-war period, 20–30 per cent of blue-collar workers have been female (nearly twice the rate of most Western countries) (Brinton, 1993, cited in Robertson, 1998). Although blue-collar work accounts for a small and diminishing pro-portion of the workforce, Glenda Roberts has documented the desire of blue-collar female workers to continue to work throughout their childbear-ing years until retirement, either because of economic necessity or a desire for financial and personal autonomy, in the face of a strong socio-cultural ideology of married women as full-time wives and mothers and the recruit-ment, promotion and retirement policies of their firm (Roberts, 1994). Women may have felt under extra pressure to leave work when they became pregnant not only because conditions were less favourable to them than before the legal revisions but also because of the widespread belief that night work is harmful to women's fertility. The National Confederation of Trade Unions (Zenroren), for example, opposed the relaxation on night work restrictions on the grounds that abnormal delivery was 40 per cent higher among women workers doing night shifts, before the revision, such as nurses and TV producers (Zenroren, 1997b). In the face of a strong social prefer-ence for mothers to work part-time or not at all, this is one additional factor to discourage them from continuing to pursue a full-time career.

The restructuring of the workforce

Although the EEOL was of limited retrospective applicability, it did have a major impact on employers' behaviour and hiring practices. The secondary position that women had filled in the regular workforce in the post-war model of Japan capitalism was formalized by the introduction of the 'dual track' system, and an increasing proportion of women were employed in an increasingly feminized non-regular workforce.

The dual track system

Just two months before the EEOL became operational, *Nikkeiren* published a book, which strongly implied that women were not expected to have similar positions to men (Molony, 1995). The book noted that the EEOL only required that companies grant women an 'opportunity', not a guar-antee, of employment. In other words, they did not have to actually employ women; merely include them in the recruitment, interview and testing process, although it added the caveat that if after 'several years' no women had been hired, then it might appear that the company was intentionally not hiring female employees (Molony, 1995: 85). In fact the Ministry of Labour specifically made firms aware that they could still discriminate, when it published an official notice which stated that it is not a violation 'to employ workers according to a system of separate numbers of men and women to be admitted, such as 70 men and 30 women in the same job classification or recruitment' (A Letter from Japanese Women Circle, 1994: 43). The revised EEOL has made it illegal to have gender quotas, but there is, as yet, little evidence of the efficacy of this. This legal loophole enabled companies to negotiate a compromise between the ideal of sexual equality in the workplace and maintaining existing gender norms. Many large companies reacted to the enactment of the 1986 version of the EEOL by introducing a dual track employment system for their employees. The system generally consists of a 'general clerical track' (*ippanshoku*) and a 'managerial track' (*sogoshoku*). In addition, specialists are employed, either intermittently or on the *senmonshoku* (specialist track), having gained specialist skills at their own, rather than at company expense. Entrants to the *sogoshoku* are usually expected to do overtime and to be prepared to accept transfers. In 1990, 99 per cent of men were on the management track, compared to just 3.7 per cent of women (A Letter from Japanese Women Circle, 1994: 40). The general clerical track is usually an almost exclusively female domain. The EEOL only applied to denying women, rather than men, job opportunities, therefore it continued to be legal to recruit or advertise for only women to fill certain (usually subordinate) positions. This was reflected in the EEOL's full title: Law Respecting the Improvement of the Welfare of Women Workers, including the Guarantee of Equal Opportunity and Treatment Between Men and Women in Employment, Law No. 45 of 1985, as amended. In the late 1990s, in approximately 52 per cent of Japanese companies with more than 5,000 employees that introduced this dual track system, the *ippanshoku* class was only for female employees (Kakuyama, 1997). Evidently this makes it more difficult for employees to complain about unequal treatment on the grounds of gender. In November 1992 Osaka Women's and Young Workers' Office decided that Sumitomo Mutual Life Assurance Company's apparent failure to promote married women, while single women and married men could get promoted, did not constitute sex discrimination since there were no married men on the general clerical track with whom the women could be compared (A Letter from Japanese Women Circle, 1994). The revised EEOL forbids the practice of employing women only in certain positions, although it does permit 'positive action' to redress discrimination.

The growth of the non-regular workforce

As explained above, the EEOL does not address the question of sex-based occupational segregation. Because there is no basis for comparison between male and female workers, it is impossible for women in an entirely female part-time workforce to bring a case of sexual discrimination. Table 6.1 shows how the labour force of non-part-timers has become increasingly diversified and flexibilized between 1975 and 2002, while Table 6.2 sets out the increase in part-time employment.

The proportion of part-time employment among female workers in Japan rose by 23.3 per cent of the female workforce between 1983 and 1996 (Table 6.2). This total percentage change is not mirrored in any of the major industrialized countries, except France, where the proportion of the female workforce working part-time grew by 46.8 per cent, and Italy, which also had a larger percentage change, but it began from a far smaller base of only 9.4 thousand, compared to Japan's 29.2 thousand. As the size of the change in the female part-time workforce in other advanced industrialized economies was not of the same order of magnitude as that of Japan, it is reasonable to assume that legal change in Japan played a large part in stimulating this rise. After the strengthened EEOL came into effect in 1999, some female regular workers appear to have been reclassified as non-regular. According to records kept by the Tokyo Josei Union (personal communication, December 1999), the majority of people calling the Working Women's Helpline were experiencing problems stemming from a change in their status from regular to non-regular employees.

The growth and characteristics of the female non-regular workforce will be examined in more detail in Chapter 7.

Women in the restructured regular workforce

This section discusses women's employment in the restructured regular workforce. It begins by examining whether the EEOL has had any evident

Table 6.1 Employed persons by employment status, 1975–2002

Year	Male			Female		
	Regular employees	*Temporary employees*	*Daily employees*	*Regular employees*	*Temporary employees*	*Daily employees*
1975	2,351	60	69	996	117	54
1980	2,476	74	67	1,109	182	63
1985	2,619	85	61	1,247	237	65
1990	2,836	108	58	1,480	286	68
1995	3,039	124	52	1,670	310	68
2000	2,995	169	52	1,689	383	67
2001	2,971	177	54	1,706	393	68
2002	2,925	191	54	1,679	417	66

Source: adapted from Ministry of Public Management, Home Affairs, Posts and Telecommunications (2004).

impact upon women's participation and tenure in the regular workforce generally, and then examines the extent and nature of women's work in the different sections of the restructured regular workforce.

Women's participation in the regular workforce

The increasing participation in the non-regular workforce and the increasing proportion of part-time work in the labour force will be examined in more depth in Chapter 7, but it will be shown to have been disproportionately large compared to participation in the workforce overall. There has also been a rise in the proportion of regular employees who are female, albeit of a far smaller magnitude. The proportion of women in the regular workforce has also risen from 29.8 per cent of all regular employees in 1976 to 36.1 per cent in 2000 (Ministry of Public Management, Home Affairs, Posts and Telecommunications, 2001). Furthermore, as Figure 6.1 shows, women's tenure in the regular workforce has also increased from 3.9 years in 1965 to 7.6 years in 1994. When this information is represented graphically, it is easy to see that the passage of the EEOL in 1986 did not lead to any sharp discontinuity in a general secular trend of lengthening participation in the regular workforce.

Japan, then, is not an exception to the general trend of the increased feminization of work, but it seems that this can more easily be attributed to the gradual social changes described in the previous chapter than to legislation that had the ostensible aim of increasing women's employment opportunities. Although the EEOL had little effect on the rates of participation and tenure of female regular workers, it did have a significant effect on the organization of work for those women. The following subsections will describe the variety of women's work in the restructured regular workforce.

Table 6.2 Part-time employment among female workers in major industrialized countries 1983–96

Country	Total number of female part-time workers, thousands			
	1983	*1990*	*1996*	*Percentage change*
Japan	29.2	32.8	36	23.3
US	28.1	25.2	26.9	−4.3
UK	41.3	42.6	42.7	3.4
Germany	30.0	33.8	33.8	12.7
France	20.1	23.6	29.5	46.8
Italy	9.4	9.6	12.7	35.1
Canada	28.1	26.8	28.9	2.8
Sweden	45.9	40.4	39	−15.0

Source: adapted from OECD, 1997.

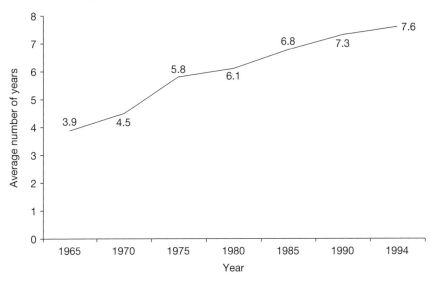

Figure 6.1 Average tenure of female workers in the regular workforce: Ministry of
Public Management, Home Affairs, Posts and Telecommunications, 2001.

Women and the sogoshoku

One of the obstacles to women entering the management track is the different educational paths traditionally followed by men and women, which were
described in the previous chapter. Graduation from four-year universities is
a usual requirement for entry into career-track jobs. The result is that the
majority of women entered non-career tracks more or less automatically,
and that this can be rationalized on the grounds of different qualifications.
When asked if there was any difference between the way they and their male
co-workers were treated, respondents to the author's 1996–7 survey replied:

> Women's wages are different and their duties are different from those
> of men. Training for the university graduates is different from those for
> junior college graduates. Male colleagues are mostly university gradu-
> ates. In this sense, training for male workers is different from women.
>   (Clerical worker employed by a radio company)

> Yes, especially because I graduated from junior college, my appoint-
> ment, position, initiation and training were separate from those who
> graduated from a four year university. . . . The time of training is totally
> different according to your academic background. For example, if you
> finished university, you'll get training right after you join the company,
> but if you are a junior college graduate, it takes 6–7 years before you
> can have training.
>   (33-year-old employee of multinational corporation)

Even those who have a four-year degree often find themselves in positions for which they are overqualified. Between 1982 and 1992, the most common career destination of women graduates from four-year universities actually changed from professional jobs to clerical and related jobs, although among women engaged in professional jobs, on the other hand, those in technical jobs increased sharply (Imada, 1994: 3), indicating that for some determined women, the EEOL might have had the positive effect of opening up more diverse job opportunities. Certainly recent trends suggest that women are increasingly equipping themselves to be eligible for such positions. Table 6.3 shows the rising numbers of female students at four-year universities.

Interestingly, Figure 6.2 shows a quite sharp discontinuity in the rate of increase in the proportion of female students attending four-year universities around the time of the introduction of the EEOL and consequent introduction of the dual track employment system. It is not possible to definitively link the EEOL/dual track system with the changing rate of female participation in degree-level education without more supporting evidence. However, it is possible that young women and their parents' decision-making about further education were influenced either by a changing discourse around sexual equality in the workplace or by the perception that, with legal change, it might be possible that a four-year degree could assist women in gaining career-track positions.

Nonetheless, the practice remains of women being automatically assigned to the *ippanshoku* regardless of their academic background. The author had the following conversation, in 1999, with a woman who had a bachelor's degree from the United States:

> Interviewer: Since you graduated from university, didn't you want to get a *sogoshoku* position?
> Respondent: Yes. I wanted to. [. . .] [But] at my company, women cannot apply for *sogoshoku* unless they have work there for a year. So all women have to start at *jimu shoku* (clerical work) first.

Table 6.3 The number and proportion of female students attending four-year universities, 1975–2000

Year	Total number of students attending four-year universities	Number of female students	Percentage of female students at four-year universities
1975	1,734,082	368,258	21.2
1980	1,835,312	405,529	22.1
1985	1,848,698	434,401	23.5
1990	2,133,362	584,155	27.4
1995	2,546,649	821,893	32.3
2000	2,740,023	992,312	36.2

Source: Ministry of Education, Culture, Sports and Technology, 2001.

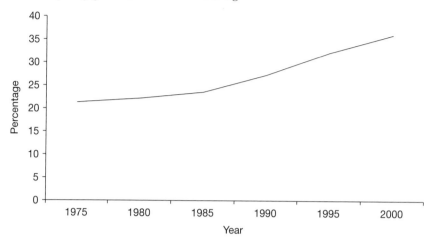

Figure 6.2 Percentage of female students at four-year universities, 1975–2000:
Ministry of Education, Culture, Sports, Science and Technology, 2001.

Interviewer: What about men?

Respondent: *Sogoshoku*. I have never met any men working at *jimu shoku*. As far as I know, all men are working at *sogoshoku*.

Interviewer: So women have a hope that they may be able to move up to *sogoshoku* after a year?

Respondent: Yes.

Later in the interview she continued:

Interviewer: So after you had worked for a year, did you ask for *sogoshoku* position?

Respondent: Yes, but I was rejected.

Interviewer: For what reasons?

Respondent: I don't know.

Interviewer: Just you were told 'no'?

Respondent: Well, my boss said that I was not capable enough for *sogoshoku*, but I don't believe so. I asked my boss to explain what kind of capabilities I was missing in details, but my boss did not tell me. In our society, it happens all the time. People in general do not say things back to their bosses once their decisions are made. We are supposed to accept whatever their orders are. So I guess he was annoyed by me for asking for the reasons.

Another woman, working for 'A' company, which deals with the provision of education and sporting facilities, explained the situation whereby some women who had shown exceptional commitment to their general track position were offered the chance to advance to the *sogoshoku*, but that it was made it clear that this was the exception rather than the rule:

> Interviewer: Is the condition of recruitment the same between men and women?
> Respondent: Well, the recruitment was for both men and women, but when we were placed, there was a division by university or by the year of university (4 years or 2 years) or by general track and career track.
> Interviewer: How about you?
> Respondent: I was at general track and . . .
> Interviewer: Were you at two-year college?
> Respondent: No, I graduated from [a] four-year university, but I chose general track and my co-workers, male co-workers were at career track from the beginning.
> Interviewer: How did your boss explain about the discrimination?
> Respondent: [Silence] I think there was not any particular explanation. I think I asked whether women could work at career track and he said that persons who had training were given chances.

She went on that she was injured at the time of her recruitment and did not apply for the career track, because she initially wanted work which was not too taxing. Unlike the previous company, there were examples of women being promoted from one track to the other, but it seemed that they needed to have demonstrated exceptional loyalty to the company before this could happen:

> Respondent: But later I realized something was wrong.
> (She explained that all the career-track members but one were men.)
> Respondent: There was a woman who worked at career track. She was at general track at the beginning and after she had a training in Tokyo . . . and after she returned, she worked at career track. After the case, I asked it there something wrong, and they said they have changed the system a little bit . . . for women who worked for a long time, they asked whether they wanted to change from the general track to career track but the condition was for more than five years . . . Only women who were at general track and worked for more than five years were asked whether they wanted to shift or not and two came to work at career track but after that there was not such a revision at all.

A woman who had succeeded in entering the management track wrote that she worked from 9.30 am to 15.25 seven days a week (*sic*) and disliked the amount of overtime she had to do. However, she still believed that she had no possibility of promotion, explaining:

> I'm the only member of the management staff among the women
> ... Trends are changing, but Japan is still a male-centred society.
> Women have to make an effort. I don't think it's possible to get a
> higher position in this company. Equal pay is only a façade. There is
> inequality in Japanese companies.

Some women, like the example above, have managed to succeed in gaining the prized *sogoshoku* jobs with large companies and receive the benefits that accompany them. One respondent had taken an MBA in the United States, then worked for a company in the US for a further five years, becoming fluent in English and gaining a further qualification as a pensions analyst. At the time of interview, in 1999, she was working in the *sogoshoku* of a prestigious Japanese company and was earning 12 million yen. However, as the following extract shows, her situation was exceptional:

> Interviewer: Is the condition of career-track workers the same between
>   men and women?
> Respondent: I think the same.
> Interviewer : How many women are there in the career track?
> Respondent: About 1 per cent.
> Interviewer: How about the general track?
> Respondent: It is . . . the opposite. About 99 per cent are women.

The practice of requiring women to make exceptional efforts before they are offered the same positions as men fits in well with the theory of statistical discrimination: the extra qualification and effort required of aspiring female managers are perhaps used by managers as a proxy for willingness to establish a permanent career. However, it is difficult for a woman to make the decision at the start of her career about whether or not she will be able to continue to shoulder the work burden of a 'salaryman'. Certainly there has been an increase in reports of women suffering from the symptoms of overwork, a phenomenon known as 'complete exhaustion syndrome' or 'superwoman syndrome' (Asakura, 1998).

Female *sogoshoku* workers, in some instances, have even heavier work burdens than their 'salaryman' colleagues. They are not only required to demonstrate as much commitment as male *sogoshoku* workers, without the support of wives carrying out reproductive work at home but are sometimes also asked to perform the same subordinate tasks as women in the *ippanshoku*.

One former OL[6] who was invited to 'try out' a management position, has written:

> I was good at it and I loved it . . . But then I discovered the reality
> of male-dominated Japan: that a woman in management is considered an 'uppity girl'. If I offered the smallest opinion I would be
> dismissed as a woman [*onna no kuse ni*].
>   (Ryuugaku taikenki, 1992: 6, cited in Kelsky, 2001: 92)

It is very difficult to combine the expectations of a *sogoshoku* worker with any domestic responsibilities, and women workers are unsure they will be rewarded for the sacrifices they make. This does not mean that women carry out work that is of the same status as that of men. While firms have been increasingly prepared to recruit skilled and qualified women, evidence seems to suggest the existence of a 'glass ceiling', that is, even for women who enter the management or technical jobs track, prospects of promotion are limited. The proportion of firms recruiting female college graduates almost doubled between 1984 and 1995 (from 33.2 per cent to 69.7 per cent or 56.3 per cent for white-collar and technical jobs respectively), and the proportion of female team leaders has risen from 4.0 per cent to 7.3 per cent, but the proportion of female section heads has grown only incrementally from 1.1 per cent to 1.3 per cent (Takahashi, 1998: 8). This indicates that the upper echelons of the regular workforce have not been significantly feminized.

It is perhaps not surprising that the high drop-out rate of women from the *sogoshoku* has become a topic of concern in Japan (Ministry of Labour, 1996). Almost 70 per cent of female graduates from the prestigious Hitotsubashi University in Tokyo, who took professional-level jobs in 1986 left their original employers (Takahashi, 1998). This does not, however, mean that women who have left the *sogoshoku* have necessarily given up their career ambitions. Renshaw (1999) cites many case histories of women who started work as a company employee, then left and began their own businesses as the 'glass ceiling' became all too visible. In fact 23 per cent of Japanese businesses are owned by women (Renshaw, 1999: 158) and 87 per cent of women entrepreneurs had worked for a company before starting their own business (Renshaw, 1999: 166).

Women and the ippanshoku

The majority of women tend to choose the general track as they are aware of the demands of *sogoshoku* work, and know that transfer between tracks is difficult (Asakura, 1998). Some women appear to have been either offered inducements or put under pressure not to apply for the career track. Some employers offer a sort of dowry: a lump-sum payment to women who opt for the *ippanshoku* and then eventually leave (Brinton, 1993). This allows companies to retain the numerical flexibility of the previous system. A 31-year-old bank worker reported:

> When I was in a pre-executive position, due to a merger with another bank, the bank forced me to write an oath to the effect that I didn't hope to have an executive position. But I passed the exam, and recovered the position.

Many companies continue to assume that women in the *ippanshoku* will follow the model of short-term regular work, followed by marriage, childbirth and non-regular work. This assumption is reflected in the attitudes displayed to those who do not follow this pattern. A 32-year-old receptionist said:

> Very often the staff (especially men) tell me I should marry early and mention about my age. I feel it's mean to say 'Why don't you marry for your age?' (*sic*) . . . I am tired of that.

A 27-year-old clerical worker had a similar experience:

> My (male) colleagues ask me why I don't get married, or if not, they think about why I'm not getting married. It doesn't force me to retire, but I think my junior colleagues feel 'sorry' for me about not getting married.

Some women are allowed to change tracks following a promotion test. However, again, it is they, rather than their employers, who are expected to show initiative, and this can lead to resentment. An *ippanshoku* worker in her twenties told me this:

> Training, only men are allowed to take the training. Women are staying at their offices. And women have to take paid leaves . . . do you know paid holidays ([. . .])? I had to take paid holidays and then I could learn something or do whatever I wanted. Even though the train[ing] was related to my professional field, I had to take paid leave and pay for the training. Men can go out when their schedule allows and when the training is accepted in their work, they can go to the training as part of their work . . . This strange system exists and I really don't like that. It won't help building my career.

Ogasawara (1998) writes that the exclusion of OLs ('office ladies') from career advancement can in some ways liberate them from office authority. She writes about how OLs use gossip, withholding of giving chocolates on Valentine's Day (see Chapter 5) and even total non-co-operation with the requests of male co-workers in order to manipulate the behaviour of their male co-workers. Ironically, this behaviour reinforces management stereotypes of women as emotional, irrational and lacking in commitment to work, and provides a further excuse not to promote women or give them responsibility.

A recent legal decision has challenged the assumption that once women have accepted a position in the clerical track, they must accept a traditionally female career. In January 2001, the Tokyo High Court ruled against the Shiba Credit Association (*Shiba Shinkin*) in a case that lasted more than 13 years from filing to final decision. Thirteen women workers filed a suit against *Shiba Shinkin* for discrimination in promotion. The company's defence was that the women had not been promoted because of a lack of ability. When the company lost the case in Tokyo District Court, they appealed to Tokyo High Court, who found that the company had – even though operating a supposedly objective promotion test system – discriminated against women. Even though there had been a test, ostensibly to decide promotion, special measures were taken to promote men who failed the exam. Significantly, it also ordered that the company should promote the women to section chiefs and pay them compensation (New Japan Women's Association, no date given).

Innovations in the tracking system

There have been adjustments to the tracking system. Firms have realized the advantages of using the full capacities of women, and, in the wake of the publicity around the drop-out rate of female workers from the *sogoshoku*, have taken into account that women continue to be charged with responsibility for reproductive labour after marriage and therefore cannot automatically be expected to be as flexible in job transfers as *sogoshoku* workers.

The gyoumushoku

One innovation in the tracking system is that some companies have introduced an intermediate track, the *gyomushoku* (business operations job) track (Japan Institute of Labour, 1999). This track does not require auto-matic long-distance transfers, which allows women to take some of the opportunities of a career track. A pensions analyst the author interviewed in 1999 explained the situation at her workplace:

> The difference between career track, semi-career track, and general track . . . They are full-time workers. Career track are required to be transferred all over the world. They have to be [in] a position of managing people as well. Semi-career track have [a] transfer system, but it is limited [to] within [a] commutable area. The job responsi-bility mainly covers office work. [The] general track doesn't have transfer and do office work.

Comprehensive management track

In 2000, Nippon Yusen, a major shipping company integrated the career and non-career tracks with the goal of promoting solely on merit and without concern for gender. In April 2002, the company appointed its first female manager, who was also the first employee among those who entered in the same year to reach this rank (*Nikkei Weekly*, 23 September 2002). Other firms, including Sony, have abolished their clerical tracks completely, allowing all employees to compete for management jobs.

The senmonshoku

Nikkeiren has advocated an increasing role for specialists in the Japanese employment system. Specialists are seen as adding flexibility to the Japanese model of capitalism, by being employed on short-term contracts and being paid according to merit rather than seniority. The career strategies of young women are increasingly being shaped by the realization that certified skills could offer them the best chance for progression within the constraints of the existing institutions of Japanese employment. Many have therefore been active in preparing themselves to become *senmonka* (specialists, who follow the *senmonshoku*, or specialist track). Shinotsuka (1994) noted that, even in 1994 a greater proportion of women (13.8 per cent) than men (11.3 per cent) worked as specialists. This appears to be becoming an increasingly popular career destination. Sixty-two per cent of women in their thirties answered that they felt the most desirable way to work was to become an expert in a certain field, compared to 12.1 per cent who thought the most desirable way to work was to work for the same company for a long time and obtain a managerial position. Respondents gave the impression that women were aware of job discrimination. By December 2000, 48.5 per cent of final-year junior college students (female students only) had a job offer, compared with 93.8 per cent of final-year higher technical school students (male students only) (Japan Institute of Labour, 1 January 2001), and felt that this was one way to ensure career success. Women, especially those at junior colleges, are more likely than men to consider that skills and specialisms are more important than the university one attends and one's degree (Economic Planning Agency, 1997). However, the requisite training is usually at the worker's own expense, rather than at the company's expense, as with the traditional employment system. An increasingly common phenomenon is that of *duburu sukuru* (double school), where undergraduates take vocational certificates at the same time as their bachelor's or associate degrees. In a focus group session, a university lecturer noted:

> Girls . . . my students are very eager to get licences and so they go to another vocational school as they study at university, because they think that girls are disadvantaged . . . Girls have to have some weapon, so they take some course, such as bookkeeping, or they become a specialist in real estate.

Another woman commented:

> I know a young woman . . . and on her name card there is a lot of qualifications [. . .]. She said, 'With these certificates, I'm just . . . I'm on the starting line with boys.'

Female students interviewed by Lee-Cunin (2004) gave the following opinions, which seemed to indicate that certification was a desired route to career success:

> I want a job that lets me use a certificate related to economics because I want to be active in society as a woman.

> I would like to get office work in accounting as the job itself will improve my ability. I would become an office lady if I can't get better work or improve myself.

> My ideal job is being a teacher, or a chartered or tax accountant but in reality my job will be an office lady.

However, specialist work too is being re-regulated. One notable feature of the re-regulation of employment has been the expansion of the 'discretionary work scheme'. Legally, if the hours worked exceed a daily or weekly maximum, then employers are formally obliged to pay an overtime premium of 25 per cent. However, Article 32–02 Paragraph 4 of the current Labour Standards Law, which was introduced in 1982, allows written agreement between employer and employee representatives which stipulates that payment is to be made for a certain length of time, regardless of how long the task specified in that agreement actually took. Initially this applied only to six types of jobs, largely in the media, design or research. From 1 April 2000 seven other 'specialist' jobs, such as certified public accountant, were added to the list. The Japan Federation of Employers' Associations (*Nikkeiren*) is campaigning for the list to be further expanded to cover jobs such as planning of business strategy, sales, finance and public relations. A woman who worked as an advertising copywriter in 1996 complained:

> I have no time. Sometimes I can't control my time. My time schedule is controlled by other people, by clients. There is no limit to how long I work. I have to work overtime at short notice often. The payment for the job is one payment for one day. So some jobs I do one hour and others I work three days for one job. The price is the same. I get paid according to my idea. Sometimes I can get a good idea very easily and quickly, but sometimes I can't, so the payment is the same.

The image and reality of working for a foreign firm

The formal tracking system that operates in large Japanese companies helps to institutionalize the secondary labour force status of most women, in comparison with most men. However, there is nothing uniquely Japanese about employing women predominantly in jobs of lower status than those of the men who work beside them. This is demonstrated by the experience of Japanese women working for foreign companies in Japan.

The transnationality index in Japan is lower than that of other advanced industrialized countries (see Chapter 4). However, even the minor presence of a foreign firm in a market can be influential in introducing changes in the organization of work (Yashiro, 1998). The entry of foreign firms into the Japanese market appears to provide slightly more attractive opportunities for high-achieving women who intend to continue working than has been the case in Japanese companies. About 60 per cent of third-year university students of both sexes express an interest in working for foreign companies and their affiliates in Japan, commonly believing that they offer chances for employees to improve their skills and to reach their full potential (Economic Planning Agency, 1999). Certainly this is a common impression held by female Japanese students seeking employment. A marketing specialist, around thirty years of age, working for a foreign company in Japan told the author:

> In my company we don't have much difference between females and males. More likely, your educational background. Sometimes we have a difference between males and females. . . . Japanese bosses – they think they can do better, you know. They think that a male the same age can do better than me. But as far as the foreigners are concerned, I don't think there is any difference. For foreign bosses – they have no . . . I don't think they judge me because I'm female. For Japanese bosses, probably they judge me because I am female. I have to treat them very well. I have to be very nice all the time. That happens. Since I moved to [X company]. [X company] was acquired about 5 years ago to [Y company] and I was one of the people who came from X to Y and they were very shocked the first time they saw me, because I was very young. I was like 25 years old, a very young girl coming to take over their business. So at that time they didn't like me at all. Because they think, you know, that if somebody comes to take over their business, they should be male, older. So when I was one of the people who was chosen to come into X . . .

Foreign-affiliate firms (*gaishikei*) do appear to be more ready than Japanese firms to hire female employees. In the mid-1990s, 70 per cent of Japanese staff at the security company Lehmann Brothers were female, while at McCann Eriksson Hakuhoudo, a foreign-affiliated advertising company, 106 Japanese women were employed compared to only 6 Japanese men (Kelsky, 2001). Although Kelsky does not state the precise levels at which these women were employed, she says that they generally occupied higher positions of authority than they would in Japanese firms. Kelsky suggests that the reason for this over-representation of female employees at foreign affiliate firms is attributable to women being more likely than men to be proficient in English (as they are far more likely to have studied overseas), and because, for educated men, taking a job with a foreign-affiliated corporation implies a risky and unknown future instead of the job security and age-related pay and promotions he is still likely to benefit from in a large Japanese corporation. Employing women therefore is a foreign company's only way of accessing highly educated employees. The fact that women are more likely than men to have achieved job-related certification and skills may be another reason.

Higuchi (1993: 176) noted that the rate of retention of female university graduates for between 5 and 10 years was 75.7 per cent in foreign-affiliated companies, compared to only 57.9 per cent in Japanese companies. However, company documents provided to the author by the union at a subsidiary of a multinational company demonstrate that, while women's tenure in the company is far longer than the average for Japanese companies, women are nonetheless greatly over-represented in the lower employment grades.

As the following anecdote shows, some Western employers may also be inclined to exploit stereotypes of Japanese women as passive and undemanding workers, in order to save on their wages bill:

> Actually I had one interview with an American person and . . . he offered me 150,000 yen for doing secretarial work for a month . . . I asked him if I could get a little bit more, because it was . . . noon till ten or five to ten at night or something like that. The time was really bad. So I asked him if I could get more, and he said, 'Well, women in Japan are not supposed to ask for money . . . Actually the average pay the women are getting is 110,000 yen in Japan, so I'm really surprised that you asked for more and you're a Japanese woman.' So I guess I gave him a bad impression of me.
>
> (Part-time worker, early 20s,
> describing search for full-time work)

Kelsky describes deeply embedded gender norms within *gaisheki* themselves, noting the reliance of young monolingual white male traders working on *gaisheki* stock brokerages in Tokyo, who are completely dependent on bilingual secretaries who contact and negotiate with clients and rival firms, filter market information, interpret at meetings, handle complex paperwork and facilitate cultural adjustment – all for a secretarial wage. Kelsky (2001: 208) quotes a bilingual legal assistant employed in a foreign affiliate law firm, who says:

> At this firm all the lawyers are white men, and all the assistants are Japanese women. It's the official policy. The partners don't want any Japanese males here. They say Japanese women are easier to control . . . It pisses me off, but what can you do? Aren't all law firms sexist?

Participation in the regular workforce and the characteristics of women's reproductive labour

The strength of the assumption in Japan that women, or at least other family members, will be responsible for all reproductive work continues to differentiate Japan from other First World countries. Japan has no developed network of paid babysitters comparable to that of the US or UK. The previous chapter also described the demands nursery schools place upon working mothers (Allison, 1996).

Women living in three-generation households, however, are somewhat less burdened than other married working women.[7] Thirty-eight per cent of Japanese working women using state childcare found that housework was a heavy or very heavy burden, a figure which dropped to only 24 per cent of those living in three-generation households and 14 per cent where the mother-in-law had the main responsibility for cooking (Stockman *et al.*, 1995: 114). A teacher the author interviewed was very enthusiastic about her work, teaching children with disabilities. She was a civil servant and thus able to take several months' maternity leave, but she said that it would have been quite impossible for her to return to work without the help of her mother-in-law, who acted as a full-time babysitter.

Nakamura and Ueda (1999) found that living with one's mother was a statistically significant positive factor in determining the likelihood of married women continuing to work after childbirth. In terms of childcare, 23 per cent of married couples with children under six lived in three-generation households and 77 per cent in two-generation households; the percentage of these households in which both partners worked was 54 per cent and 33 per cent respectively (Headquarters for the Promotion of Gender Equality, 2000). However, as Japan becomes increasingly urbanized and family size decreases there are fewer sons and daughters able or willing to accommodate an elderly parent (Ochiai, 1997).

Feminist theorists have observed that the potentially 'freeing' aspect that globalization has had upon an elite class of First World women, in that they have been able to pursue cosmopolitan professional careers, has been facilitated by the emergence of a class of female overseas contract workers carrying out personal services, such as domestic labour, for this cosmopolitan elite (Chang and Ling, 2000). Although this has been a notable feature of other East Asian economies, such as Hong Kong and Singapore, it is not at all characteristic of Japan, although the flow of female migrant workers in other sectors of the workforce has increased. No female undocumented workers (i.e. foreign migrants working without the necessary papers) have been found to be working as maids or providers of childcare since 1991, compared to 45,229 hostesses, 18,562 factory workers, 63,791 prostitutes, 8,817 dishwashers and 14,898 waitresses (Sellek, 2001: 53). There is pressure on women to show that they can 'cope' with housework and childcare, even if they hold jobs.

A questionnaire respondent wrote:

> There are many talented housewives and others who want to go out and work around me. But their present situation is such that, because of their husbands' disapproval, they have no choice but to give up their dreams. The situation gets worse as a woman gets married, gives birth to a child and becomes a mother. It's still difficult for women to do whatever they want in this society. *Because people take it for granted that the woman working outside should be able to manage her work at home perfectly, it's important for them to manage things efficiently.* I studied abroad for a month with my child. My husband had opposed the idea very strongly and it took me more than six months to persuade him. When I came back, people said that I was a bad wife because I did what I wanted to. On the other hand, my husband's stock rose and he was seen as a sympathetic husband. It wasn't fair.

Conclusion

In Japan, as elsewhere, neo-liberal globalization is presented by political elites as an inevitable process to which national states must react by reforming their domestic institutions.

The globalization of Japanese production, increased global regulation of women's rights, and increased flows of information, have exposed Japan's institutions to global scrutiny, and increased reflexivity about appropriate gender roles in Japan. Japanese women's rights campaigners have helped to construct a global standard concerning equal treatment of men and women in the workplace, and have been assisted in their cause by the development of that standard and by international organizations concerned with labour conditions. This is helping them to put pressure on the Japanese government to reduce the more obvious aspects of sexual discrimination in employment practices, via legislation such as the 1999 version of the Equal Employment Opportunities Law. The publicity surrounding the passage of this law and its 1986 predecessor has raised the consciousness of the Japanese public generally about women's labour rights. However, as most women are constrained by the expectation that they carry out reproductive work in the household as well, it is difficult for them to insist on entry to the same positions as their male colleagues – unless they have the help of a family member who will carry out reproductive work in their place. For a minority of highly skilled specialists, professionals, and totally dedicated *sogoshoku* employees, legal changes and restructuring may have some positive benefits, despite frequent violations of the spirit of the law.

Dominant ideologies can lead to the state and existing institutions to negotiate a compromise between encouraging change and maintaining the current gender order. This has in fact been the result of the way the

EEOL has been implemented. According to Hanami Tadashi, Chairman of the Central Labour Standards Council, companies are increasingly dividing workers into two discrete groups: core workers and:

> a large number of peripheral workers who can readily be displaced . . . It is obvious that women and immigrant workers are expected to constitute the latter group. The gist of the problem is that laws such as the Equal Employment Opportunity Law fit in perfectly with this design.
>
> (Osawa, 1998: 160)

Although some companies are taking steps to recruit skilled and qualified women by introducing a new employment track, what the EEOL has hastened overall is the institutionalization of a gender-based dual economy, where educated women continue to work in less-skilled jobs than their male counterparts, then leave the workplace to raise children. They then re-enter the workforce as non-regular workers under conditions which will be discussed in the next chapter.

7 Deregulation, restructuring and women working in non-regular positions

Introduction

One of the most significant effects of workforce restructuring in response to globalization in Japan is the increased use of 'non-regular' workers, that is, workers who do not have the same security of tenure or regular salary and other benefits that are enjoyed by full-time 'regular' employees. These non-regular workers include part-time, temporary and agency workers, as well as homeworkers, and are overwhelmingly female.[1]

In Chapter 3, the following observations were made about globalization and gender:

- States respond to the challenges of globalization by marketization and the adoption of neo-liberal policies. These policies have impacts which increase the reproductive work of women.
- There has been a 'feminization of labour'. A higher proportion of the workforce is female and a rising proportion of jobs available have those characteristics associated with female employment: relatively low pay; little job security; short-tenure; and part-time, temporary or home-based.

This chapter will show how these outcomes of globalization are particularly relevant to the situation in Japan, and thereby:

- contribute to the debate about the impact of globalization upon women by bringing in insights from the case of Japan into the wider academic discourse;
- examine the impact of restructuring upon women's employment in Japan.

This analysis will be restricted to non-regular workers in the formal, rather than informal, economy.[2] Analyses of the impact of globalization upon women in the Third World often focus on the growth of informal work and the articulation of women's work in the formal and informal economies (Gills, 2001; Carr and Chen, 2001). In Japan, a far higher proportion of economic activity is formally recorded than in Third World countries (although as the last chapter made clear, some sexual and service work is carried out by undocumented migrant workers). Even in comparison with other industrialized countries, Japan appears to be rather adept at recording employment. It is one of only seven countries in the world to include homeworking in its statistics on employment and production (International Labour Organization (ILO), 2002). Frey and Schneider (2000) attribute the small size of the informal economy in Japan, to Japan's relatively low public sector spending, compared to other First World nations. Low public spending is reflected in lower taxation, and therefore in a reduced incentive for workers to take on work to gain untaxable income.

The previous chapter described how an important outcome of the regulation of work was the employment of women in non-regular jobs. The growth of non-regular work has also been stimulated by the deregulation of employment as part of Japan's general move towards laissez-faire economic reforms. The first section of this chapter describes how government deregulation and marketization of the economy is predicated upon the assumption that women's reproductive work will render unnecessary increased state provision of welfare. It also shows how the continuation of Japanese norms about women's reproductive work is decisive in women's increased entry into non-regular work. The second section explains how globalization has increased companies' motivation to reduce costs and increase workforce flexibility, while the next section shows how the flexiblization of employment is facilitated by state deregulation of non-regular work. To show what impact this has on the women who constitute the vast majority of non-regular workers, the characteristics of important categories of non-regular work are then examined, looking particularly at the experiences of part-time, dispatched workers and homeworkers.

Deregulation and women's reproductive work

Deregulation has played an important part in the increase of women's reproductive work. As seen in Chapter 4, Japan had begun the process of marketization and deregulation in the 1990s, under pressure from the Clinton administration to facilitate the entry of foreign firms in Japan, and under pressure from the global economy to reduce production and transaction costs. With the formation of the second Hashimoto administration in 1990, a second period of deregulation began, characterised by Keidanren as the reform of 'traditional systems in the areas of administration, finance, and the economy to secure further economic development in harmony with the international community' (Toyoda, 1997). The six specified targets of reform were the administration, the financial system, the fiscal, economic and social security structures, and education. In his address to the Council for Gender Equality[3] on 16 June 1997 Prime Minister Hashimoto announced:

The kind of [Japanese] society I aim to create through the six reforms in preparation for the coming twenty-first century is one in which each and every citizen has a dream and objectives for the future and is able to fully display their creativity and spirit of challenge. This society that generates values to be shared with people throughout the world, when viewed from the perspective of men and women, is essentially a gender-equal society. The realization of this kind of society is the urgent demand of these times in which we grapple with rapid changes taking place in the socio-economic environment – *the ageing population*, the low birth rate, and the *maturation and internationalization of the economy* – in our quest for a prosperous and vigorous nation. Realization of this goal will be the key to Japan's future. For that reason, it is my belief that building a gender-equal society can be considered a form of social reform and that gender equality will be one of the pillars of 'reform and creation' in every field of society.

(Osawa, 2000: 3)

Upon initial examination, the administrative reforms did not obviously promote gender equality because they had the potential to increase the burden of women's reproductive work. In particular, the move towards a more laissez-faire economic policy is having harsh consequences for social welfare, as a gap has appeared between government spending requirements and government revenue. Taxes and economic stagnation have lowered Japan's revenue from 60,000 billion yen in 1990 to a predicted 46,800 billion yen in the fiscal year beginning April 2002 (*Financial Times*, 2002a: 12). The tax burden in Japan as a proportion of national income is the lowest in the G7 countries (at 22.9 per cent compared to 26.5 per cent in the US, 40 per cent in the UK, 31 per cent in Germany and 40 per cent in France (*Financial Times*, 2002b: 12). As noted in Chapter 4, Japan's spending on welfare was already, by the standards of advanced industrial economies, rather low, and women's reproductive work is expected to fill the gaps in state-provided welfare.

The previous two chapters have discussed the expectation that mothers will provide the largest proportion of care for children in Japan. There is not only social, but also legal, pressure for families to compensate for any shortfalls in state-provided care for the elderly. Even though three-generation co-residence has been decreasing with the move towards the nuclearization of the Japanese family, in 1999 23 per cent of married couples with children under six lived in three-generation households (Gender Equality Bureau, 2002). The improvements in living conditions of the Japanese people since the end of the Second World War has been accompanied by a remarkable rise in life expectancy.[4] This rise in life expectancy means that there are many elderly Japanese who will need care for a decade or more, and as infirmity tends to increase with age, the intensity of this care will be greater than in the past. The result is that there has been a remarkable increase in public spending on care for the elderly, and this is predicted to rise still further.[5]

Day care for the elderly, while not totally free, is heavily subsidized through taxation. Rises in costs therefore have important implications for those who pay taxes. Tax and social security contributions from firms account for 13.8 per cent of Japan's national income, a proportion which, if current trends continue, is set to increase to 20 per cent by 2025 (Ministry of Health and Welfare, 1999). The Japanese government has come under pressure to reduce these costs from the business lobby. *Nikkeiren*, for example, commissioned a study which showed that large Japanese firms paid the equivalent of US$10,000 per employee per year in welfare costs (*Nikkeiren*, 2001).

The Japanese government had instituted the Ten-Year Strategy to Promote Health Care and Welfare for the Elderly (commonly known as the Gold Plan) in 1989 (before the administrative reforms). However, the total amount of money budgeted by local governments for the health and welfare of elderly persons was, as of the end of 1993, more than that envisaged in the original Gold Plan. This plan was therefore revised in 1994 under the name New Gold Plan. The New Gold Plan stressed the increasing role of family members in providing care to elderly relatives. However, while government discourse might have played a role in encouraging women to undertake the traditional role of providing care for the elderly, continued shortfalls in publicly provided welfare have meant that there continued to be a 'care gap'. The Japanese government has removed local authorities' responsibility to produce the service infrastructure to care for elderly people and has encouraged a market-based system, as part of the government's more general moves towards marketization. Many local authorities continue to lack short-stay and day services for the elderly (Yoshida, 2002).

In 1995, the Child Care and Family Leave Care Law came into effect, entitling workers to a full year of leave after a child's birth and up to three months to care for infirm family members. While the provisions of the Law are theoretically open to both men and women, in reality it is almost exclusively women who use this provision. Between 1 April 1995 and 31 March 1996, only 0.6 per cent of the male workforce took childcare leave following the birth of a child (Sato, 2000: 3). The implications of this expectation of care from family members is reflected in this statement by the Ministry of Health, Labour and Welfare:

> In order for workers to lead a fulfilling career life through their life-time amid the ageing of the population and the declining birth rate, *it has become extremely important to create an environment where they can make good use of their abilities and experiences while combining work with childcare and the nursing of family members.*
>
> (Ministry of Health, Labour and Welfare, 2001, my italics)

It is then evident from this pronouncement and changes in legislation that the 'joint participation' of men and women in society is differentiated according to gender. Non-regular work allows firms to make use of women's 'abilities and experiences', while also leaving women sufficient time to be unpaid carers of Japan's growing elderly population. Women's unpaid care of the elderly represents a considerable saving in public expenditure. The annual per capita assessed value of unpaid elderly and nursing care accounts for 21.5 per cent of women's unpaid work (Fukami, 1999: 8), and has a replacement value of 1.475 billion yen (Economic Planning Agency, 1998).

The restructuring and 'flexibilizing' of the Japanese workforce are presented as the answer to the twin challenges of an aged society and economic globalization in Prime Minister Ryutaro Hashimoto's policy speech to the 136th Session of the National Diet:

> Reform is Japan's most pressing need today. When I was first elected to the Diet back in 1963, there were only 153 people 100 [years old] or older nationwide. Today, there are over 6,000. In the same period, the number of babies born every year has plummeted from 1.65 million to about 1.20 million. By the start of the next century, one in five Japanese will be 65 or older, and this will soon be one in four. *We are clearly becoming an aged society. With this outlook and the unprecedented speed at which the Japanese society is aging, it is imperative that we overhaul those social arrangements* premised upon a life span of twoscore and ten [*sic*] to suit our new expected life span of fourscore. At the same time, *there are also many changes that must be made, like it or not, in all aspects of Japanese society to cope with the collapse of Cold War structures, the borderless-action of the economy, Japan's enhanced global status, and other international changes.*
>
> (Ministry of Foreign Affairs, 1996, my italics)

Caregiving for the elderly is one of the most frequently given reasons for women to quit work after child rearing, but it does not seem, as yet, to be a major reason for taking on part-time work. The supply of women willing to accept part-time work is increasing for other reasons associated with shortfalls in welfare funding, though. The most frequently cited principal reason for taking a job given by part-time workers in a survey carried out by the Working Women's PAW (Part-timers Analysis and Watch)[6] was 'to supplement living expenses' (see Table 7.1). This was followed by 'to pay for children's education and mortgage', cited by around 14 per cent of part-time workers. Women's perceived need to pay for their children's education costs can also be attributed to shortfalls in state funding for secondary schools[7] and the increasing marketization of university funding.[8]

The Japanese government is facilitating reform through deregulation and marketization of the economy. It is evident from government pronouncements that women's reproductive labour is expected to cover

Table 7.1 What is your reason for working? Most important reason

	Regular public sector	Regular private sector	Non-regular public sector	Non-regular private sector	Total
To earn living expenses	70 (44.0%)	197 (50.0%)	158 (26.0%)	303 (30.0%)	886 (38.0%)
It is proper to work	40 (25.0%)	46 (12.0%)	43 (7.0%)	47 (5.0%)	176 (8.0%)
I want to be economically independent	17 (11.0%)	48 (12.0%)	18 (3.0%)	26 (3.0%)	109 (5.0%)
To improve myself and get a feeling of satisfaction	11 (7.0%)	17 (4.0%)	45 (7.0%)	55 (6.0%)	128 (6.0%)
I want links with society and other people	8 (5.0%)	12 (3.0%)	46 (7.0%)	30 (3.0%)	96 (4.0%)
To pay for children's education and the mortgage	5 (3.0%)	17 (4.0%)	65 (11.0%)	95 (10.0%)	182 (8.0%)
To supplement living expenses	5 (3.0%)	36 (9.0%)	180 (29.0%)	404 (40.0%)	625 (27.0%)
Money for shopping, travel etc.	0 (0.0%)	10 (3.0%)	27 (4.0%)	19 (2.0%)	56 (2.0%)
I want to pursue studies/hobbies	1 (1.0%)	8 (2.0%)	30 (5.0%)	15 (2.0%)	54 (2.0%)
Other	2 (1.0%)	5 (2.0%)	6 (1.0%)	4 (<1.0%)	17 (1.0%)
Total	159 (100.0%)	396 (100.0%)	460 (100.0%)	695 (100.0%)	2,329 (100.0%)

Source: Working Women's PAW, 1999: 88.

the subsequent shortfall in the provision of state-funded welfare for the elderly. Caring for the elderly though, does not, *as yet*, seem to be a major reason for women working in non-regular positions. According to the reasons that women themselves give, the potential supply of non-regular workers is partially determined by women's continued responsibility for childcare and housework, combined with their perceived need to contribute to household expenditure, particularly expenditure on their children's education (Table 7.1). The costs of education are rising as the Japanese education system becomes increasingly marketized.

The increased demand for non-regular workers

The previous section has examined why the supply of women ready to accept part-time employment is increasing. This section will examine why globalization is leading to an increased demand among firms for non-regular employees. It will then look at how government policy has facilitated firms' hiring of non-regular workers.

Globalization and the demand for a larger non-regular workforce

Companies receive a number of benefits by hiring non-regular or periph-eral workers, including part-time and contract workers. The non-regular workforce provides companies with greater flexibility in responding to market requirements. In addition, the hiring of non-regular workers is often cheaper for companies as wages, fringe benefits and legal protection of non-regular workers are often less than those of regular workers. The gradual growth of Japan's part-time labour force has been traced in Chapter 5, but as economic globalization has progressed, the rate of growth of non-regular work has intensified, as, in common with firms in many other First World countries, Japanese companies have attempted to reduce costs and increase the flexibility of labour. This process was accelerated by the East Asian economic crisis of 1997. In 1998, Japanese manufac-turers were suffering badly from the after-effects of the East Asian financial crisis.[9] During this time, the number of general workers fell by 0.8 per cent compared to 1997, while the number of part-time workers increased by 4.2 per cent (Ministry of Health, Labour and Welfare, 1998).[10]

Statements in the Ministry of Labour's *General Survey on the Diversified Types of Employment*, Tokyo: Ministry of Labour (1996) clearly indicate that com-panies' primary goals in taking on non-regular workers are the desire to reduce costs and attain flexibility (Figure 7.1). When companies were asked why non-regular workers were hired, the most popular reasons given were to control personnel costs (46.1 per cent), to meet personnel costs on a daily or weekly basis (29.1 per cent) and to meet personnel costs given the chang-ing business environment (21.5 per cent).

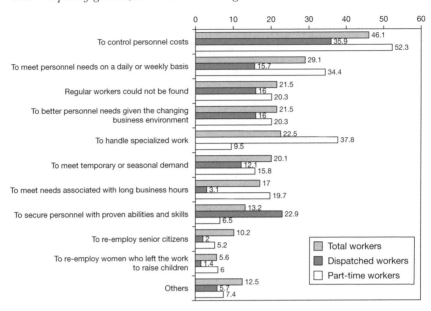

Figure 7.1 Reasons cited by establishments for hiring non-regular workers: Ministry of Labour, 1999 and Japan Institute of Labour, 1999: 24.

There is another possible reason for the growth in the non-regular work-force. As manufacturing jobs are increasingly 'exported' to low-wage economies, new jobs in First World countries are increasingly concentrated in the service sector (see Chapter 2). There have indeed been changes in the industrial structure of Japan. Like many other industrial countries, Japan has seen a growth in employment in the tertiary sector (even after the collapse of the Bubble economy) from fewer than 10 million employees in 1985 to more than 14 million in 1998 (Management and Coordination Agency, 1999b). The fact that the retail and service sectors, by their very nature, tend to have a higher share of part-time employment has contributed to this trend. However, according to Houseman and Osaka (1998: 246), only 6 per cent of the increases of part-time employment can be accounted for by changes in the industrial composition of employment, while 92 per cent can be attributed to increases in the rate of part-time employment within industries.

To the Japanese way of thinking, the Japanese style of (regular) employment offers 'three treasures': lifetime employment, payment according to seniority and enterprise unionism. Although some firms have laid off regular workers during the current recession, reluctance to lay off or fire regular workers is strong in Japanese culture. When forced to lay off workers, large firms often attempt to find new positions at different companies, usually those further down the *keiretsu* chain, for workers they can no longer employ (see Chapter 4). Public response and media coverage following the collapse of Yamaichi Securities Company, Japan's oldest and fourth-largest brokerage, and the resulting mass redundancies in 1997, demonstrate that job security is still a strong component of the Japanese concept of employment, at least for men. Non-regular work for married women, on the other hand, is far more acceptable socially, as it can be rationalized in terms of the compatibility of work and family life. In 1998, 39 per cent of Japanese people agreed or somewhat agreed with the sentiment that 'Women working full time will have a negative impact on their families' (NHK, 1998).

In many firms then, the non-regular workforce is entirely female. One 47-year-old interviewee was a homeworker. She worked for a company which produced practice tests for schoolchildren. She marked English papers and returned them to the company, which then redistributed the corrected tests to pupils. She said:

> There are almost no men – we have about 2000 people in the Osaka area, but only a few men. This job is not good for men, because the salary is low. It's a woman's job [. . .] My current job is very good for women, because I need to work only two days per week and I don't have to work longer hours, so I can use the rest of my time as I like. Only women can do this . . . Only married women can do this.

The deregulation of the airline and banking industries

The cases of the airline and banking industries provide two clear examples of how globalization has led to the restructuring of the workforce, and how restructuring has particular implications for female employees. The airline industry has been progressively deregulated since 1986. Reforms have included permitting Japanese airlines to compete against each other; allowing ANA (All Nippon Airlines) to enter international markets; permitting code-sharing with US airlines; and allowing discount tickets to be bought through legitimate channels. This shift from national protected business to one of international alliances competing with other alliances both globally and locally has led to a substantial worsening of conditions for the overwhelmingly female workforce of flight attendants in Japan.

In 1994 Japan Airlines announced a reorganization of personnel. All regular workers would be assigned to international flights, while temporary workers on short-term contracts, earning approximately half the wages of regular workers, would work on domestic flights. Consequently, many female regular workers who had domestic or childcare responsibilities left work, rather than be reassigned to international flights (Japan Airlines (JAL) Cabin Attendants' Union, 1995; Nakura, 1997). Meanwhile, the annual working hours of regular workers increased from 840 to 900 hours. Uchida Taeko (1998: 7), a flight attendant and activist in the aviation industry labour union, also claimed that as contract employees are paid by the hour, they tend to report to work even when unwell and that Japan Airlines was taking on a higher proportion of attendants from Singapore,

Hong Kong, Germany and Britain as women from these countries could be hired for up to 75 per cent less than their Japanese counterparts. Unlike most private companies, where there is a clear division between full-timers and others, contract workers can be upgraded to the status of full-timers, but this depends partly on the evaluations of their full-time colleagues, with obvious implications for workforce solidarity.

With the impact of 'Big Bang', the substantial deregulation of Japan's financial markets which came into effect on 11 March 1998, Japan's banking and financial services industry has become subject to increased foreign penetration from the likes of Merrill Lynch and Citibank (*Business-Week*, 1997). Big Bang has also made Japanese capital markets far more liberal. The result is that the Japanese financial sector is far more vulnerable to international flows. The speed with which foreign institutions entered Japan became a matter of political concern, particularly to Prime Minister Keizo Obuchi and Finance Minister Kiichi Miyazawa (Rowley, 1998). Japan's banks, including Asahi Bank, Chuo Trust Banking, Dai-ichi Kangyo Bank, Fuji Bank, Industrial Bank of Japan (IBJ), Long Term Credit Bank of Japan (LTCB), Mitsui Trust and Banking, Sumitomo Bank, Tokai Bank and Yasuda Bank, have acted defensively by forming mergers. The post-war system of cross-shareholding of banks and other firms, which facilitated long-term planning and stability (see Chapter 3), is also rapidly declining (*BusinessWeek*, 1997). It had been generally believed in the post-war period that banks could not fail. However, in 1997, the government showed its commitment to a more laissez-faire banking system when it failed to rescue Hokkaido Takushoku Bank, Yamaichi Securities, Sanyo Securities and Tokuyo City Bank.

Japan's domestic banks have been responding to increased competition, integration into the world economy and growing insecurity by attempting to reduce costs and increase the flexibility of their workforce so that they might respond more quickly to fluctuations in the international economic environment. This has impacted heavily upon women working in banking. One of the disadvantages for employers of hiring short-term or part-time workers rather than regular workers is that there are certain fixed costs associated with recruiting, such as the costs of recruitment, hiring and training. Many banks and security companies (as well as major trading and manufacturing firms) took steps to overcome this disadvantage, by setting up their own agencies in the 1980s. Mitsubishi, for example, is served by Diamond Staff Services, Sumitomo by Izumi Office Service and Daiwa by Daiwa Office Service. Female regular employees are encouraged to register with the firm's subsidiary agency when they leave upon childbirth or marriage. In this way, experienced and skilled workers continue to work for the same firm, but no longer benefit from the *nenko* system, and employers replace female regular workers with non-regular workers (Nakura, 1997). Recently, most major banks and general trading companies have stopped hiring regular clerical workers, most of whom were women. Part-time and agency workers are filling their places (Kuroiwa, 2001). One respondent described the situation of acquaintances who were differentiated from full-time workers despite carrying out the same job:

> It's a part of restructuring. I have three, four or five friends, um . . . at least three or four friends, who are working at a bank [. . .] part-time for almost ten years or more than that, but you can't see who is a part-timer and who is not. [. . .] And my friend said she is a little bit depressed because she knows better than the new, I mean, full-time worker[s] and still she is paid [less] . . . I mean, very low [wages] and she is treated as, of course, [a] part-timer so her [. . .] is quite unstable.
> (English Discussion Society focus group, 1999)

One securities firm did not even wait for women to resign, announcing that all female regular employees would be seconded to a worker dispatching company[11] and that the firm would from then on only recruit dispatched women workers (Sakai, 1999).

Women have not only been highly concentrated in the non-regular sector but their concentration within it is increasing, as Figure 7.2 shows. While 30.7 per cent of female employees were classified as irregular in 1982, that figure had risen to 50.7 per cent in 2002. The equivalent figures for men were 7.6 per cent and 14.8 per cent. Japanese employers' organizations had been keen to increase the non-regular proportion of the workforce,[12] but the rise in *effective* demand for non-regular workers was encouraged and facilitated by government policy.

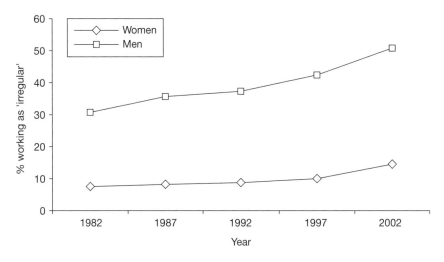

Figure 7.2 Trend in proportion of employees classified as 'non-regular', 1982–2002, by sex: Ministry of Public Management, Home Affairs, Posts and Telecommunications, 2002.

Government policy and the increased demand for female non-regular workers

The previous chapter described the impact of the EEOL and its revisions upon regular workers, and also the way it acted as an incentive for employers to increasingly employ women as non-regular workers. The employment of non-regular workers was further facilitated by the legalization of 'dispatched work'.

The Worker Dispatching Law

The progressive deregulation of worker dispatching activities is part of the Japanese government's overall deregulation policy, which aims to activate the external labour market (International Reform Monitor, 2001). The growth of a particular sub-category of non-regular work, that of dispatched work, has also been facilitated by legal change. The 1947 Employment Security Law prohibited private employment agencies from supplying companies with temporary workers to ensure employment security of workers and to break the hold of criminal gangs *(yakuza)* on the supply of casual manual labourers. The limited legalization of worker supply agencies (known as *hakenkaisha*, or 'dispatching' companies) in 1986 was therefore controversial, although an illicit worker dispatch industry had flourished since the late 1970s, supplying mostly white-collar female workers. This type of service grew rapidly, and the number of dispatched workers increased from 145,000 to 654,000 between 1986 and 1992 (Araki, 1994: 1), and by FY 1999 this number had increased to 1.07 million dispatched workers (*Japan Times*, 2001).

By 1994 there were 2,300 temporary employment agencies, which supplied mostly workers for basic computer operating, filing and general office work, accounting and finance (Hulme, 1996). The Worker Dispatching Law originally limited worker dispatching to a very limited range of specialist activities, such as legal services, accountancy and acting, in which workers were, by the nature of the activity, only required for specified limited time periods. The list of activities that can be carried out by dispatched workers has gradually been expanded until in 1990 the proportion of professions for which fee-charging agencies could legitimately supply workers accounted for 18 per cent of the workforce. Revisions in the Worker Dispatching Law effective from 1 April 1997 listed only six classes of occupation which could *not* be carried out by dispatched workers:

- clerical workers, within one year of school graduation;
- sales work, within one year of school graduation;
- service workers, with the exception of housekeepers, barbers, hairdressers, kimono dressing helpers, laundering and cleaning technicians, cooks, bartenders, waiters and waitresses at formal restaurants, models, and demonstrators of retail goods;

- security guards;
- agriculture, forestry and fishery workers;
- transport and communication workers, with the exception of bus tour conductors.

After these revisions came into effect, the jobs of 40 per cent of Japanese employees could be carried out by dispatched workers (Morito, 1999). With a revision of the Employment Security Law which came into effect at the end of 1999, the procedures by which worker dispatching agencies can gain the necessary operating licence have also been eased.

Japanese companies, then, have, in line with companies elsewhere, responded to the challenges of globalization by the feminization of employment and an increase in part-time, temporary and home-based work, predominantly carried out by women. The employment of non-regular workers has been encouraged and facilitated by legal change. Evidence from other countries (see Chapter 3) suggests that this work will tend to be characterized by less favourable conditions than those prevailing in the shrinking regular workforce. The next section will describe the characteristics of such non-regular work in Japan, concentrating particularly on the cases of female part-time and dispatched workers,[13] with the aim of clarifying whether this is the case in Japan.

The characteristics of non-regular work

Few regular workers seem to envy the lot of non-regular workers: 77.3 per cent of non-regular public-sector workers and 46.2 per cent of non-regular private-sector workers wanted to work as regular workers (Table 7.2) while only 10.1 per cent of regular public-sector workers and 10.3 per cent of regular private-sector workers wished to work as non-regular workers (Table 7.3).

This section examines why non-regular work seems to be viewed so unfavourably. It describes the formal and informal segregation of non-regular workers from their regular counterparts, and the wages non-regular workers can expect to receive. It also looks at the age and gender profile of non-regular workers, shows how non-regular work is changing, and why, in spite of its apparent disadvantages, women tend to be concentrated in the non-regular workforce.

Part-time work

The largest category of non-regular work is that of part-time work. Part-time work is generally paid by the hour, and does not have the guarantee of job security that is expected from employment in the regular workforce. Most *paato* work in manufacturing or in retail. Very few Japanese women are members of what is known in Japanese English as the *paalite* – or part-time elite, of consultants, researchers, or programmers etc. (Molony, 1995). Most part-time work, therefore, tends to be low-paid, relative to regular work.

Table 7.2 I want to work as a regular, not a non-regular worker

	Regular public sector	Regular private sector	Non-regular public sector	Non-regular private sector	Total
Yes	71 (80.7%)	220 (90.2%)	650 (77.3%)	230 (46.2%)	1,171 (70.1%)
No	17 (19.3%)	24 (9.8%)	191 (22.7%)	268 (53.8%)	500 (29.9%)
Total	88 (100.0%)	244 (100.0%)	841 (100.0%)	498 (100.0%)	1,671 (100.0%)

Source: Working Women's PAW, 1999: 93.

Table 7.3 I want to work as a non-regular, not a regular worker

	Regular public sector	Regular private sector	Non-regular public sector	Non-regular private sector	Total
Yes	11 (10.1%)	26 (10.3%)	166 (28.1%)	202 (55.0%)	405 (30.8%)
No	98 (89.9%)	226 (89.7%)	423 (71.8%)	165 (45.0%)	912 (69.2%)
Total	109 (100.0%)	252 (100.0%)	589 (100.0%)	367 (100.0%)	1,317 (100.0%)

Source: Working Women's PAW, 1999: 93.

Table 7.4 What kind of satisfaction do you get from your job?

	Regular public sector	Regular private sector	Non-regular public sector	Non-regular private sector
Possibility of working long-term	8.5	6.1	4.6	6.3
Working environment	6.8	5.9	6.2	6.3
Wages for the amount of work	7.3	5.3	5.0	5.6
Authority in charge	6.8	5.5	4.1	5.2
Relations with co-workers	7.2	6.8	7.0	7.3
Chances for education	6.3	4.6	3.3	4.5
It is worthwhile	6.4	5.5	5.6	5.9
Working hours	7.5	6.7	7.0	7.3
The amount of work	6.8	5.9	5.9	6.3
Arrangement of flexibility	6.2	5.4	5.3	6.1
Good relations with superiors	6.3	5.6	6.0	6.3
Possibilities of promotion	6.0	4.0	2.0	2.9
Future prospects of company	5.7	4.6	4.5	5.2
Total	87.8	71.9	66.5	75.2

Note: All figures in percentages.

Source: Working Women's PAW, 1999: 87.

Formally and informally differentiated from regular workers

The International Labour Organization (1997) cite as one of the benefits of part-time work for employees the idea that it can make it easier for workers to enter or leave the labour market. However, in Japan the opportunities to use part-time work as a stepping stone to establishing a career seem to be very few. Although there has been an expansion in the tasks allocated to part-time workers, generally regular and non-regular workers have very different career paths. Most companies do not allow staff to transfer from non-regular to regular status. A 57-year-old consumer credit worker answered the question 'Have you ever considered taking a full-time job with the company?' by saying: 'Regardless of whether I want to do a full-time job or not, there is no system like that. I can't transfer from a part-time worker basis to a full-time worker basis.'

Only 2 per cent of non-regular workers in the public sector and 2.9 per cent of non-regular workers in the private sector claimed to derive job satisfaction from 'possibilities of promotion' (female regular workers also showed little anticipation of promotion, with only 6 per cent in the public sector and 4 per cent in the private sector gaining satisfaction from the possibility of advancement; see Table 7.4). When asked about her chances of promotion, a 45-year-old worker at a childcare centre, wrote, 'Not applicable because I'm a part-timer.'

Part-time workers (and other non-regular workers) do not enjoy the same legal rights and work benefits as regular workers. Labour protection and maternity protection in the Labour Standards Law apply solely to regular employees and there have been an increasing number of cases where employment contracts have been cancelled when a worker takes maternity or childcare leave. Regular (51.1 per cent) and non-regular workers (61.3 per cent) in the public sector agree that regular workers can more easily take time off under various holiday systems; 31.1 per cent of non-regular private-sector workers agreed, while 24.3 per cent disagreed and 44.6 per cent were unsure. Only regular private-sector workers dissented, with 25.6 per cent agreeing, 36.6 per cent 'unsure' and 37.9 per cent disagreeing (Table 7.5).

This is exemplified by the case of Matsushita Electrical, where 71 part-timers over the age of fifty were dismissed in 2001, to solve the company's problems of over-production of magnetic-heads for discs. The part-time workers were sufficiently skilled to instruct new full-time employees and many had worked for the company for more than ten years. The employer said to part-timers when he dismissed them, 'Those whose children have grown up should retire or those who have taken more paid leave should retire first.' (Zenroren, 2001a). In the case of Matsushita Electric, workers set up their own union to protest against the dismissals, as the union at their workplace did not permit part-time workers to join. Lack of union protection had been one of the factors which had exacerbated the relatively unstable and poorly rewarded situation of peripheral workers (see Chapter 5). This does not mean that all non-regular workers are necessarily happy with the situation of exclusion from trade unions. A 43-year-old worker at a childcare centre explained that she was not a trade union member, but would like to be because: 'I [could] join activities to improve working conditions.' A 39-year-old worker at a consumer credit company said that if she were able to join a trade union, then she would because:

> I want a wage rise. (Laughs) My contract is renewed every two months, so I would like a longer term contract than this. I don't get any fringe benefits like unemployment benefit and I don't get any health benefits, because I am a part-timer. Nor a pension.

As well as this formal differentiation, where part-time workers do not have the same legal rights, terms of employment and access to trade unions as their full-time counterparts, there is also a degree of informal segregation.

Some full-time workers in the survey conducted by the Part-Time Research Group to Consider Women's Working Life appeared to show a degree of hostility to non-regular workers: 35.7 per cent of regular workers felt that regular workers tackled their jobs more positively than their non-regular colleagues (Table 7.6).

These attitudes might well reflect a lingering prejudice against working mothers (see Chapter 5), even when only working part-time. Many Japanese believe that a mother should devote herself to bringing up her children before the age of three (*Japan Labour Bulletin*, 1 July 2001).

Part-time workers are also aware that the differentiation between their status and those in the regular workforce is at least partially determined by their gender. For example a 40-year-old worker for a social and educational association responded to the question 'Was there a difference between the way you were recruited and the way your male co-workers were recruited?' with the reply, 'I can't answer because I'm a part-timer.'

Pay

The average hourly wage of female part-timers in 2001 was 886 yen, which was only 68.4 per cent of the average wage for female workers or 44.25 per cent of that of male workers (Kuroiwa, 2001: 4). Furthermore, part-time workers are far less likely to be eligible to receive a bonus or other fringe benefits. It is doubtful whether women working part-time could earn enough to live an independent life. According to a survey of 2,319 working women (excluding dispatched workers) conducted by the Working Women's PAW, no non-regular workers gave as their most important reason for working 'to earn living expenses' compared to 44 per cent of regular public-sector workers and 49.7 per cent of regular private-sector workers (see Table 7.1). That does not mean that the wages they earned were unimportant to household income: 39.1 per cent of non-regular workers employed in the public-sector and 58.1 per cent employed in the private-sector were working to supplement living expenses and 14.1 per cent and 13.7 per cent respectively were working to pay for their children's education or for their mortgage (see Table 7.1).

Not only do non-regular workers seem dissatisfied with the money they receive for their work (79.4 per cent of non-regular workers in the public sector and 57.1 per cent in the private sector felt that their wages were 'rather low' or 'too low') but there appears to be considerable support among their full-time colleagues for the idea that part-timers' pay is unsatisfactory: 54.6 per cent of full-time public-sector workers and 34.7 per cent of full-time private-sector workers felt that part-timers' pay was 'too low' or 'rather low', compared to just 2.9 per cent and 3.7 per cent respectively who felt that part-timers' pay was 'rather high' (no respondents felt it was 'too high') (Table 7.7).

There is, however, some evidence that the average wages of part-time workers are increasing at a faster rate than those of regular non-managerial workers. The average hourly wages of part-timers in manufacturing and services rose by 54.3 per cent and 54.2 per cent respectively between 1984 and 2000, while the average annual contractual wages of non-managerial regular employees rose by only 33.3 per cent in the same period (see Figures 7.3 and 7.4).

Table 7.5 Regular workers can more easily take time off under various holiday systems

	Regular public sector	Regular private sector	Non-regular public sector	Non-regular private sector	Total
Yes	71 (51.1%)	79 (25.6%)	543 (61.3%)	178 (31.1%)	871 (45.7%)
Cannot say which	48 (34.5%)	113 (36.6%)	250 (28.2%)	255 (44.6%)	666 (34.9%)
No	20 (14.4%)	117 (37.9%)	93 (10.5%)	139 (24.3%)	369 (19.4%)
Total	139 (100.0%)	309 (100.0%)	886 (100.0%)	572 (100.0%)	1,906 (100.0%)

Source: Working Women's PAW, 1999: 92.

Table 7.6 Regular workers tackle their jobs more positively

	Regular public sector	Regular private sector	Non-regular public sector	Non-regular private sector	Total
Yes	50 (35.7%)	111 (35.7%)	150 (16.9%)	88 (15.5%)	399 (20.9%)
Cannot say which	81 (57.9%)	180 (57.9%)	572 (64.6%)	369 (64.9%)	1,202 (63.1%)
No	9 (6.4%)	20 (6.4%)	164 (18.5%)	112 (19.7%)	305 (16.0%)
Total	140 (100.0%)	311 (100.0%)	886 (100.0%)	569 (100.0%)	1,906 (100.0%)

Source: Working Women's PAW, 1999: 92.

Table 7.7 What do you think of the wage rate of part-timers and non-regular workers, compared to regular workers doing the same job?

	Regular public sector	Regular private sector	Non-regular public sector	Non-regular private sector	Total
Too low	50 (36.4%)	66 (18.9%)	629 (63.7%)	241 (37.4%)	986 (51.7%)
Rather low	25 (18.2%)	55 (15.8%)	155 (15.7%)	127 (19.7%)	362 (19.0%)
Appropriate	11 (8.0%)	66 (18.9%)	87 (8.8%)	116 (18.0%)	280 (14.7%)
Rather high	4 (2.9%)	13 (3.7%)	7 (0.7%)	8 (1.2%)	32 (1.7%)
Too high	0 (0.0%)	0 (0.0%)	1 (0.1%)	2 (0.3%)	3 (0.2%)
Don't know	47 (34.3%)	149 (42.7%)	108 (10.9%)	151 (23.4%)	455 (23.9%)
Total	137 (100.0%)	349 (100.0%)	987 (100.0%)	645 (100.0%)	1,906 (100.0%)

Source: Working Women's PAW, 1999: 86.

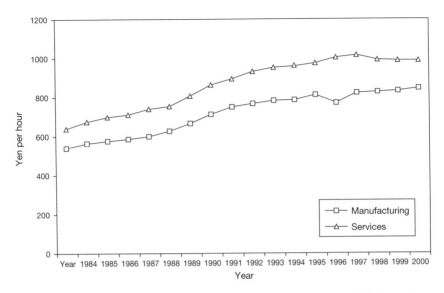

Figure 7.3 Hourly earnings of female part-time workers, 1984–2000: Ministry of Health, Labour and Welfare, 2001.

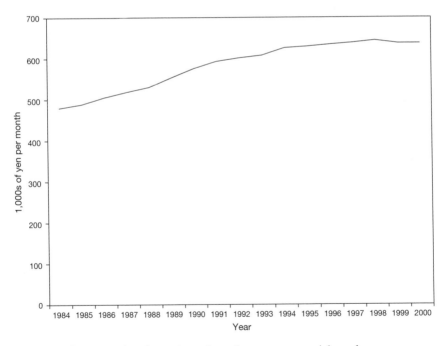

Figure 7.4 Contractual cash earnings of regular non-managerial employees, 1984–2000: Ministry of Health, Labour and Welfare, 2001.

Increased diversification in the part-time workforce

The rise in the wages of part-time workers could be partially attributable to the emergence of a class of workers known as *kikan ga paato* (key part-timers): long-tenure part-time employees, who have been increasingly trusted with some of the same tasks as regular workers, e.g. ordering stocks in the retail sector. In the past, it was widely felt that differences in compensation for non-regular workers would cause resentment at work. This is reflected in Iwao's analysis:

> What makes [non-regular] jobs so popular among women and employers are the advantages they offer for both sides. From the employer's standpoint, part-time jobs are a way of obtaining additional workers *without having to spend more on employee benefits or worry about people vying for promotion* . . .

> (Iwao, 1993: 173, my italics)

However, in recent years there has been increased acceptance of the idea of merit-based pay. Takeishi (2000) investigated 16 companies in the retail sector and found that 7 had 'drastically' revised their pay and promotions structure for non-regular workers. A supermarket had introduced incentives in the form of bonuses based on store, department and individual performance. The promotion of part-time workers to regular workers in the retail trade has also been reported. One women's apparel retail store in Takeishi's survey had even extended promotion opportunities to non-regular workers (Takeishi, 2000).

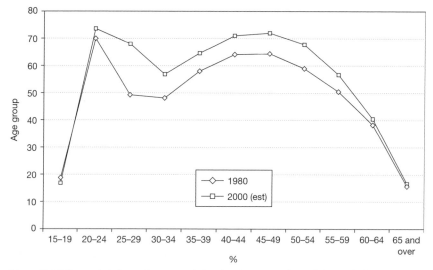

Figure 7.5 Women's labour force participation by age: adapted from Cabinet Office (2001a – downloaded date).

Age and gender profile of part-time workers

Figure 7.5 shows how women's labour force participation has increased between 1980 and 2000. However, when the figures are broken down into full-time and part-time employment (see Figure 7.6) it becomes apparent that from the age group 25–29 until 45–49, i.e. the years where one is most likely to be caring for children, or perhaps undertaking other family or elder care, the proportion of women working part-time rises. Indeed, the proportion of part-time workers surpasses full-time workers in the age group 40–49. Conversely, the proportion of women working full-time begins to fall after the age group 20–24, and does not significantly rise again. One interviewee used the Japanese English phrase *paato no obachan*, literally, 'auntie part-timer', indicating part-time work has a very specific gender and age profile. It is interesting to note that when part-time work is carried out by students (of either sex) it is customarily referred to as *arubaito* (from the German work 'Arbeit') rather than *paato* work.

Combination of reproductive work and part-time employment

The age profile of part-time workers shown above indicates that most women turn to part-time work at times in their life course where they are most likely to be carrying out reproductive work. The most popular reason given for working part-time by female part-time workers is wishing to work only when convenient, which was chosen by over 60 per cent of participants in the Ministry of Labour's (1990) *Comprehensive Research on the Actual*

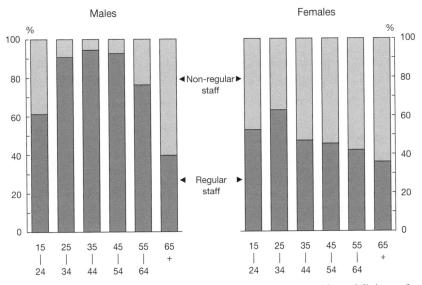

Figure 7.6 Ratios of regular to non-regular employment by age and sex: Ministry of Public Management, Home Affairs, Posts and Telecommunications (2003).

Conditions of Part-time Employees. However, the second most common answer chosen by nearly 45 per cent of female part-time employees between 30 and 39 was 'cannot work full-time due to housework and childcare' (Ministry of Labour, 1990). Part-time employment can indeed help workers to balance work and family life. However, there are a couple of important caveats which make it difficult to judge the extent to which taking a part-time job for this reason is really a free 'choice'. First, people might have assumed the responsibility for reproductive work because they are aware that they have limited opportunities for paid work. Sakai (1999) makes the point that the work available to women depends on age: 25 is the usual limit for regular employment. Furthermore the need for individuals to provide childcare and care for the elderly is at least partially determined by political decisions about how much social care is provided by the state. According to a survey of 2,319 working women (excluding dispatched workers), 34.5 per cent of non-regular workers in private companies and 56.4 per cent of non-regular workers in the public sector said they were doing non-regular work 'involuntarily' (Working Women's PAW, 1999).

In some cases part-time work does not necessarily even guarantee flexibility to organize one's domestic work, as working hours can be the same as those of full-time workers (see Chapter 5), or can lack flexibility. A part-time worker also explained the difficulty she had in determining her own working hours:

> In the beginning it was only four hours a week, so there was no difficulty with the children. The only one difficulty was during the weekend, there is no . . . it is not certain that I will be able to get days off in the weekend . . .

This is somewhat ironic. Workers who are often working in non-regular jobs because of childcare responsibilities do not have the same flexibility to take time off to supervise children as their full-time colleagues.

Dispatched work

Another form of non-regular work, which is becoming increasingly important in Japan is that of 'dispatched' work. There has been a boom in the agency worker business, with the number of dispatched workers doubling from 1,140,000 in 1992 to 2,040,000 in 1997 (Rengo White Paper, 1999: 77).

Formally and informally differentiated from regular workers

Like *paato* workers, dispatched workers are formally and informally segregated from regular workers. One interviewee who used to work as a dispatched worker gave an example of her isolation from regular workers:

What I didn't like was that . . . although there were several dispatched workers, all . . . the whole group were [called] *Haken-san* (Ms Temp) . . . I mean, we didn't say '*Seishain-san*' (Ms Regular Worker) . . . It wasn't discrimination but . . . for example . . . sometimes in Japanese companies there are sweets. A customer comes and brings sweets as a present. In the office they would hand them round, but when they got to a *haken-san*, they would skip you. It's unbelievable isn't it? . . . That's really dreadful, isn't it?

(34-year-old former dispatched worker)

It is possible that this can be attributed to fear of being replaced by dispatched workers. Certainly, this was a fear at the time the Law was passed. When the Worker Dispatching Law was voted on by the Social Labour Committee of the House of Councillors in May 1985, the Committee also resolved that the Government should pay attention to harmonizing the worker dispatching business with Japanese customs of employment and take measures to ensure that dispatched workers would not replace regular workers (Goka, 1998).

A 31-year-old dispatched worker at a multinational accounting firm though, was less distressed by not being part of a cohesive group at work. She wrote on a questionnaire about whether or not she socialized with her co-workers, 'I don't expect them to socialize and I don't want to do it.' Similarly, a discussion group participant found that having a status that meant she was not a true 'member' of the company could be quite liberating, at least in the short term:

still at that time people were paid about 700 yen for regular part time job[s], but I got 1200 per hour, so that was very good. So I enjoyed it very much and I had no responsibilities whatsoever. And I was like a guest. (Laughter from the rest of the group) So that was good. But now, thinking back, if I had to work as a . . . that kind of worker, then I wouldn't continue to do that more than one year, so . . . That would be too bad, because I . . . Maybe if I stayed there for more than one year I would have felt isolated from other workers. And I would have noticed many discrimination against me, but I stayed there only six months. They treated me very well.

However, in some cases, in contrast to the situation of part-time workers, work as a dispatched worker can lead to entry into the regular workforce. Revisions to the worker dispatching legislation, which came into effect at the end of 1999, prohibit a client company from receiving a dispatched worker in the same position in the workplace for more than one year; this also applies to the dispatching agencies. If a company wishes to continue to employ a worker after that time, it must employ them directly. Yoshikazu Hashiguchi, head of the marketing headquarters at Manpower Co. Japan says, 'Foreign-affiliated firms show a particularly high level of interest.' (*Japan Times*, 2001). Three-quarters of workers placed by the agency Girl Friday with foreign firms became permanent, suggesting that these firms are using agencies as a way of 'checking out' workers, rather than risking immediately taking on the responsibilities associated with employing full-timers in Japan. However, only 1 per cent of employees of Tempstaff, whose customers are predominantly Japanese, are retained in this way (Hulme, 1996).

Pay

In contrast to the trends in the wages of part-timers, the job of a dispatched worker is becoming less well rewarded. A survey conducted by the Dispatching Network found that the 1,706 yen average hourly wage in 1994 had decreased to 1,660 yen in 1998 (Sakai, 1999). There are additional hidden costs. Dispatched workers are expected to have skills, such as computer proficiency or the ability to speak English, which must be gained at their own expense. Agencies charge applicants an 'acceptance fee' when they are chosen for a position. Few dispatched workers receive social insurance of any kind, which means that employees of 'general worker dispatching enterprises', which tend to supply computer operators, clerks and so on, do not receive pay or benefits between assignments. The employees of 'special worker dispatching agencies' which focus on providing highly skilled professionals who, for example, design computer systems or machinery continue to be paid between assignments. In addition, most are not reimbursed for travel expenses (which is standard practice for employees in Japan). Being dispatched to a distant location therefore involves considerable expense for them. Although Japan has been criticized for not signing the ILO Convention on Dispatched Work (Goka, 1998), Japanese domestic courts have begun to establish some minimum rights for dispatched workers with regard to pay. In November 1999, Nagano District Court judged that temporary workers doing the same work as regular workers were entitled to 80 per cent of the pay of regular workers, and were entitled to the same standards of bonus and pensions. It remains to be seen to what extent this judgement will be used as a precedent for dealing with the treatment of other non-regular workers.

'Deskilling' of the dispatched work sector

The falling wages of dispatched workers can also be attributed to the changing nature of dispatched work. As the list of jobs dispatched workers may do has expanded, dispatched workers have increasingly been recruited for less-skilled jobs. (Wages do vary considerably between different types of dispatched work. In 1993, the highest average daily wage was 18,824 yen for interpretation, translation and shorthand, while the lowest was

5,562 yen for cleaning service for buildings. The wage commonly paid for filing or classification of papers was 8,818 yen (Goka, 1998).) Anecdotal evidence, however, suggests that the law was merely regularizing what had been common practice for a long time. One former dispatched worker said:

> if they can't find [an] appropriate person within the company, then they can hire the temporary workers as skilled labour. But in reality they hire the workers without skills, without, you know, special skills. I mean, workers as a clerk. But if they call them clerk, it's illegal, so they call them 'operator' or. . . . different names [. . .] When I worked as an assistant [. . .] in the document my position was 'Operator for English documents' or something. I was just an assistant, doing nothing particular.
>
> (31-year-old former dispatched worker)

It is, of course, difficult for vulnerable employees to complain about this practice. For instance, workers formally allocated to specific secretarial work can find upon arrival at a firm that they are to work in warehousing (Kondo *et al.*, 1999).

Age and gender profile of dispatched workers

The profile of workers of dispatching companies is a little different from that of a 'typical' non-regular worker. There is often a limit of 35 years for registering as a dispatched worker, and dispatching companies often exhibit a preference for young and attractive women (Sakai, 1999). Client companies often ask the supplying agencies for photographs or for interviews. One company ranked their employees' appearance in three categories. When the information later appeared on the Internet, a lawsuit was brought against the company. A former dispatched worker complained about seemingly being selected according to characteristics other than her skills, as follows:

> [E]ven if you have both computer and English skills . . . it's hard to get a job. But I . . . I think it's really a stupid thing, because . . . why . . . you know, I've already registered in this agency, and before the registration it takes about two or three hours, you know, you know, because I have to have an interview with the um with the manager or personnel of the agency . . . [Y]ou have to take exams on computers. You have to [. . .] show your skill of computers. So you have to take exams . . . tests, computer tests or English tests or have interview with that person. So it's . . . you have to have . . . to do these kinds of things already. So they know how skilful you are already . . . but still you can't get a job. Several months later I got a quite good job in a pharmaceutical company [. . .]

but at the time, I was selected out of more than 10 people from differ-ent agencies [. . .] I was lucky at that time, but other . . . in other times, I was failed, you know. I failed to be selected and other person was selected. It's [a] kind of thing [that] happen[s] every day for everyone. And every time I ask the people in agency, 'What was wrong with me? Why I wasn't be selected?' But always time, they say, 'Oh there noth-ing wrong with you. *It's just a, you know, chemistry.' (Laughs) Or the . . . or if you are good for you know, . . . if you will go well with the atmosphere of the com-pany or something. Or if the personnel or the people who you are working for like you or not. It depends on these things [. . .] (Laughs)* (my italics)

Furthermore, in the context of the 'Ice Age' of employment for female university graduates (see Chapter 6), many young women are signing up for dispatched work in the hope of regular work, which they could previ-ously have expected to find anyway with little difficulty: 'There are widespread complaints by female students who say that since it will be hard for them to get regular jobs after graduation, they have no choice but to find temporary employment' (Goka, 1998).

Homeworking

Part-time and dispatched workers are not the only non-regular workers in Japan. Women are over-represented in almost all areas of non-regular work, including homeworking.

In many countries, it is difficult to carry out research on homeworking, because of its hidden nature, and, often, the uncertain legal status of such work. Japan is unusual in its recording and regulation of homework-ing (*naishoku*). Following a campaign by homeworkers in 1959 (when some homeworkers were poisoned after using the adhesive benzine) the Japanese government recognized the sector in the Industrial Homework Act of 1970, which regulated the conditions of such workers. Committees were established in each prefecture, which set the wage rates of homeworkers in each province and appoint labour inspectors who monitor whether these rates are observed (ILO, 2002). Furthermore, the Kanai Soren union of homeworkers in shoe and boot making was successful in winning free medical examinations and subsidized unemployment insurance for industrial homeworkers.[14]

In spite of what is, compared to homeworking in other countries, a rela-tively high degree of regulation, homeworking is even more poorly paid than other forms of non-regular work. The hourly average wage of home-workers is 478 yen (on top of necessary expenses). When wage rates are disaggregated by gender, men receive 865 yen per hour and women 452 yen (Zenroren, 2001b). In addition the Industrial Homeworking Act (in contravention of the recommendations of the draft ILO Convention on Homeworking) classifies homeworkers as self-employed, which means that they are eligible to pay a higher tax rate than employees.

According to a Ministry of Labour survey in 1995, there were 657,300 homeworkers. Of these, 93.4 per cent were not classified as the primary earner in the household (i.e. were probably married women), 5.6 per cent were professional male homeworkers and 1 per cent were side workers with another primary occupation (Zenroren, 2001b).

Counter-intuitively, and very differently to the case in the UK (Greater Manchester Low Pay Unit, 1998), homeworkers in Japan are rather well organized. There are community-based associations of homeworkers who act as subcontractors. They are responsible for quality control and for negotiating contracts with employers, and often have small offices, with a van for delivery of the work to homeworkers (Women in Informal Employment Globalizing and Organizing (WIEGO), no date). Examples are the Homeworkers' Friendship Associations in Kyoto which provide a network of support for homeworkers. This support includes providing training and finding work for homeworkers, delivering and collecting work, quality control and collective bargaining over rates of pay (Tate, 2000).

Homeworking in Japan is becoming increasingly diversified, to include industrial homeworkers in relatively 'new' industries, such as the women who put together circuit boards at home, to teleworkers. One interviewee worked for a company which set practice tests in mathematics, Japanese, English, science and social science, in order to improve exam performance. She marked the tests and then returned them to the company who distributed them to the children. Like other non-regular workers her paid work choices were constrained by responsibility for childrearing. She explained: 'I took this job because I had two children so I couldn't go outside. I couldn't find a job outside.' As she liked the job, she had continued doing it even after her children had grown up, and used her wages to send 'pocket money' to her child at university. She found satisfaction from social activities with other homeworkers for the same company. She said she was '[n]ot isolated: Sometimes we meet at Christmas and go hiking or go shopping or go to a restaurant – one or two times a month (laughs) – it's good for relaxing and getting rid of frustration . . . get rid of stress.' However, in line with the suggestion in Chapter 5 that non-regular work may have retarded change and to have institutionalized women's 'dual burden' of productive and reproductive work, she added:

> I worked three or fours days a week before I got married. I quit when I got married. Returning to work was difficult, because I have to do everything. My husband doesn't help. *I don't work* (sic) so I do the housework.

Conclusion

Japanese firms have attempted to restructure their workforces in order to cut costs and increase flexibility, in the face of globalization. This is especially notable in the airline and banking sectors where the impact of globalization has been particularly marked. The goal of restructuring is being supported by the Japanese government. A non-regular or part-time workforce helps the government to achieve its joint goals of:

- keeping public spending on social services to a minimum, as it increasingly adopts a more neo-liberal, Anglo-American model of economic governance (see Chapter 4); and
- making use of the skills and experience of Japanese women in the workplace.

The increasing desire of women to work, combined with government encouragement for women to combine caring and reproductive work with outside employment has meant that there is a pool of women available to meet the increasing demand for 'non-regular' workers. With the passage of the EEOL, there is an additional incentive for employers to take on women as non-regular workers, as occupational sexual segregation means that employers are not obliged to provide them with the same pay and fringe benefits as male regular workers.

The image of a non-regular worker is generally very 'gendered'. *Paato* and homeworkers are expected to be married women, with family responsibilities, and consequently there is little pressure to pay them wages to cover the costs of reproduction. There is some evidence that dispatched workers, too, are expected to be young, attractive and have a personality that fits in with the firm's expectations.

The regular and non-regular workforces in Japan are strictly differentiated. Non-regular workers can expect to receive lower wages, fewer fringe benefits and less legal protection than their full-time regular co-workers; and to be excluded from trade union membership. There is also anecdotal emphasis that they are to some extent excluded from the workplace community.

The position of non-regular workers, though, is not static. As the non-regular workforce has grown, so it has diversified. In the retail sector particularly, part-time workers are increasingly being graded and offered a range of responsibilities dependent on their abilities and the length of their tenure. The range of positions open to dispatched workers is also growing, although the corollary of this is a fall in the average wages of such workers. In some cases, dispatched work can lead to regular job opportunities. In the main though, an increasing number of women are being concentrated in a secondary labour market, with few of the benefits that 'core' workers have enjoyed in the post-war Japanese model of employment.

8 Globalization and women's activism in Japan

Introduction

As Chapter 4 shows, Japan has played a pro-active role in the globalization of production (Hatch and Yamamura, 1996; Hasegawa and Hook, 1998). This strategy has had significant reciprocal dynamics, in the shape of the 'hollowing out' of Japanese production (Hasegawa and Hook, 1998: Eades *et al.*, 2000) and of pressure on companies within Japan to reduce the cost of production (Ohmae, 1995). Companies therefore are attempting to reduce the costs of labour in the Japanese workforce by increasing the segmentation of the Japanese workforce (Chapters 5 and 7). Although equal opportunities legislation, passed to meet UN commitments, has been passed, companies have generally restructured their labour forces in ways that institutionalize the secondary status of many female regular employees (see Chapter 6). Non-regular employment, in the form of part-time and temporary contract work, has expanded, with the new jobs largely filled by women, who are increasingly entering the workforce, but under conditions very different to those typically enjoyed by male regular employees (see Chapter 7). This has been facilitated by government deregulation of employment in Japan (Araki, 1994, 1998, 1999). However, the government and corporations are not the only actors in the Japanese, or any other, political economy. We need also to consider organized actors outside the state and business.

Cox (1999) defines civil society as autonomous group action, distinct from both corporate power and the state. Cox further points out that, as a response to globalization, there has been a revival of civil society, such as the French strikes of 1995 and the South Korean protests of 1997, and the growth of NGOs in Japan and other Asian countries which often build links and mutual aid relationships with similar organizations in other countries. A difference can be made between bottom-up action, in which civil society acts as a conduit for those disadvantaged by globalization to mount protests and propose alternatives, and 'top-down' activity, where states and corporate interests can try to co-opt civil society and encourage actors towards conformity (Cox, 1999). Chapters 6 and 7 have largely described the latter process of globalization, while this chapter will describe the former.

An obvious example of the effectiveness of the action of civil society in shaping the institutions of a society is that of the Japanese trade union movement in the period following the Second World War. Workers took industrial action resulting in the achievement of lifetime employment and other benefits so strongly associated with the regular workforce in Japan (Inoue, 1999; see also Chapter 4). Japan has an active and long-standing feminist movement. However, it has seldom achieved the formal institutional recognition of the male-dominated trade union movement, although Japanese women workers have taken action to improve their conditions of work. Previous chapters have recorded women continuing to work despite pressure from managers and co-workers to leave, women part-timers organizing themselves into unions, women bringing court cases against companies which practise discrimination in recruitment and promotion, and women who carry out infrapolitical resistance against higher status male employees. This chapter will explicitly focus on women's activism in order to describe the actions women are taking individually and collectively to resist or campaign for change in their working environment and the laws and practices regulating it.

The strategies of actors will be shaped by institutions, and actors will adapt their strategies to accommodate changes in those institutions (March and Olsen, 1989; Thelen and Steinmo, 1992). This has certainly been the case in Japan. Feminist labour activists in Japan have adapted their strategies to the existing national and international institutions, and changed their strategies as the processes of globalization have altered the relative power of these institutions. Chapter 3 referred to the fact that globalization has facilitated the development of a global women's movement by:

- increasing the salience of non-state identities;
- opening up opportunities for effective political activity at a local level;
- raising the international profile of women's rights;
- allowing activists to use international law and organize transnationally.

Globalization has impacted upon women's activism in Japan, as this chapter will illustrate. However, it will also show how the institutions of Japanese governance impact upon the strategies pursued by supporters of Japanese women workers. These institutions include a political party and trade union system which is constituted in such a way that women are effectively excluded and a homosocial normative order which dictates that activism is usually structured along gender lines.

Although Japanese feminists campaign around a multiplicity of issues,[1] the focus of this book is women workers in Japan, so I shall concentrate on feminist activities in support of women's labour rights. The first two sections in this chapter examine the lack of influence that women labour activists have traditionally had in party and trade union politics, and how changes in these institutions are affecting the way women engage with them. The next section looks at the alternative way campaigners for women's labour rights actually do organize: through active networking, using Women's Centres, and publishing *minikomi*.[2] Finally, the chapter examines the way women's groups are increasingly directing action at international bodies and sharing information and activities with activists overseas.

Women in electoral politics

This section will show how the institutions of Japanese politics have been difficult for women to penetrate, therefore encouraging extra-parliamentary activism. However, as explained in Chapter 3, one of the ironies of democratic representation and globalization is that, just as the power of the nation state is declining (Held, 1995), the proportion of liberal democracies and the number of female parliamentary representatives is increasing (Walby, 2003). This has been the case in Japan, as Figure 8.1 (later in this chapter) shows.

Another observation commonly made about globalization is that governance has become more multi-layered as policies are increasingly formulated at a sub-state or suprastate level (Strange, 1996). Women activists in Japan have, in recent years, concentrated their activities at the local state level or at the transnational level.

Political representation

In Japan's first post-war election a record number of female deputies were elected: 39 out of a total of 464. However, this number has never been equalled and has in any case been attributed to the very specific circumstances prevailing at the time: women had just attained suffrage amid great publicity and many voters believed that they were obliged to vote for one male and one female candidate; women were more closely associated with peace than men; and voters could not tell from the names on the ballot paper which candidates were male and which female (Ogai, 2001). The majority of the female candidates represented the left or centre-left. However, the change from large to medium-sized electoral districts when the Japanese political system was reformed in 1947 disadvantaged the Social Democratic Party (SDP) and the Japan Communist Party (JCP), and consequently female left-wingers lost their seats.

The political priority of the Liberal Democratic Party (LDP), and its undoubted success, was Japan's economic growth. With this end in mind, its election tactics consisted predominantly of establishing strong links with the corporate elite, an elite from which, for reasons discussed earlier in this book, women were largely excluded. Ideologically also, the LDP did not appear keen to encourage female candidates and for one period of ten years had no female deputies at all.

Even within centre-left parties, however, there were institutional reasons why women were less likely than men to be selected. With the exception of Doi Takako, who was Japan's first female political party leader in 1986, female SDP candidates were only successful if they had the support of trade unions. Women account for only 28 per cent of trade unionists in Japan (Miura, 2001) and with the decline of union membership in the 1970s, the number of Diet seats fell, so there were fewer seats available. Ironically, the decline in political influence of trade unions may also have negatively affected the proportion of women standing. In the past, unions used to undertake to support unsuccessful candidates whom they sponsored until the next election. Now this is less and less frequent, so only those who are either financially secure or very sure of winning can afford to stand. This disproportionately disadvantages women, who are less likely to be able to garner electoral funds and less likely to be elected.

The contribution of social norms may also play a part in excluding women from parliamentary power. Voters are, at first sight, apparently reluctant to vote for women. In the general election of 25 June 2000, only 17 per cent of women who stood for election were returned, compared to 37 per cent of men (Mikanagi, 2001: 212). However, this does raise the question, as in the UK, of the extent to which women are allowed to contest winnable seats. Furthermore, Komatsu (2002, personal communication) attributes women's lack of electoral success to insufficient resources, adding: 'In Japan, we say it needs 3 "ban" to win the election: they are Kaban (money), Kanban (publicity), or [being] well-known, Jiban (many supporters in the constituency).'

The judicial arm of government is also male-dominated. The conservative way that labour laws have been interpreted in test cases (see Chapter 6) might also be partly attributed to the total absence of female judges in the Supreme Court.

As well as the institutional factors working against women, Mikanagi (2001) attributes the lack of representation of women's interests in the formal political sphere to the characteristics of those interested in feminist politics. Particularly, she decries the influence of radical feminism in Japan – a brand of feminism, she claims, that has encouraged Japanese feminists to keep a distance from the 'patriarchal state'. Campaigning for equal labour rights in the 1950s to the 1970s appeared to have a lower profile than anti-nuclear and environmental movements because, according to Eto (2001), Japanese women's labour market participation at this time was less than in Europe and the US, and therefore Japanese women were less conscious of the gender-based division of paid labour than their Western counterparts.

A variety of women's groups have, however, been active in lobbying the government. In particular the administrative reforms of the mid-1980s discussed in Chapter 7, where the Nakasone government cut education, welfare and environmental spending, excited the anger of women's groups. Cuts in spending for day care centres and school lunches, which increased the reproductive work done by women, were particularly controversial (Iwamoto, 2001). In 1981 cutbacks were introduced in public service provision, and in 1982 a group of women who had been forced to leave their jobs or give up social activities because of increased caring obligations held a symposium to publicize this issue in Tokyo (Eto, 2001).

Some Japanese women have also been disproportionately affected by changes in agricultural policy in the wake of globalization. Women now constitute over half of the formal agricultural labour force (Gender Equality Bureau, 2000), and, probably account for a considerably higher proportion, once the informal labour of family members, such as farmer's wives, is taken into consideration. The liberalization of US agricultural imports caused a backlash against the LDP as did the party's decision to open the rice market to foreign competition (Ogai, 2001; Iwamoto, 2001).

Electoral and parliamentary institutions in Japan have generally been male-dominated and, perhaps as a result of this, have tended to pursue policies which work to the detriment of female workers. Institutions and social norms are, however, dynamic. Historical institutionalists, such as Hall and Taylor (1998), accept the role of ideas in politics and acknowledge that the introduction of new ideas can alter the basic and strategic preferences of actors. This phenomenon was observed through the introduction of new ideas through the intervention of the United Nations and its associated conventions and conferences, which were followed by an upsurge in feminist activities in Japan and an increased awareness of issues of gender equality in the general population. The increased representation of women in the Diet and local assemblies (see Figures 8.1 and 8.2) is a sign that Japanese voters are more willing to accept female politicians. Women's rights activists are taking advantage of this by increasingly attempting to enter formal political institutions.

The high profile and positive image of Doi Takako, the first Japanese female political party leader (1986–1991) and Ogata Sadako, United Nations High Commissioner for Refugees (1991–2000), has led to popular enthusiasm for female politicians. This has recently been shown in the widespread accusations of gender bias, following the sacking of Foreign Minister Tanaka Makiko.

In the wake to the anti-LDP backlash the SDP gained 21 seats in the Lower House in 1989, of which women held 7 (with 6 of the women winning a seat for the first time). The image of sleaze and corruption, and the scandal caused by the LDP Prime Minister's extra-marital affair, had led the SPD to deliberately choose female candidates, whom it dubbed 'Madonnas'. The subsequent electoral success of these candidates became known as the 'Madonna Boom'. This success was not welcomed by all, though, and some popular newspapers ran headlines such as 'Ritual of the Witches' and 'These Women Will Ruin Japan' (Iwao, 1993: 238).

Women have gradually increased their representation in both the Diet and local assemblies, as shown in Figures 8.1 and 8.2. Furthermore, there are signs of representatives making positive efforts to recruit more women.

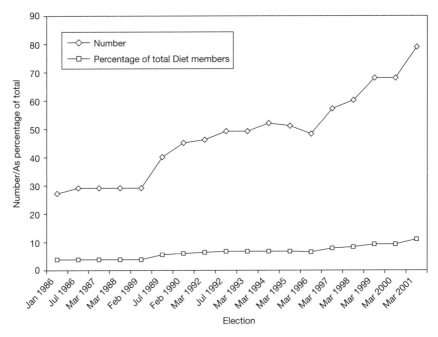

Figure 8.1 Number and percentage of women Diet members, January 1986–March 2001: Cabinet Office (2001b).

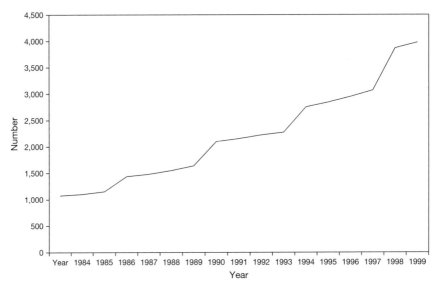

Figure 8.2 Number of female local assembly members, 1984–99: Cabinet Office (2001b).

In February 1992 the Feminists Assemblymen's (*sic*) Federation, whose membership is made up of 65 female and 5 male national and local government representatives, resolved to campaign for a membership quota of 30 per cent for women in each prefectural assembly (Iwao, 1993).

Women's traditional marginalization from electoral politics can give them the freedom to act more independently, once they gain a seat in Parliament. As Tripp commented, when referring to female political actors in Uganda, 'Because women have been more marginalized politically than virtually any other sector of society, they have had more to gain and less to lose by altering the status quo' (Tripp, 2000: 7).

Moriya Yuko, the founder of a school for female politicians, claims, 'Women do not feel restrained to ask questions in the assembly. This stimulates their male colleagues to ask more questions. Thus a more open style of decision making is being implemented rather than the elitist "over-dinner-and-drinks" sort of decision-making style' (Foreign Press Center, 2001). Certainly, Ms Doi was criticized by male politicians for her blunt 'unfeminine' style; and Tanaka Makiko, the foreign minister who lost her job in a high profile sacking on 29 January 2002, was fantastically popular with the general public for her outspoken and flamboyant style. However, within the political class itself, behaving in a manner different from male colleagues can also lead to a backlash. In the week before her sacking Ms Tanaka was reported to have had tears in her eyes following a meeting, prompting Mr Koizumi to remark, 'When women cry, men cannot compete with them.' The prime minister's remarks enraged female MPs, 18 of whom handed over a letter demanding a retraction of the statement (Mainichi, 30 January 2002).

A 1991 study by the Centre for the American Women and Politics at Rutgers University found that, regardless of party or ideology, female politicians tend to have a different agenda to men (Fujimura-Fanselow and Kameda, 1995: 373). Women in the Japanese assemblies do seem to be perceived as being allied to a feminist agenda. In 1992 the National Federation of Feminist Legislators was established as a non-partisan national network of 130 male and female legislators with an interest in feminist concerns. Senator Nakanishi Tamako, for example, promulgated and backed Japan's equal employment opportunity law to open up jobs to women, and claimed: 'My purpose for coming into politics was to write bills that protect women, to raise the status of women, eliminate discrimination in the workplace and so forth. And for the care of children and care of the elderly' (PBS online, 2002b).

Tokyo Assembly woman Mitsui Mariko has, since proposing the inauguration of sexual equality ombudsman in her 1987 maiden speech, taken up the causes of working women, gender inequality in education and the portrayal of women in the media (Kaya,1995). There are nearly 30 extra parliamentary groups which aim to put women's issues on the Japanese political agenda. Most of them are activist groups. Some support specific candidates while others aim to raise the profile of women's issues. *Onna kara Onnatachi e: Ichinichi Juen no Kai* (From Woman to Women: Ten-Yen a Day group), for example, has the goal of electing a female district councillor to focus on women's issues (Khor, 1999).

According to *Women 2000: Japan NGO Report*, however:

> One of the serious obstacles to create (*sic*) a gender equality society is the ignorance of gender issues among local government officers and members of local assemblies. Local government officers have to obey decisions made at assemblies. Therefore, consciousness raising of those officers and assembly members by gender training is important. Consciousness of the civil society itself which elects those assembly members should also be raised.
>
> (Japan NGO Report Preparatory Committee, 1999: 67)

In Japan local governments have come to be the focus of initiatives towards gender equality as, supported by women's networks, feminist deputies gain representation. In June 1999, the Basic Law for a Gender-Equal Society came into effect. Like the EEOL, the Basic Law was the indirect outcome of Japan's participation in UN initiatives, and Chapter 4 of the Law states the intention of '[a]dopting and absorbing international standards in Japan' (Gender Equality Bureau, 2000). The Platform for Action of the Fourth World Conference on Women called for governments to develop plans of action for gender equality. The Japanese Council for Gender Equality submitted its report *Vision of Gender Equality – Creating New Values for the 21st Century* to the Prime Minister on 30 July 1996. This was followed by a new national plan of action entitled 'National Plan for Gender Equality toward year 2000' on 13 December 1996.

The aim of the Basic Law for a Gender-Equal Society was to clarify basic concepts pertaining to the formation of a gender-equal society and indicate the direction these should take. Under the Law, the central government, local governments and Japanese citizens are required to make efforts towards the achievement of a gender-equal society in all areas. In Tokyo the local government can request private companies to report on the status of their implementation of gender equality. Gifu prefecture has conducted research on the sexual division of labour in the workplace and in the home, and Fukui City has concentrated on improving women's political participation.

The diffusion of power to local assemblies has resulted in the entirely pragmatic decision by feminist activists to intentionally target local government. Strategies include joining advisory committees or attempting to aid the election of candidates who will champion feminist causes. Moriya Yuko worked for 20 years after university graduation, and in that time came to feel that women would be empowered if they entered the decision-making fields from which they were largely excluded. In 1993, she resigned from her job with a research and planning firm and launched the Society for Discussing Women and Politics. However, she was further radicalized by her participation in the World Conference on Women in Beijing, where she was 'stimulated by the energy of assembly women from the West and elsewhere' (Foreign Press Center, 2001).

In 1996 Moriya set up the World Women's Conference Network, Kansai, to promote international exchange among women, and founded a school for aspiring female politicians. This non-profit-making organization (NPO) based in Osaka is run by Fifty Net, which aims to achieve a situation where 50 per cent of councillors are women. Two hundred women applied for the initial 30 places to learn about policy-making, the workings of parliament and know-how regarding elections from lectures by politicians and women's activists. Seventy-four were accepted, and by 2001 25 graduates of the course had become councillors.

Nonetheless, in 2000, the United Nations Gender Empowerment measure, which records women's participation in political and economic decision-making, still ranked Japan only 41st out of 70 countries judged to have 'high human development' (United Nations Development Programme, 2000). Ironically, just as women are organizing to accede to formal political power, opponents of neo-liberal economic globalization are arguing that concentrating on conventional electoral politics is futile, where the main parties accept the discipline of global capital (Falk, 1997b).

Women in trade union politics

An obvious avenue to campaign for women's labour rights is through the trade union movement. However, women account for only 28 per cent of the membership of Japanese trade unions. Chapter 4 explained how, after the deflation of the 1940s, unions moved from including all non-managerial employees to a membership limited to those whose job security was assured. The corollary of this is that as non-regular forms of employment have increased, the proportion of labour which is unionized has fallen from around 34 per cent in 1975 to an all-time low of 22 per cent in 1999 (Choy, 1999b).

Some unions have recently made an effort to recruit non-regular workers. Part-timers account for 24.3 per cent of the membership of the Japan Federation of Commercial Workers' Union (*Shougyou Rouren*) and 17.4 per cent of the National Union of General Workers (*Zenkoku Ippan*) respectively. However, other unions, even in highly feminized sectors, recruit few part-timers. Only 5 per cent of members of the Japanese Federation of Textile, Garment, Chemical, Food and Allied Industries Workers' Union (Zensen) are part-time workers. Rates of unionization of dispatched workers are even lower (Miura, 2001).

One response to the lack of female representation in mainstream unions has been the formation of small, predominantly female, unions. For example,

71 part-time workers employed by the magnetic-head section of Matsushita in Kumamoto were laid off in 1996, following Matsushita's shifting of magnetic-head production to Malaysia and the Philippines. The trade union at their workplace did not permit part-timers to join, so the workers formed their own union, which entered collective bargaining with the company and demanded a withdrawal of their notices of dismissal (Zenroren, 1996).

Tokyo Josei Union was established in March 1995. It has 18 committee members and charges a membership fee of 2,000 yen per month. Between its establishment and July 1999, the union has recorded 3,383 consultations from women, mainly concerned with restructuring and change of status from regular to non-regular status. The union operates by recording women's complaints on their Working Women's Helpline. They then encourage the complainant to join the union and to fill out an application form for 'collective bargaining' with the company. According to the union, most collective bargaining actions are completed within six months. In the period covered, Tokyo Josei Union had dealt with almost 200 cases, of which the majority were resolved by compensation and continued employment (Tokyo Josei Union, 1999).

Japanese feminist movements

Extent and nature of group membership

The preceding sections have demonstrated the reasons why formal politics has been a largely male preserve. Women who are politically active tend to be politically active in a realm outside the male formal polity.

The fact that Japanese cultural norms often structure activism and political participation along gender lines means that women's social and political life is often organized around women's organizations, which provide an autonomous basis on which to challenge women's exclusion, and to challenge the existing political hegemony. Passy (2000) claims that networks fill a vital gap between structure and agency in that they *socialize* and build individual identities, *recruit* individuals who are sensitive to a particular political issue, and allow them the chance to participate, and *shape individuals' preferences* before they decide to join the movement.

Although this chapter emphasizes the importance of outside influences, networks and the use of foreign institutions to put pressure upon the Japanese government, Japan has a long history of indigenous women movements. Just after the 1880s a popular rights movement stimulated strikes by female workers. The 1920s saw the emergence of an active women suffrage movement that succeeded in getting a Bill passed in the House of Representatives that gave women the vote in 1930, but the House of Peers session ended before it could be ratified, and with the Manchuria Incident in 1931 and subsequent events, it became indefinitely postponed (Iwao, 1993). During the Second World War, women's activist groups were either banned or co-opted:

the women of the Greater Japan Women's Patriotic Association (*Dai Nippon Aikoku Fujin Kai*), for example, were active in supporting Japan's war effort (Fujieda, 1995). The Occupation Forces were keen to encourage women's emancipation and particularly a new women's movement, associated with progressive, labour-related policies. Its connections with the JCP, however, caused disquiet in SCAP, and the administration tried to revive the old community groups association with the Patriotic Association, and 'rehabilitate' its leaders after some cursory 're-education' (Matsui, 1996b: 24). This seems to be a clear example of attempts at top-down organization of civil society. There were therefore two major strands to the women's movement in the immediate post-war period. The JCP Central Conference on Working Women movement clung to the Marxian idea that the oppression of women would be solved with the achievement of a socialist society, and thus concentrated on organizing women into trade unions rather than analysing or protesting against the more complex conditions of women in post-war Japan (Tanaka, 1995). The rump of the Central Conference on Working Women is still active today, particularly in campaigning for part-time workers' rights (Zenroren, 1997a). There was also a more conservative network of women who organized non-challenging cultural activities, such as taking language or cookery classes. The latter were supported by women's centres (*fujin kaikan*), usually built by public organizations and operated by local women's groups. By the 1960s there were more than 100 private and state *fujin kaikan*.

There was little high-profile activism around women's labour rights until the 1970s, when the *uuman ribu* (women's lib movement) burst into public consciousness on 21 October 1970. *Uuman ribu* activists marched in the streets of Tokyo carrying placards with slogans protesting about a range of issues. Placards read, 'Mother, are you really happy with your married life?', 'A housewife and a prostitute are raccoons in the same den' (Tanaka, 1995). The majority of the *uuman ribu* activists were disillusioned young female workers and students who had been active in the New Left, anti-Vietnam War movements, and had been dissatisfied by the cognitive dissonance of male activists who rejected authority, yet permitted female activists only such stereotyped roles as typing. Some *uuman ribu* activists experimented with collectives for women and children, consciousness-raising groups and staging high profile 'zapping' activities, such as targeting individual men at their places of work. Several of the *uuman ribu* activists participate in the feminist movement even today. However, their high profile activities, such as marching in pink helmets, demanding the legalization of the contraceptive pill, while attracting significant media coverage, were often ridiculed and attracted little public sympathy.

Nonetheless *uuman ribu* did reflect a growing interest in women's issues at the time. This had been occasioned by the following:

• Economic growth leading to women's greater participation in the workforce (see Chapter 5). An increasing number of women, therefore, were bearing the double load of paid employment and household chores (Tanaka, 1995). A number of academics, such as Komatsu Makiko, became interested in the problem of women in the labour force and of sexual discrimination in the workplace.

- The establishment of academic women's studies. Female academics that had studied in the US or Europe returned to Japan and introduced women's studies in the Japanese Academy. Japan *fujinmondai kouwakai* (discussion group on the woman question) member, Inoue Teruko member introduced the ideas discussed in 'Women's Studies' in the US as '*Joseigaku*'. Iwao and Hara wrote a book called *Joseigaku nyuumon* (*Introduction to Women's Studies*) (Komatsu, 2002: personal communication).

The groups which emerged in the second half of the 1970s were more likely to be lawyers, Diet members, labour movement activists and members of political parties. They were more directly focused on 'working within the system' and influencing government policies and actions (Tanaka, 1995). They were lent more legitimacy in the eyes of the public and among elites when the UN International Women's Year forced the Japanese government to act on the problem of sex discrimination. In 1975 the Japanese government set up the Headquarters for the Planning and Promotion of Policies Related to Women. Fifty-two NGO groups came to make up the liaison group for the Implementation of the Resolution from the International Women's Year Conference on Japan (*Kokusai Fujin-nen Renraku-kai*).

Chapter 3 cited the case of Russian groups who intentionally use the language of international organizations to gain legitimacy for their own struggles (Sperling *et al.*, 2001). The UN is extremely well regarded in Japan, and therefore campaigning using UN documents and protesting at UN conferences have proved to be effective strategies for women's groups with little formal influence at the domestic level (a strategy referred to in Chapter 1 as a 'boomerang' strategy (Keck and Sikkink, 1998)). Attending the UN Women's Conferences has also proved to be inspirational to several activists who were interviewed.

Although Japan was not permitted to join the United Nations until 1956, the Women's and Young Workers' Bureau of the Ministry of Labour, impressed with the UN Commission on the Status of Women, has been sending observers since 1950. As stated in Chapter 6, the United Nations Decade of Women (1975–85) and International Women's Year (1975) also stimulated much popular and media debate in Japan, and impacted upon public opinion (National Institute of Employment and Vocational Research, 1988). In the late 1970s the Japanese government established the National Women's Education Centre and the 1970s and 1980s saw a state-led building programme of women's centres. These have proved to be more of a focus for overtly feminist activities than the *fujin kaikan*. This is indicated in the choice of name: *josei sentaa* rather than *fujin kaikan*. While *josei* and *fujin* both mean 'woman', the Chinese character *'fu'* depicts a woman carrying a broom, and therefore does not indicate a challenge to traditional roles for women.

In July 1985, 27 delegates led by the Vice Minister of Foreign Affairs, 13 advisory female Diet members and 700 NGO members who were to attend the NGO forum went to Nairobi to the UN conference where the Nairobi Forward-Looking Strategies for the Advancement of Women was passed. Professor Komatsu Makiko has long been active in campaigning and research on women's labour issues, and she wrote the second-ever women studies textbook in Japan. She spoke about the effect the conference had on her, by encouraging her to be active and introducing her to feminists from other countries:

> Interviewer: Did the International Decade of Women have a high profile in Japan?
>
> Komatsu Makiko: Yes, because the Japanese government began to develop Gender Equality Policy from 1975, the year of the first UN conference on gender equality in Mexico City.
>
> Interviewer: Did you go?
>
> Komatsu Makiko: No I didn't go. The second time I went – to Nairobi.
>
> Interviewer: What were your impressions?
>
> Komatsu Makiko: That's so vigorous, brilliant and [. . .] Power!
>
> (Interview, 19 January 2001)

She added that she had been deeply impressed by 'the power of African women' and had come to deeply consider the relation between multiculturalism and human rights.

The year before the UN conference in Beijing, the Japanese government established the Headquarters for the Promotion of Gender Equality within the Prime Minister's Office, with the function of 'gender mainstreaming', integrating a gender equality perspective across all areas of government policy (True and Mintrom, 2001). Approximately 6,000 Japanese women attended the Beijing Conference (Convention on the Elimination of All Forms of Discrimination Against Women (CEDAW), 2000). Moriya Yuko, founder of the school for female politicians referred to earlier in this chapter, said:

> It was the Beijing Conference in '95 (the 4th World Women's Conference) that made me start the network. I saw many women involved in the political scene before my eyes and I thought, 'Hey, we need this in Japan too!'
>
> (Wings, 2001)

After Beijing, attendees from Japan set up new NGOs and pushed for national and local governments to work in accordance with the Beijing principles. One of the highest profile groups is the Beijing Japan Accountability Caucus (Beijing JAC), with branches in Tokyo, Kansai, Hiroshima, Sendai, Shizuoka and Yamaguchi. The World Women's Conference Network, Kansai, was begun in 1996 by Kansai women who had attended the Beijing conference, to 'make good use of the results of the conference and to enlarge the public role for women'.

The point has been made in previous chapters that it was the UN Convention on the Elimination of All Forms of Discrimination Against Women (CEDAW) that formed the basis for the passing of the EEOL. The Japanese Association of International Women's Rights (JAIWR) developed various programmes to publicize the Convention, which Japan agreed to ratify in 1980. JAIWR's programmes are based on drama performances and questionnaires to check gender bias. Twenty years after the Convention was signed, the term CEDAW was known to 37 per cent of a July 2000 survey conducted by the government for the July 2000 White Paper on Women (compared to only 13.6 per cent who had heard of 'affirmative action' and 7.1 per cent who understood the concept of 'unpaid work' (Dales, 2001)).

Unlike *uuman ribu*, the new groups tended to be more oriented towards single issues. There is no Japanese equivalent of the American National Organization of Women. However, groups do tend to be long-lasting and active, usually meeting frequently and producing *minikomi*. Khor (1999) analysed 590 groups from an initial list of 1,000 on the *Onna no Nettowakingu* (Women's Networking) list for Japan. About 50 per cent, she found, could be classified as activist. However, it could be argued that 'research/study' groups on the list also play a role in creating pressure for change, and conducting independent research seems to be a core activity for groups in Japan. A group of lawyers and academics calling themselves the Women Workers Research Group (*Fujin Roudousha mondai kenkyuukai*) reported that 80 per cent of women surveyed in 1988 said the EEOL had had little effect on their workplace (1995). Working Women's PAW (Part-timers Analysis and Watch) (*Josei no waakinguraifu wo kangaeru Paata kenkyuukai*) began in 1993 with the aim of having the government ratify the ILO Part-Time Work Convention and to improve legal protection of part-time workers. In 1999, it conducted a survey of 2,319 working women (excluding dispatched workers). The group liaises and shares information with other women's labour organizations elsewhere in Asia. Female students in the Kansai area (Osaka, Kyoto, Kobe and Nara) have conducted surveys on their experiences job-hunting, and from 1986 (the start date of the EEOL) have published the details of discriminatory experiences they have had while job-hunting and the names of the companies involved in their book *Girls be Ambitious*. Furthermore, one of the most high-profile activities of the women's movement has been, the publication of counter-reports to the Japanese government's periodic reports to CEDAW in July 1992 and August 1999. Countries that have ratified or acceded to the Convention are legally bound to put its provisions into practice, and to submit national reports at least every four years on measures they have taken to comply with their treaty obligations. In March 1999, after the 43rd session of the Commission on the Status of Women in New York, NGOs were advised that while there would be no NGO Forum at the Women 2000 Special Session of the UN General Assembly, NGOs would be encouraged to compile an alternative report on their country's implementation of the Beijing Platform for Action. Twelve organizations in Japan obtained responses from 300 organizations and individuals and finalized the report at a public meeting.

There is also a general expectation that those involved in research about women should be committed to the women's movement, and that 'women's studies' should not be an elitist, narrowly academic pursuit. The Women's Studies Association of Japan (*Nihon Joseigaku Kai*), for example, was formed in 1978, and has 600 members, including researchers, students, housewives and company employees (Khor, 1999; Worldwide Organization of Women's Studies, 2000) Komatsu Makiko commented:

> We should not say women's studies without movement. If you can say women's studies specialist, you have to be active. . . . Maybe 60 or 70 per cent of the scholars are involved in women's movement, but recently, academic only, I saw.
>
> (Komatsu, 2002, personal communication)

Several of the groups have a dual focus: perhaps particularly specific to Japan are English discussion groups, whose members initially come together to discuss current topics in English. In an all-female group members undergo a process of socialization/consciousness raising, which leads to the group or the individuals becoming keener to be involved in activism. Women's Messages, for instance, began in 1988. Its members come together to discuss topical news articles in English on a biweekly basis, as well as hosting talks about 'world issues' and 'women's issues'. The group produces a bilingual magazine which is sent to about 600 individuals/organizations in 87 countries and highlights sex discrimination in the Japanese workforce as well as forging links with, and supporting the campaigns of, women's groups overseas. Usui Yuki joined Women's Messages to practise her English language but became increasingly interested in the articles she read. She is now a regular contributor to and translator of the *Women's Messages Newsletter*, and she eventually went to Dublin to take an MA in Women's Studies. She now is very involved in Working Women's International Network and Women Helping Women.

Similarly, the English Discussion Society has published two books, *Japanese Women Now I* (English Discussion Society, 1993), and *Japanese*

Women Now II (English Discussion Society, 1996), in which they provide previously unavailable information about the situation of Japanese women in the home and in the workforce, in English.

Khor (1999) notes that there are 50 groups which are concerned with women's employment. Around 50 per cent of these provide support for part-time workers re-entering paid employment, while the other half are 'activist' groups which aim to redress issues of discrimination, balancing productive and reproductive work and issues of sexual harassment. There are, according to Khor (1999) a further 50 groups concerned with women's businesses, either pragmatically to create work which fits in with domestic labour or to challenge male domination of paid work by offering flexible work hours, providing services or teaching women such traditionally 'male' skills as refurbishing.

Many of these women's groups make use of the *josei sentaa* to meet for 'Self-enlightenment and teaching, collection and distribution of information, consultation, surveys and research, exchange of views among individual women and groups' (Uno, 1997: 2). While in Japan, the author frequently attended meetings, seminars and lectures at one such *josei sentaa*, the Dawn Centre in Osaka. This 11-storey building was established in November 1994 by Osaka Prefectural Government, under the administration of the Osaka Gender Equality Foundation. It is open six days per week from 9.30 am to 9.30 pm and attracted nearly one million people in its first two years. While some feminist groups were less than enthusiastic about the women's centre building programme, complaining, for example, that there was a greater need for refuges for women fleeing domestic violence (Uno, 1997), in recent years, women's activists, rather than being co-opted by the relatively institutional nature of the women's centres, have used them for explicitly feminist aims. Usui Yuki said in an interview with the author:

> They [i.e. women's centres] help work effectively to play a supportive role, because they have places, so lots of women can have a meeting there and also lots of events are organized. So . . . the thing is these women's centres are all over Japan, and their policy or strategy is greatly affected by the boss . . . top people's awareness . . . understanding.

She agreed that *josei sentaa* are not necessarily feminist, but added:

> recently a lot of NPO groups, women's groups, specially if they have power in local area, then this government or this *gyousei* [administrative body] contact this group to get some idea from the group, because they don't know well about their strategies . . . So this kind of situation happens quite a lot. Actually I was asked by one of the *josei sentaas* to talk about the issues of organizing women's centres.

As the centres are a focus for women, activists can even make use of physical proximity to the centres. Three lawyers that were active in the Kintou Hou Network have recently formed an independent practice situated in front of the Dawn Centre, where women can consult them on their labour rights.

The globalization of women's activism

As well as using an international stage as a base for campaigning, Japanese women's groups have built links with other women's labour campaigners to add to foreign pressure on the Japanese government, to pragmatically share information and to build solidarity with women workers elsewhere in the world. Chapter 5 recorded the joint organizing of women's groups in Japan and in other Asian countries to protest about Japanese sex tours to countries hosting Japanese FDI. In 1995, the Asia-Japan Women's Resource Center was established in Tokyo to extend and provide a basis for the activities of the Asian Women's Association (AWA), one of several women's organizations in Japan which has adopted a critical view of Japan's role in Asia since the 1970s. It acts as a bridge to link Japanese women with women's groups elsewhere in Asia in order to share information and engage in joint activities around the issues of migrant women, prostitution and trafficking of Asian women, Asian brides and international marriages, Japanese–Filipino children and women workers employed by Japanese multinational companies.

Another example, referred to briefly in Chapter 6, is the case of transnational activism around sexual harassment. Japanese women's groups in 1996 sponsored the week-long visit to Japan of the US National Organization for Women (NOW)'s Vice President Rosemary Dempsey. The aim of the trip was to raise awareness of sexual harassment. The more than 50 Japanese groups involved also intended to show solidarity with US women workers who had filed sexual harassment charges against the Japanese TNC Mitsubishi Motor Manufacturing. It seems indisputable that *gaiatsu* (foreign pressure) enabled the feminist groups to win their case. Dempsey met feminist groups, business leaders, parliamentary representatives, trade union leaders, the Minister of Labour and representatives of Mitsubishi. The visit was widely publicized and the Minister of Labour reversed his previous stance and came out in support of a tougher EEOL, which included prohibitions on sexual harassment (Corbin, 1996).

Prior to the World Conference on Women in Beijing, several regional meetings were organized in Asia. At the Asia Pacific NGO Symposium held in Manila in 1993, women from East Asia held a regional workshop which resulted in the formation of the East Asia Women Forum, with the first meeting held in Japan the following year. This was rather significant as:

> Despite the fact that women in East Asia share the experience of the rapid economic growth in the region, the common cultural background

of Confucian patriarchy and the history of Japanese military rule, it was the first gathering of activists from different women's groups in East Asia.

(Moriki, 1997: 1–2)

Women's activists became increasingly aware of the link between their own situation and the globalization of Japanese production. In fact, one of the rationales for opposing the revision of the Labour Standards Law was that regulations would be similarly relaxed in Japanese companies overseas, as this extract from the 1999 Counter Report to the UN makes clear:

> In addition, we are afraid the abolition of the restriction for the protection of female workers will have a bad influence on Asian women Worker's (*sic*) working conditions. It is necessary to watch carefully that the working conditions of Asians does not worsen in Japanese enterprises.
>
> (Japan NGO Report Preparatory Committee, 1999: 51)

Similarly, Shiozawa Miyoko, Director of the Asian Women Workers' Center, explained that initially she was reluctant to contribute to Hiroki Michiko's collection of stories of Japanese women, as a companion volume to the publication of stories of Korean and Filipino working women, as she felt that the vast material differences between the lives of women in Japan and those elsewhere in Asia would make it difficult for women outside Japan to appreciate the difficulties women in Japan faced (Hiroki, 1986). However, she decided to contribute to the book because she believed that women workers in Japan were subject to the double burden of responsibility for housework and childrearing, in addition to a job outside the home and discrimination, meaning that 'although their suffering may be mitigated by enjoying occasional extravagances, their human growth is seriously hindered, probably in a way very different from our Asian sisters' (in Hiroki, 1986: i). In addition, whe felt that the export of 'the Japanese method of labour control, which is becoming increasingly sophisticated and is now being introduced into Asian countries through Japanese-owned corporations' and the trade friction caused by long working hours and labour intensity causing the market expansion of export-oriented low-cost projects convinced her that 'the struggle for liberation from the bitter exploitation of capital is common and can be shared, although the forms of struggle may be different in each country' (ibid., 1986: ii).

Again, groups in Japan have attempted to raise consciousness through research and publicity. The Association of Asian Women (*Ajia no onnatachi no kai*) between 1977 and 1991 published *Ajia to josei kaihou* (translated as 'Asia in Everyday Life', but literally meaning 'Bulletin of Asia and Women'), in which they considered food, cosmetics and manufactured goods produced in Asia and brought to Japan so that Japanese women could see the way in which they were direct beneficiaries of exploitation of their Asian sisters. The related journal *Asia no Kaihou* (*Asian Bulletin*) focused on political repression in Asian countries, Japanese cultural imperialism, liberation movements in Asian countries, the economic activities of Japanese companies in Asian countries, and international tourism industry and its links with prostitution (Mackie, 1999). The emergence of the ethical consumer is perhaps a sign of the links between the economic and cultural aspects of globalization.

Recently such organizations as the Asian Women's Association have paid attention to Japan's role as a major donor of foreign aid in the region and the increased emphasis on support for tourism-related projects.

Working Women's Network: an example of an activist group

Working Women's Network (WWN) has a long history. It started in October 1995, having grown out of a smaller group (Kintou Hou [EEOL] Network) which was set up in 1986 to discuss and raise awareness of the EEOL. Kintou Hou Network itself grew out of a study group with an interest in women and labour issues. In 1995 around 100 women came together to form WWN in support of core members who were suffering from discrimination in the workplace. WWN's inaugural meeting at the Osaka Dawn Centre attracted a large number of company workers, civil servants, lawyers, researchers, and the organization now has a membership of over 800. WWN supported the core members, who are plaintiffs in a number of sex discrimination cases against various branches of the Sumitomo Corporation.

Members commit a great deal of their own money and time to the organization. The Japanese government report to the International Labour Organization that women in Japan earned on average 80 per cent of average male earnings was countered by a visit of 12 WWN members to give evidence to the Committee of Experts on the Application of Conventions and Recommendations of the ILO in September 1997 with their own statistics and information about their cause. The same month the delegates made representations to the United Nations and the European Union (Working Women's International Network (WWIN), 2001a). These activities were well covered in the Japanese press, as was the visit of Dr Marsha A. Freeman, Director of the International Women's Rights Action Watch, who, at the behest of WWN, in 1999 submitted to the Court her statement on the issues in the case of *Shirafuji Eiko and Nishimura Katsumi* versus *Sumitomo Electric and the Government of Japan*. The Japanese government had claimed that Japanese tradition was an obstacle to the immediate implementation of CEDAW, and argued for a culturally based gradualist implementation of the standard of sexual equality in the workplace, while Dr Freeman pointed out that the language of the convention required immediate implementation of the non-discrimination provision (WWIN, 2001b).

WWN is backed by a subsidiary organization, Working Women's International Network (WWIN), consisting of Japanese activists and a fluctuating number of foreign women living in Japan. When the author attended there were usually about ten members and Dales (2001) reports that there are now around seven regular attendees. Meetings are conducted in English and Japanese. Foreign members were encouraged to network with people in their own countries to collect signatures from overseas for a petition supporting the Sumitomo women. The movement also produces an English version of their *minikomi, Working Women's International Network: A Message from Japan,* which mainly provides details of the progress of the court cases. WWN places a high value on using international exposure of the Japanese situation to attain their goals. Usui told the author:

> They organized a symposium about informal discrimination . . . indirect discrimination and I think speakers from abroad came to Japan and did several symposiums. Also . . . yeah, I think these kind of symposiums to deepen the understanding of women's working situation, and especially they have a network with other countries, because their activities is introduced in foreign countries too. For example they brought a counter-report of their working situation, which is totally different from the government report, so they brought this to New York and revealed the situation . . . it was a kind of *gaiatsu* (foreign pressure), because Japanese government or Japanese legal system does not deal with these issues seriously, so women go abroad directly and appeal more sympathetic organization in foreign countries, and then they give some comment to the Japanese government. [This] embarrass[es] the government quite a lot. . . . it gives the impact, so in that sense their strategy to appeal to the outside of Japan organization has a great impact to raise the awareness . . .
>
> (Usui, personal communication)

The author asked about the size of audiences at symposia, and Ms Usui claimed that, depending on the size of the meeting room, meetings attracted up to 450 participants. Despite their efforts, those court cases which have so far been decided have ultimately resulted in defeats for the plaintiffs. However WWIN did mount a striking protest, hiring a helicopter to advertise their protest and then forming a human chain around the courthouse. This, too, was covered on television and in the newspapers. After high-profile campaigning activities, an out-of-court settlement, on terms largely favourable to the plaintiff in the Sumitomo Electric case, was finally agreed.

Conclusion

Campaigners to improve the position of working women in Japan are active and well informed. However, the institutional sexism of the parliamentary system and the mainstream trade union movement, as well as the homosociality of Japanese society, means that formal politics has not been the main means of engagement for politically active women. There are signs that parliament and local government are opening up to women, and those women who have entered formal politics have tended to have both a high profile and a feminist agenda. The impact of economic globalization in causing Japanese corporations to alter their employment practice and legislators to pass laws facilitating this has been well-documented (Dore, 2000; Hasegawa and Hook, 1998). However, the processes of political globalization, including the development of supranational governance, transnational activism and foreign pressure (or at least the perception of foreign pressure), have also affected Japanese government policy. Particularly, Japanese national and local governments have passed more rigorous sex discrimination legislation and built a physical network of women's centres.

Although these changes are making electoral politics more accessible than previously, most campaigners for women's labour rights continue to concentrate on activities within women's groups. Their aims are typically to raise public awareness of women's disadvantage in the workplace and to campaign for tighter regulation of companies. There is a perception within these groups that Japan's high degree of involvement with international organizations and the positive view in Japan of internationalization can work to women's advantage. This is to some extent a correct perception as Japan's equal opportunities legislation and increased public awareness of women's labour rights are strongly associated with the UN and the ILO. Women's groups are increasingly working with their counterparts overseas both to share information and also out of a feeling of national responsibility towards the situation of women workers in Asia.

The example of Working Women's Network shows several characteristics of a Japanese women's activist group. It has proved durable; core members combine research with protest, and it places a high priority on creating effective international links. It makes use of institutional facilities for women, and is exercising an increasing influence within Osaka Dawn Centre. It has been successful in recruiting members and publicizing issues, but has not, as yet, achieved direct success in achieving its goals.

Conclusion

9 Conclusions and discussion

Introduction

This book has analysed the relationship between gender and globalization in one specific national context: Japan. Japan's position as an affluent, industrialized liberal democracy, with a distinctive national model of capitalism, means that Japanese women's experiences of globalization differ from those of women both elsewhere in Asia and in other First World countries. The actions of the Japanese state and Japanese companies have been instrumental in the globalization of production, which is now having reciprocal effects upon the Japanese national model of capitalism. In response to global economic change, the Japanese model of capitalism is being intentionally restructured through company practice and legal change. This restructuring impacts differently upon men and women, as the liberalizing processes associated with globalization interact with specific local institutions, including the ideal of the three-generation family and the position of women in the Japanese national model of capitalism.

The theoretical background for the analysis drew upon insights from mainstream theoretical analyses of globalization and the role of state and non-state actors in a globalizing political economy, as well as upon gendered analyses of globalization, to explain how the processes associated with globalization are changing the gendered national model of capitalism in Japan. Chapters 2 and 3 were a critical review of this literature. Chapters 4 and 5 described how the institutions of the Japanese model of capitalism emerged in the specific conditions of the post-war political economy of Asia, how men and women had very different roles in this model, and the pressures for change upon that model. Chapters 6 and 7 described how this model is changing, with different consequences for men and women, under the exigencies of a globalizing political economy. Chapter 8 described how women activists are both reacting to the restructuring of employment and how globalization is presenting new opportunities for activism around feminist concerns.

Three central aims have steered the research for this book:

- to contribute to the debate about the impact of globalization upon women by bringing in insights from the case of Japan into the wider academic discourse;
- to examine the impact of restructuring upon women's employment in Japan;
- to describe the actions women are taking individually or collectively to resist or campaign for change in their working environment and the laws and practices regulating it.

This chapter will summarize the arguments running through this book, to show how it has met the latter two aims. It will set its findings in a wider academic context, showing how the case of women working in Japan reinforces, contradicts, or adds to hypotheses about gender and globalization.

A summary

Analytical framework

There are many definitions of globalization, and debates about the extent to which it has been realized. Chapter 2 argued that there have indisputably been moves towards global economic interdependence, with the result that national control over economic forces for most countries in the world has become less feasible. There has also been an international convergence in social and cultural practices. That is not to say that globalization has been uniform throughout the globe, or that the world is 'globalized': it is in the process of 'globalizing'. One of the areas in which economic integration and social change have been most striking is East Asia.

The state has played an important role in the economic development of East Asia, as East Asian governments have encouraged FDI, particularly from Japan. However, the state plays an ambivalent role in the process of globalization. Globalization is generally taken as implying that the nation state has been superseded by the forces of transnational capital and/or supranational organizations. However, as Rai (2002: 199) argues, 'the nation state continues to be a critically important actor in the international political economy and, as such, it is not simply a victim of globalizing forces, but a participant in the refashioning of itself and the world we live in'.

The Japanese state, in particular, has been a very pro-active player in the process of the globalization of production as, for strategic geo-political and economic reasons, it has forged closer links with East Asia, Europe and the United States. This has facilitated the globalization of Japanese production, which has had reciprocal effects on the Japanese economy. The relatively low cost of producing manufactured goods outside Japan has undercut Japan's export-oriented economy. Japan has also come under pressure from the US to open its markets and even restructure its institutions to facilitate foreign penetration. While imports have entered Japan, very little FDI has; this net flow of capital and jobs out of the country has provoked concern in Japan about *kudouka*, or 'hollowing out'.

Japanese industry has tried to counter this challenge by attempting to cut the costs of domestic production, and by reducing labour costs and making the workforce more numerically flexible. Representatives of Japanese business have successfully campaigned for the state to deregulate labour in ways that make it easier to achieve a more numerically flexible workforce, and has pursued policies itself (as well as supporting measures to make it easier to invest overseas, thereby increasing hollowing out). This deregulation is happening in the context of an internationally hegemonic discourse in favour of free trade and laissez-faire capitalism. Nonetheless, the particular policy mix each state chooses varies according to its political, social and cultural complexion, and, of course, according to its level of strategic power in the international political economy. The Japanese state has generally adopted liberalizing measures, such as the deregulation of agency work, the repeal of protective legislation for women and reductions in taxation, which have had differential effects on men and women in the Japanese labour force.

Gender and capital in post-war Japan

Labour markets are socially constituted (Polanyi, 1944). The institutions shaping a labour market will include its existing political and economic institutions and its social norms. One of the strongest social norms in post-war Japan has been that of the male breadwinner, where both blue- and white-collar male employees have shown commitment to their employers, and in return have job security, seniority-related pay increments and promotion and training, as well as more 'social' benefits, such as welfare benefits, grants on marriage/childbirth/illness/death, provision of company housing and subsidized shopping facilities that in other countries might have been provided by the state. The role of women in this model has been to provide a temporary, peripheral labour force, until marriage, and then domestic labour and care for children. The persistence of the ideal of the three-generation family in Japan means that a higher proportion of women provide care for elderly family members than is the case in most Western countries.

Firms, particularly the larger companies associated with the Japanese national model of capitalism, relied upon the temporary nature of the employment of women peripheral workers to provide numerical flexibility in the workforce and to allow men to rise upwards through the company and take on more responsibility as the *nenko* system required. The system has evolved as a result of labour shortages, combined with the availability of an educated and experienced workforce of older women who desired to work outside the home. From the late 1970s, it has become more and more common for women to first work part-time, then leave the work-force to raise children, and then to return as lower paid part-time workers, their part-time status being encouraged by the tax and pensions system as well as their continued responsibility for reproductive work.

These norms of the employment system are not solely attributable to unique Japanese cultural traditions. The Japanese national model of capitalism developed in response to choices made by political and economic actors in the first few decades following the Second World War: particularly the passing of the 1947 Labour Standards Law and the character of Japanese enterprise unions. However, once institutions have been developed, they tend to persist as the values and preferences of political actors develop within those institutions. Institutions can become dysfunctional and unstable as a result of exogenous change, and it is in times of change that they are particularly likely to be transformed. The success these actors have in achieving reform will depend on their power, and the strategies they employ. This book has argued that globalization is just such an exogenous force, and that different actors within Japan are reforming Japanese institutions in reaction to it. These actors include economic and business interests, feminist campaigners and politicians and working women in all sectors of the workforce.

Globalization and the restructuring of women's employment in Japan

Mainstream theories of globalization have largely been gender blind, although the impact of globalization has been shown to be heavily differentiated according to gender. This has certainly been the case in Japan.

Globalization is producing two kinds of apparently countervailing pressures for change to the Japanese national model of capitalism, both of which have different implications for men and women. There are pressures for labour market deregulation, to increase the international competitiveness of Japanese production. There are also pressures for the 're'-regulation of labour to establish a principle of sexual equality at work. The deregulation of employment, including the removal of sex-specific protective legislation, has made it increasingly difficult for many women to pursue full-time careers.

Japanese companies are responding to challenges to the Japanese national model of capitalism brought about by globalization, especially those occasioned by structural change (particularly a decline in manufacturing) and increased vulnerability to cyclical forces (embodied in the threat of capital flight). They are doing so by segregating the regular workforce into discrete and gendered groups, and, like employers elsewhere, increasing the size of the non-regular workforce.

Although a combination of activism within Japan and the development of a global standard concerning equal treatment of men and women in the workplace has put pressure on the Japanese government to reduce the more obvious aspects of sexual discrimination in employment practices, the equal opportunities legislation which has been passed, such as the EEOL, has often been counterproductive for working women. Within the regular workforce, women continue to be largely confined to clerical positions with very limited chances of advancement. Many firms have reacted to the introduction of the law by formalizing informal segregation in employment, based on gender. Having a different job category to their male colleagues makes it more difficult for women to sue their employers for discriminatory treatment. Furthermore, advances in formal equality have been accompanied by a loss in protective legislation, such as limitations on night work for women, that have resulted in some women finding difficulty continuing in their current jobs. It has, however, provided new opportunities for a minority of determined elite women to find jobs in the management track of companies. In this changing labour market, an increasing number of young women appear to be investing in training to become certified as *senmonka* (specialists). For society in general, there is also some evidence that the publicity surrounding the Equal Employment Opportunities Law has helped to change attitudes about working women. Transnational activism has also been shown to be effective in raising awareness of sexism in the workplace. Globalization may also have resulted in change in the attitudes of employers and employees towards regular female employees: as more Japanese managers and students have diverse and internationalized careers, they are exposed to different models of workplace social relations, including relations between men and women.

The size of the regular workforce relative to that of the non-regular workforce is decreasing, particularly in sectors that have been highly affected by the exigencies of globalization, such as the banking and airline industries. The past ten years have seen a remarkable growth in part-time work, dispatched work, and other forms of non-regular employment. The increasing desire of women to work, combined with government encouragement for women to combine reproductive work with paid employment outside the home, has meant that there is a pool of women available to meet the increasing demand for 'non-regular' workers. The EEOL creates an additional incentive for employers to take on women as irregular workers, as occupational sexual segregation means that employers are not obliged to provide them with the same pay and fringe benefits as male regular workers.

Paato and homeworkers are expected to be married women, who are financially supported by their husbands, and consequently firms do not appear to pay them wages to cover the costs of reproduction. Dispatched workers are generally expected to be young, conventionally attractive and have a personality that fits in with the firm's expectations. Some anecdotal evidence exists that these non-regular workers are excluded from the workplace community.

As the irregular workforce has grown, so it has diversified. In some sectors, particularly retail, the experience of long-term part-time workers is being recognized by their employers, who are increasingly grading them according to their abilities and offering some of them increased responsibility in the workplace. The variety of employment open to dispatched workers is also growing, albeit that one consequence of this has been a fall in the average wages of such workers. In some cases, dispatched work can lead to regular job opportunities.

Globalization and women's activism

There is an active feminist movement in Japan. However, the parliamentary system and mainstream trade union movement have largely been closed to women and thus have not proved fruitful avenues for attaining feminist demands. Activists therefore have tended to concentrate their energies on women's groups, with the aim of consciousness-raising about women's position in the workforce and campaigning for change. These groups are characterized by their longevity and their mixture of scholarship and activism. Some have recently begun to take advantage of legal changes to gain formal representation for women in national and local assemblies and a higher profile for women workers. The prestige that international organizations such as the ILO and the UN have in Japan has meant that Japanese women's groups have also made these sites of protest, in the knowledge that this strategy will ensure a high profile in the Japanese domestic media.

Japan's relative wealth has enabled a relatively high proportion of feminist activists to travel to UN Women's Conferences, which have had a profound influence in Japan, and have increased awareness of the impact of globalization upon women overseas. Japanese women's groups increasingly work together with foreign women in Japan and abroad, to share information and awareness of the impact of Japanese companies overseas.

The implications of the Japanese case for current debates on gender and globalization

Although the mainstream literature on globalization, the state and historical institutionalism has been a useful framework for analysing the impact of globalization upon Japan, these are incomplete literatures, in that, with few exceptions, they neglect the gendered nature of globalization. Literature about gender and globalization has filled an important gap in these literatures by analysing how globalization impacts differently upon men and women. It has also shown how globalization has different impacts upon women depending upon their nationality, ethnicity and social class. This book has examined a particular case study of gender and globalization: that of the restructuring of work in Japan in response to globalization, and the way this affects women. This section will show how this case study relates to the themes uncovered in feminist critiques of globalization (cited in italics), and discusses which findings are generalizable, and which result from an interaction of global forces and local institutions and are therefore specific to the Japanese case.

Globalization is presented in a gendered and natural phenomenon in political discourse, in a way that suggests nation states are powerless to resist its exigencies.

Chapters 4 and 7 cite evidence from key players in the Japanese economy to show that, in Japan as elsewhere, the discourse of globalization employed by elites presents the phenomenon as natural and irresistible and recommends a neo-liberal economic strategy as a necessary response to its challenges.

States respond to the challenges of globalization by marketization and the adoption of neo-liberal policies. These policies have impacts, which increase the reproductive work of women.

The neo-liberal economic strategies adopted by the Japanese government include both the deregulation of labour, introducing higher charges for tertiary education and encouraging families to provide care for the elderly. The result of these policies is that women with young children or elderly parents continue to provide the largest proportion of care for family members, but this is combined with going out to work part-time to contribute towards living costs, education costs for their children, and perhaps the provision of care for elderly people. Furthermore, deregulation has made it more difficult for some women to pursue full-time careers, as the removal of gender specific social protection legislation has made it possible for them to be asked to work unfeasibly long hours, which are difficult to combine with reproductive labour.

Dominant ideologies can lead a state and existing institutions to negotiate a compromise between encouraging change and maintaining current gender orders.

Kelsky (2001) has argued that it has become almost axiomatic to present women – particularly non-Western women, as the 'victims' of globalization. While recent work is far more nuanced than this (cf. Rai, 2001, ILO/ SEAPAT, 1998b), Japan is certainly a case where globalization has had complex and contradictory effects. On the one hand, it has produced an increasing acceptance of the 'global standard' of gender equality and produced new arenas where women can campaign for improved labour rights. On the other hand, it has encouraged the movement towards a less regulated and more segmented labour market, where women are more likely to find employment than has previously been the case, but, in most cases, are likely to find employment that is less secure and less well-remunerated than has, until very recently, been the case for most Japanese men since the 1940s.

The promulgation of the EEOL is a prime example of a dominant ideology of leading state and institutions to negotiate a compromise between encouraging change and maintaining gender orders. A detailed examination of the impact of the EEOL shows that this legislation has led to the formalization of the gender-based segregation of regular workers and encouraged employers to employ an increasing proportion of women in non-regular positions.

> *There has been a 'feminization' of waged work, as an increasing proportion of jobs are taken by women, and an increasing proportion of jobs are irregular, part-time and/or service sector jobs which have typically been filled by women.*

In Japan's period of rapid economic growth, women actually became less likely to work outside the home than men, even as their standard of education increased. There is nevertheless a long tradition of women in Japan undertaking paid employment, a tradition which declined during the 1950s and 1960s, but in recent decades, Japan has, like most other countries in the globalized economy, seen a feminization of the workforce. Chapters 5, 6 and 7 provide quantitative data to support the proposition that the processes of economic, social and political globalization are strongly associated with an increase in the number of women working, a diversification of the positions women hold, and growth in the proportion of non-regular jobs in the economy.

> *The entry of the workforce of many First World women into professional positions is facilitated by the domestic work of poorer migrant women.*

Recent studies (e.g. Chang and Ling, 2000; True, 2000) have shown that a minority of elite women have found that globalization offers them opportunities for travel and a professional career comparable to that of elite men, but that for many women, the experience of migration is one of providing domestic labour for other women. Japan is an exception to this case. In Japan, as elsewhere in East Asia, there has been a significant growth in the number of women seeking professional careers. However, despite increasing inward migration, Japan has not seen the emergence of a class of foreign female domestic workers. On the other hand, increasing numbers of Japanese women are choosing to work or study abroad generally out of desire for advancement or self-fulfilment rather than economic necessity.

> *Globalization can weaken local patriarchal structures by exposing culturally specific practices to global scrutiny, while flows of information and ideas increase reflexivity within cultures.*

In Japan, as elsewhere, the increase in women in the workforce and the adoption of a global norm around the idea of gender equality, has led to an intensification of women workers' struggles for labour rights. Japanese women have, in recent years, succeeded in gaining increased representation in local and national assemblies and have also founded their own trade unions, which have had some success in negotiating settlements for their members in industrial disputes. However, the emergence of new institutions of global governance, and the esteem in which these are held in Japan, has provided Japanese campaigners for women's labour rights with new sites of resistance to gender inequality. Japanese women have also formed networks and alliances with women in other countries, particularly in those regions that are the hosts for overseas production by Japanese corporations.

Suggestions for further research

This book has by no means been a comprehensive analysis of globalization and the restructuring of women's employment in Japan. Its goal was to gain a broad overview of the situation of women in Japan. Studies from other countries, though, have shown that not only does globalization impact differently upon men and women but it also impacts differently upon women according to their class and 'race'. Understanding of the impact of globalization in the Japanese workforce would be greatly enriched by studies of the situation of women from the *Burakumin* group or from the permanent residents from Korea. Similarly, the flow of women who do come to Japan to work as migrants bears closer examination. Japanese-Brazilians, for example, can claim Japanese citizenship on the basis of having a Japanese heritage, but are differentiated by culture and language from the majority of the population.

I have concentrated on the experiences and actions of Japanese women resident in Japan. A study of the migration of Japanese women, the experience of such women working or studying overseas, the positions they later occupy and the opinions they hold if and when they return to Japan would throw considerable light on the development of transnational identities in a globalizing world, and on the role of structure and agency in the constitution of such identities.

A third factor to note is that the non-regular workforce is not solely composed of women. The increasing marketization of higher education has led to more students taking *arubaito* (part-time jobs), which contribute to Japan's growing service sector. Furthermore the growing number of young people of both sexes, known as *freeter*, who choose to take short-term or irregular jobs (a phenomenon which has been the cause of much critical comment in the press) points to a growing diversity of Japanese attitudes to work and leisure. This may have implications for the degree of commitment that companies can reasonably expect of their male regular workers in the future. These phenomena, too, merit examination.

Appendix A

Details of 1996–7 pilot study

From mid-1996 until March 1997, while working as Visiting Foreign Lecturer at the University of Shiga, I conducted a scoping exercise using semi-structured interviews and questionnaires. As personal introductions are very important in conducting research with Japanese respondents (Pharr, 1981), the participants in this survey were found through a 'snowball' technique. Initial interviewees were found through personal recommendation. Both initial and subsequent interviewees were asked to recommend others who would be willing to answer questions about their work experiences. In total, this technique yielded 214 usable responses. While this method does not produce a statistically representative sample, the respondents did represent a reasonably wide range of ages, educational backgrounds and working situations. Respondents varied in age from 19 to 64, enabling me to collect anecdotal data about different work experiences of women throughout much of the post-war period. The mean age of respondents was 34.7 years, with a standard deviation of 10.33. The marital status of the respondents at the time of the interview was as follows: 52.6 per cent single, 39.4 per cent married, 0.9 per cent cohabiting with a partner, 4.2 per cent divorced, 0.9 per cent separated, and 2.8 per cent widowed. Sixty-eight respondents (31.8 per cent) had children, of whom 12 (5.6 per cent) had children under five years of age. The educational background of respondents and their employment status is presented in Tables A.1 and A.2 respectively.

Table A.1 Educational backgrounds of respondents

Highest qualification achieved by respondent	Number of respondents	%
Junior high school	3	1.4
High school	44	20.6
Junior college	40	18.7
Four year university	71	33.2
Post-graduate degree	10	4.7
Professional qualification	10	4.7
Other	4	1.9
Total	182	85.0
No response	32	15.0
Total	214	100.0

Table A.2 Employment status of respondents

Employment status of respondent	Number of respondents	%
Self employed/freelancer	4	1.9
Small business owner	7	3.3
Full-time with job security	123	57.5
Part-time	36	16.8
Freeter*	6	2.8
Working in family business	2	0.9
Homeworker	4	1.9
Other	23	10.7
Total	205	95.8
No response	9	4.2
Total	214	100.0

* The term 'freeter' usually refers to someone who is working at one or more part-time jobs and moves between jobs freely.

Appendix B

List of working women respondents

Most respondents in the 1996–7 survey filled out questionnaires, but some agreed to speak at greater length in face-to-face interviews. Interviewees were employed in the categories below:

laundry worker (1)
local government employee (part-time)
homeworker (1)
owner of translation company (1)
consumer researcher
journalist
antiques dealer
advertising copywriter
teachers (2)
lecturers (4)
kimono-wearing instructor
building manager
tourist company worker
family business worker
general office work (3)
OL (3)
website specialist
record company worker
dentist
export sales
ticket sales (part-time)

It is difficult to separate 'elite' from 'non-elite' interviews, as in the course of interviews, court plaintiffs and activists often told me of their working lives. (In this case, the term 'elite interviewee' refers to a respondent with a specialist knowledge of the research topic, rather than a 'non-elite' informant who relates their own experience of the changing Japanese workforce.) However, the following women granted interviews about their work lives during the period from October 1999 to March 2000.

Group interview:
    women working in trading companies (7)
    university administrators/union activists (3)

Individual interviews:
    flight attendant (1)
    civil servants (3)
    (former) dispatched workers (2)
    ippanshoku/jimushoku workers ('OLs') (3)
    office worker
    sogoshoku worker (pensions analyst) (1)

Appendix C
Elite interviews

October 1999
Focus Group Interview with English Discussion Society/writers of *Japanese Women Today* and *Japanese Women Today I*, Kyoto

November 1999
Interviews with stewards of Osaka City Trade Union, Osaka

December 1999
Yunoki Yasuko – Showa Shell Union Representative, Tokyo
Group interview with Board of Tokyo Josei Union, Tokyo

January 2000
Group interview with Shosha ni Hataraku Josei, Osaka

February 2000
Shirafuji Eiko – plaintiff in Sumitomo lawsuit, Osaka
Ms Kageyama – plaintiff in Sumitomo lawsuit, Osaka
Ms Watanabe – plaintiff in Sumitomo lawsuit, Osaka

March 2000
Interview with Koedou Shizuko – activist and co-ordinator of Women Helping Women, Osaka

February 2002
Usui Yuki: activist and writer on *Women's Messages*, Sheffield
Professor Komatsu Makiko, Professor of Women's Studies, Mukogawa Women's University, Newcastle upon Tyne

Notes

1 Introduction: aims, methodology and structure of the book

1 In the 1950s and 1960s, economic growth in Japan averaged 10 per cent per annum in real terms (Maruo, 1997).
2 In 2001, 41 per cent of the Japanese workforce was female (Ministry of Public Management, Home Affairs, Posts and Communications, 2002).
3 The number of births per woman has fallen from 4.54 in 1947 to 1.3 today (Ministry of Health, Labour and Welfare, 2002).
4 Although this is becoming less common in reality, the ideal persists and impacts upon policy and expectations of women's reproductive labour.
5 Some of the most illuminating studies of women's work in Japan have come from anthropologists using a participant observation method. Glenda S. Roberts (1994) and Jeannie Lo (1990) both worked alongside Japanese female factory workers and Lo (1990) and Ogasawara (1998) worked with white-collar employees, without drawing attention to their role as researchers. This method of data collection has several advantages. It is flexible, in that the researcher can constantly reflect upon and adjust the focus of research in the light of new observations, while in a more structured and formal survey it may not be possible to change or add to the questions if they do not seem to be working. The observer also gains a richer understanding of research participants though the proportionally higher (compared to other methods of data-gathering) 'indices of subjective adequacy' (Bruyn, 1966). These are:

- *Time*: spending more time with a group will enlighten the researcher about how deeply subjects feel about or are affected by social phenomena.
- *Place*: the researcher will be aware of the physical setting in which actions take place.
- *Social circumstances*: if the researcher has varied opportunities to interact with different individuals in a variety of settings, this will deepen his or her comprehension of how a phenomenon is enacted.
- *Language*: as the researcher becomes increasingly aware of the language employed in a social setting, the more fully he or she will understand the meaning of what is being said.
- *Intimacy*: if a researcher is personally involved with a group of people, she or he is more likely to understand their actions.
- *Social consensus*: the index of 'social consensus' refers to 'the extent to which the observer is able to indicate how the meanings within a culture are employed and shared among people' (May, 1997: 146).

Participant observation does, however, raise ethical problems about the extent to which all those who are observed can really give valid consent (particularly if the research is covert). If research subjects are being observed over a period of time in their everyday lives, they do not have the same control over the information a researcher gleans about them that they would have if they had just filled in a questionnaire or agreed to take part in a one-hour interview.

6 Although Prime Minister Nakasone Yasuhiro, in 1986, described Japan as a 'homogenous community', there are several minority communities in Japan. The largest minority ethnic community is made up of around 700,000 North and South Korean nationals, who have permanent resident status in Japan. They represent about 1 per cent of the population of Japan. Many of these are fourth- or fifth-generation descendants of those who came to Japan in search of work during the period of Japanese colonization of Korea (1910–45) (Fukuoka, 2000). This community usually adopt Japanese names and are indistinguishable from Japanese citizens. However, as they do not hold Japanese nationality, they are barred from certain government employment, and, if they attend Korean schools, they may find that their high-school graduation is not recognized by tertiary level educational institutes, and therefore they suffer disadvantage in pursuing further studies. Another community, known as *Burakumin*, is ethnically Japanese. *Burakumin* are descendants of former hereditary occupational outcaste groups. Despite legislation, and well-organized campaigns from *Burakumin* activists, these communities continue to suffer socio-economic and educational disadvantage. The indigenous communities known as Ainu are geographically concentrated in Hokkaido. They are physically distinct from the ethnic Japanese. Ainu people are three times more likely to be living on benefits than the majority population, and high-school enrolment among Ainu children is only 78.4 per cent compared to a national average of 94 per cent, with obvious negative consequences for their future employment (Keira, 1996: 12).

7 The 'boomerang strategy' refers to a situation where State A blocks redress to organizations within its boundaries. These organizations activate transnational networks, in an attempt to persuade members to pressurize their own states and (if relevant) a third party organization, which in turn pressures State A (Keck and Sikkink, 1998).

8 I am particularly grateful to Professor Komatsu Makiko and Ms Usui Yuki for the insights they provided during and after the fieldwork period.

9 The extent to which this change has altered the position of female regular workers in Japan is examined in more detail in Chapter 6.

2 A critical analysis of globalization

1 There is a counter-example. In late 1998, the Japanese Miyazawa initiative did help the Malaysian government to reflate the economy and impose exchange controls against the expressed wishes of the IMF.

2 The Washingon Consensus refers to the programmes of fiscal austerity, privatization and market liberalization that formed the basis of IMF advice to debtor countries, particularly those in Latin American in the 1980s and 1990s.

3 Or indeed to mitigate its effects: Kaneko Masaru, author of *Han-gurobarizumu: Shijo kaikaku no senryaku-teki shiko* [Anti-globalism: Strategic Ideas of Market Reform] (1999), for example, appears to accept that some adaption of Japanese institutions is necessary, but sets out an essentially social democratic plan to cope with economic problems resulting from global change. He argues against labour flexibilization and in favour of an asset tax and a restructuring of the social security system to facilitate people's moves between jobs (Kaneko, Jinno and Nomura, H., 2000; Kaneko and Kaneko, 2003).

4 Although dubbed 'anti-globalization protestors', it would be more accurate to describe the actions of these protestors as 'anti neo-liberal economic globalization'. The networks they establish are facilitated by the global processes described by Keck and Sikkink (1998) and Cohen and Rai (2000). Furthermore, their protests are aimed at policies, institutions and companies which they see as violating an (implicitly) global standard of human rights and working conditions, of the type described in the works of Keck and Sikkink (1998), Sassen (1996) and Neysmith and Chen (2002).

5 The All China Women Federation and its local branches, for example, work on domestic violence in urban and rural areas, the employment problems of migrant women workers in Special Economic Zones and urban areas, and organize public education around the phenomena of female infanticide and the abandonment of baby girls. Yet they reject the label 'feminist' as being 'Western' and inapplicable to China (China Rights Forum, 1995).

6 The liberal intergovernmental position would argue that this is a positive sum game and that by 'pooling' sovereignty, states can act in concert to implement policies that they would have been unable to implement as individual units. However, this still implies a reduction in the power of action of individual states.

7 Of 150 regulatory changes made by 69 countries, 147 made the regime more favourable to FDI (United Nations Conference on Trade and Development (UNCTAD), 2001: 6).

8 As described in Chapter 1, note 7.

9 President Jomo Kenyatta, for instance, famously defended the tradition of female circumcision/genital mutilation in Kenya (Greer, 2000).

3 Gender and globalization: a critical review

1 I am aware that my use of the term 'feminist' to describe some of the analyses cited in this chapter, particularly those of male theorists, may be contested. To clarify: I am using the term 'feminist' to describe texts which: put gender at the centre of any analysis of individual lives and economic, political, social and cultural institutions; see most men as having more privilege and social power than most women within social groups; and appear to find this problematic.

2 The reasons for this are examined in more detail in Chapter 4.

3 The word *maquiladora* is derived from the Spanish verb *maquilar*, meaning to submit something to the action of a machine. It usually refers to factories that import and assemble duty-free components for export. See, for example, Diane Elson and Ruth Pearson's 1981 article 'The subordination of women and the internationalization of factory production' and Patricia Fernandez-Kelly's 1983 work *For We Are Sold, I and My People: Women and Industry in Mexico's Frontier*, focusing on women working for US companies in *maquiladora* on the US–Mexican border.

4 More sophisticated analyses than this do exist within neo-classical economics, for example the collection of essays in Schultz's (1995) edited collection *Investment in Women's Human Capital*. However, they do not represent the dominant view in mainstream economics.

5 Australia, France and New Zealand, for example, all require both public and private employers to write a plan outlining how they propose to attain gender equality among their employees. In all three countries women earn, on average, over 80 per cent of men's wages. In Canada, where the scope of equal pay legislation is far narrower, and women cannot, for example, ask for legal comparisons to be made between their remuneration and that of men working at a different branch of the same company, the ratio is only just over 60 per cent. In India, where, as in many other developing countries, women work in the

informal sector where it is very difficult to enforce equal pay legislation, and, in the formal sector, small firms are exempted from compliance, this figure drops to 52.7 per cent (Määttä, 1998).

6 Although J. K. Gibson-Graham is a pseudonym for two writers, in their texts they refer to themselves using the first person singular. I am therefore following their usage.

7 The impact of unreciprocated FDI upon the Japanese national model of capitalism will be examined in Chapter 4.

8 This is also discussed in more detail in Chapter 4.

9 There are, however, exceptions to these general trends. Where countries have traditionally been highly regulated and women's economic and social rights have been well established, such as Central and Eastern Europe and the People's Republic of China, integration into the world economy has led to a decline of women in paid employment. Foreign firms entering the Czech Republic, for example, have been reluctant to hire female employees (with the exception of young women who are competent in foreign languages), as women take between two and four years' maternity leave (True, 2000); Acsady (1999) points out that in Hungary, market liberalization has led to a mass exit of women from full-time work.

10 As traditional 'male' jobs decline in number, some men are more willing to accept 'female' jobs. For example, in the early years of the *maquiladora* on the US–Mexican border, women accounted for around 85 per cent of the workforce. By 1975, that had fallen to 78 per cent, and by 1998 to 64 per cent (Bayes and Kelly, 2001: 164).

11 Here I am using Hall and Taylor's definition of an institution, as cited in Chapter 2: '. . . formal or informal procedures, routines, norms and conventions embedded in the organizations . . . [and] . . . structure of the polity or political economy' (Hall and Taylor, 1996: 938).

12 Korean female activists were successful in winning reforms in the changes to the custom of female workers in banks being required to sign a contract in which they agreed to leave jobs upon marriage, and to gender specific discriminatory retirement ages in 'women's jobs': 28 for typists, telephone operators and assistant nurses, 20 for lift operators, and 25 for administrative assistants (Yoon, 2001).

13 Rai and Livesley (eds) (1996) offer wide-ranging treatment of the relationship between the state, women's organizations and women's struggles in *Women and the State: International Perspectives*.

4 The Japanese model of capitalism and the globalization of Japanese production

1 There are various definitions of the East Asian region, but where the phrase is used in this book it refers to the newly industrializing countries (Taiwan, Hong Kong, Singapore and South Korea), the key members of ASEAN (Thailand, the Philippines, Malaysia, Brunei, Cambodia, Myanmar and Indonesia) and China.

2 This phrase was used explicitly by the US Secretary of War in a speech in January 1948 (Itoh, 2000).

3 Examples of rare sackings cited by Abegglen were a man who had been absent for several weeks, following a series of similarly lengthy absences, and another accused of repeated thefts.

4 The precarious position of smaller companies was evident in the recession caused by the East Asian crisis. Not only were job losses during the recession likely to

come from smaller firms, but these have also been slowest to recover. By March 2004, the number of those working at large companies with at least 500 employees had increased by 300,000 on the year to 12.21 million; in firms with 30 or more employees, the number increased by 180,000 to 17.89 million, while companies with 29 workers or less saw a steep drop of 670,000 (*Nikkei Keizai Shimbun*, 1 May 2004).

5 Trade unions had been active during the Taisho (1912–26) period. Following a decline in the real wage of workers between 1914 and 1919, the number of independent unions increase fourfold, and the number of strikes fourfold. In the 1930s, however, the state introduced new and more restrictive labour laws, at the same time co-opting and centralizing co-operative unions (Sil, 2002).

6 This will be explored in Chapter 5.

7 As a result of government restructuring on 6 January 2001, MITI has been replaced by the Ministry of Economy, Trade and Industry (METI).

8 UNCTAD's transnationality index (TNI) is a composite index of the following ratios: foreign assets/total assets; foreign sales/total sales; and foreign employment/total employment outward FDI stock to total inward FDI stock of the economy.

9 The Bubble economy refers to the period from 1980 to 1989 when large-scale bank lending to companies, guaranteed by the extensive use of land at inflated prices as collateral, left financial institutions very exposed to asset price deflation. The Bubble burst in 1989, leaving many banks with unrecoverable loans.

5   Women workers in the post-war model of capitalism in Japan: continuity and change

1 i.e. the setting up of employment agencies to supply casual or temporary labour.

2 A fuller explanation of these concepts can be found in Chapter 3.

3 In reality, life expectancy in pre-war Japan was so low that it seems unlikely that much of women's reproductive labour was accounted for by caring for the elderly. Life expectancy at birth stood at 47 years for men and 50 years for women in 1935 (Ministry of Health, Labour and Welfare, 2000). As life expectancy has lengthened so has the nature and extent of care required, as Chapter 7 will explore more fully.

4 The increased education attainment of Japanese women, and its relationship to social and legal change wrought by globalization, will be discussed in Chapter 6.

5 Today this term is only likely to be used ironically.

6 *Senmonka* is often translated as 'expert' or 'specialist', but tends in practice to mean someone with a skill, often a certified skill, and would include people who carry out professional work such as accountants, computer programmers or translators.

7 From 1884 women were allowed to become doctors through taking the national licensing exam in Medical Arts. This was seen as appropriate to women's supposedly natural 'nurturant' qualities. Fifty-three per cent of working women who were college graduates in 1965 worked as teachers (Iwao: 1993). Knipe Mouer refers to the debates of the early twentieth century, where the increasing number of female teachers was controversial, but gradually accepted as those who favoured their employment argued, '. . . their gentle and patient dispositions make them perfectly suited for teaching'. (Knipe-Mouer, 1976: 163).

8 The fertility rate in Japan fell from 3.65 in 1950 to 1.35 in 2001 (Ministry of Public Management, Home Affairs, Posts and Telecommunications, 2003).

9 Companies are really exercising *statistical discrimination* here (Koike, 1995). Statistical discrimination refers to the case where an employer does not have, and finds it prohibitively expensive to find out about, the attributes of a particular member of a social group, and believes that members of that group are, on average, less desirable employees in terms of qualifications, reliability, tenure of employment etc. (Phelps, 1972). On this basis, the employer might treat all members of this group less favourably than other groups either by not hiring them or by hiring them under less favourable conditions. In this case, the employers take into account that most women will leave work after a short period and are therefore treating all women as short-term employees, although some individual women will wish to work for considerably longer periods than the average. Koike (1995) feels that a possible solution to this problem, which suits both the companies and more tenacious women, has been the introduction of promotion tests and tracking systems within larger companies. In the dual tracking system most women are placed in short-term semi-skilled positions, but particularly gifted women who express an interest and show ability can be employed on the same basis as men. However, this system too has complex and contradictory results, which will be discussed in Chapter 6.

10 The English Discussion Society met regularly to discuss current issues in English. They had also published two books of essays on women in Japan (English Discussion Society, 1993, 1996).

11 The two workforces are treated separately because, as this chapter has shown, they tend to be firmly differentiated, socially and demographically, and are differently regulated.

12 The *yakuza* are organized criminal gangs.

13 *Japa-yuki-san* literally means 'Ms Going to Japan' and is a play on the euphemistic term *Karayuki-san* (Ms Going Overseas), a phrase used to describe Japanese women who went to work in the sex industries in the US and South-east Asia in the first half of the twentieth century.

6 'Re-regulation', restructuring and women in the regular workforce

1 UK equal pay legislation, for example, was passed to ensure Britain's conformity with the Treaty of Rome.

2 The obvious English etymology of the phrase is evidence of the role played by global networking in attaining discursive change.

3 This case will be discussed in more detail in Chapter 8.

4 Some women also take less formal paths of resistance. One respondent told me how she lost her job when she refused to apologize to a client over whom she had thrown a drink when he attempted to put his hand up her skirt. Another respondent described how, when sharing a cab with her boss after an evening's eating and drinking with colleagues, he suggested that the taxi driver take them to a 'love hotel'. Despite her protestations, the cab driver started to drive towards the section of town where love hotels were situated until she began hitting him over the head with her shoe, at which point he stopped the car.

5 Molony writes: 'Daycare is widely available, subsidized in most locations, and high in quality. But the hours of the best programs usually range from 8.00 am to 5.00 pm or 6.00 pm, times that are inadequate for women on the fast track in their companies. Moreover, elementary schools and kindergartens pressure mothers to attend frequent school functions' (Molony, 1995: 295).

6 OL is the common abbreviation for 'office lady', a term which appears to refer to female office workers in the whole range of administrative positions.

7 At least this is the case in those three-generation households where parents or in-laws are sufficiently young and able bodied not to require care themselves.

7   Deregulation, restructuring and women working in non-regular positions

1   An important exception is the class of day labourer, who wait on certain streets in large cities in the hope of being taken on by the day to carry out casual manual work.

2   The informal economy encompasses all the productive work which goes unrecorded in a country's GDP.

3   In 1994 the Council for Gender Equality (CGE) was set up within the Prime Minister's Office. The CGE is charged with producing recommendations for how Japanese society can achieve the state of *danjou kyoudou sankaku*. This term has been translated officially as 'gender equality' in English versions of official government documents. In contrast to the more commonly used Japanese term for gender equality (*danjou byoudou*), this term has the sense of 'joint participation by men and women'. In other words, 'the term seemed to allow for a recognition that equality did not have to mean identity, that women could take a role in society just as important as men's without necessarily adopting masculine lifestyles'. (Osawa, 2000: 6). The view of equality as 'women participating in society, but in a way different than men' is implied in other Japanese government policies and pronouncements of the 1990s, as this chapter shows.

4   Life expectancy at birth had risen to 77.5 years for men and 84.6 years for women by 2000 (Ministry of Health, Labour and Welfare, 2000).

5   The number of elderly people in Japan is predicted to rise from 2 million in 1996 to 5.2 million in 2025 (Headquarters for the Promotion of Gender Equality, 1996).

6   Although the ostensible purpose of this research group is to study 'part-time' work, the study respondents are classified according to whether they are regular (*shain*) or (*hishain*) non-regular. Possibly this conflation reflects the usage of the term *paato* in Japan to refer to employees who do not receive the benefits of regular employees, regardless of the hours worked.

7   Although 96 per cent of the relevant age group go to secondary school, only about one third qualify to attend state academic schools. The remainder attend, in roughly equal proportions, state vocational or private academic schools. As vocational schools tend to have relatively low status, the consumer-led private sector provides academic education at a price (Benjamin and James, 1993).

8   The main source of funding for private universities and junior colleges is tuition and other fees. Private funding is also playing an increasing part in the funding of state universities. In FY 1971 transfers from the general budget accounted for 83.5 per cent of the Special Account for National Educational Institutions, which provides for the operation of national educational institutions including universities. By 1995 this had fallen to 62 per cent. Universities have increasingly been raising revenue from commissioned research and rising student tuition fees as 'due to the severe budgetary constraints facing the Government' (Ministry of Education, Science, Sports and Culture, 1995).

9   As Chapter 4 noted, Japanese multinationals have significant investments in South-east Asia. Japanese companies supplying intermediate goods to such companies initially received fewer orders in the crisis, and then suffered, as the depreciation of local currencies ultimately led to rising onshore production. In the first half of 1998, the number of bankruptcies reached 10,173 (Altbach, 1998).

10   This is in contrast to the oil crisis of the 1970s, when most jobs lost were part-time (see Chapter 5).

11   A worker dispatching company (*hakenkaisha*) is an agency supplying temporary workers to other firms.

12 In 1995, for example, *Nikkeiren* published a report entitled *Japanese Management for a New Age* in which the goal was set to reduce full-time workers to 70 per cent of the workforce (Sakai, 1999).

13 Japanese people refer to workers sent from agencies to carry out temporary work as 'dispatched workers' (*hakensha*).

14 Unusually for homeworking, the shoe industry in Japan is dominated by men (Women in Informal Employment Globalizing and Organizing (WIEGO), no date.)

8 Globalization and women's activism in Japan

1 Issues that were particularly salient when the author was in Japan in 1999–2000 were supporting Korean 'comfort women' and campaigning for married couples to be able to keep their pre-marital surnames.

2 *Minikomi* are newsletters that are often used by activist groups to publicize the issues with which they are involved. The word implies the opposite of 'mass communications'.

Bibliography

A Letter from Japanese Women Circle (1994) Counter-Report to The Japanese Government's Second Periodic Report to the Convention on the Elimination of All Forms of Discrimination Against Women (9 July 1992) Osaka: A Letter from Japanese Women Circle.

Abegglen, J. (1958) *The Japanese Factory: Aspects of its Social Organization*, Glencoe, IL: The Free Press, MIT.

Abegglen, J. and Stalk, G. (1985) *Kaisha: The Japanese Corporation*, New York: Basic Books.

Acsady, J. (1999) 'Urges and obstacles: chances for feminism in Eastern Europe', *Women's Studies International Forum*, 22 (4): 405–9.

Akaha, T. (1999) 'Three faces of Japan: nationalist, regionalist and globalist futures' in Yamamoto, Y. (ed.) *Globalism, Regionalism and Nationalism: Asia in Search of its Role in the 21st Century*, Oxford: Blackwell, pp. 171–98.

Aksu, E. and Camilleri (eds) *Democratizing Global Governance*, London: Palgrave.

Albert, M. (1993) *Capitalism vs. Capitalism*, New York: Four Wall Eight Windows.

Allison, A. (1996) 'Producing mothers' in Imamura, A. (ed.) *Re-Imaging Japanese Women*, Berkeley, CA: University of California Press, pp. 135–55.

Altbach, E. (1998) *Crushed by the Crunch: Small and Medium-Sized Business Suffer from Stagnant Economy, Loan Freeze*, Washington, DC: Japan Economic Institute Report, No. 30 A.

Amin, S. (1997) *Capitalism in the Age of Globalization*, London: Zed Books.

AMPO (eds) (1996) *Voices from the Japanese Women's Movement*, New York: M. E. Sharpe.

Andersen, J. and Siim, B. (eds) (2003) *Politics of Inclusion and Empowerment: Gender, Class and Citizenship*, Basingstoke: Palgrave.

Aoki, M. (2000) *Information, Corporate Governance, and Institutional Diversity: Competitiveness in Japan, the USA, and the Transitional Economies*, Oxford: Oxford University Press.

Aoki, M. (2001) *Toward a Comparative Institutional Analysis*, Cambridge, MA: MIT Press.

Appadurai, A. (1990) 'Disjunction and difference in the global cultural economy' in Featherstone, M. (ed.) *Global Culture: Nationalism, Globalization and Modernity*, London: Sage, pp. 295–310.

Araki, T. (1994) 'Characteristics of regulations on dispatched work (temporary work) in Japan', *Japan Labour Bulletin*, 33 (8), 1 August 1994, www.jil.go.jp.bulletin/year/1994/vol33-08/05.htm, downloaded 22 September 2001.

Araki, T. (1998) 'Recent legislative developments in equal employment and harmonization of work and family life in Japan', *Japan Labour Bulletin*, 37 (4), 1 April.

Araki, T. (1999) 'Revisions of employment security law and worker dispatching law: drastic reforms of Japanese labor market regulations', *Japan Labour Bulletin*, 38 (9), 1 September, www.jil.go.jp/bulletin/year/1999/vol38-09/06.htm.

Arat, Z. F. Kabaskal (2002) *The Women's Convention and State Reservations: The Lack of Compliance by Muslim States*, paper prepared for the Annual Convention of the International Studies Organization, New Orleans, Louisiana, 24–27 March.

Ariffin, R. (1999) 'Feminism in Malaysia: a historical and present perspective of women's struggles in Malaysia', *Women's Studies International Forum*, 22 (4): 417–23.

Arimura, J. (1996) 'The Japanese saurus eating up the earth', *Women's Asia 21: Voices from Japan*, no. 2, August: 15–18.

Asakura, M. (1998) 'Current legal problems concerning women workers in Japan' in Beauchamp, E. R. (ed.) *Women and Women's Issues in Post World War II Japan*, New York: Garland Publishing, pp. 309–31.

Bacon, A. (1902) *Japanese Girls and Women*, Boston, MA: Houghton Mifflin.

Badgett, M. V. L. and Folbre, N. (1999) 'Assigning care: gender norms and economic outcomes', *International Labour Review*, 138 (3): 311–26.

Baker, D. (1999) 'The real importance of a global economy', *NIRA Review*, Winter, www.nira.go.jp/publ/review/99winter/baker.html, downloaded 15 October 1999.

Bakker, I. (ed.) (1994) *The Strategic Silence: Gender and Economic Policy*, London: Zed Books.

Banno, J. (ed.) (1998) *The Political Economy of Japanese Society, volume 2: Internationalization and Domestic Issues*, Oxford: Oxford University Press.

Basu, A., Grewal, I., Kaplan, C. and Malkki, L. (eds) (2001) *Signs* Special Issue: 'Globalization and Gender', vol. 27, Summer 2001.

Bayes, J. and Kelly, R. (2001) 'Political spaces, gender, and NAFTA' in Kelly, R. M., Bayes, J. H., Hawkesworth, M. E. and Young, B. (eds) (2001) *Gender, Globalization and Democratization*, Oxford: Rowman & Littlefield, pp. 147–70.

BBC (26 April 2002) 'Japan Unemployment Falls', news.bbc.co.uk/i/hi/business/1952314.stm, downloaded 12 August 2004.

Beauchamp, E. R. (ed.) (1998) *Women and Women's Issues in Post World War II Japan*, New York: Garland Publishing.

Befu, H. (2000) 'Globalization as human dispersal: from the perspective of Japan' in Eades, J. S., Gill, T. and Befu, H. (eds) *Globalization and Social Change in Contemporary Japan*, Melbourne: Transpacific Press, ch. 2, pp. 17–40.

Benedict, R. (1989) *The Chrysanthemum and the Sword*, Boston, MA: Houghton Mifflin.

Beneria, L. and Lind, A. (1995) 'Engendering international trade: concepts, policy and action', full-text [online] *The Gender, Science and Development Programme and the UN Development Fund for Women*, GSO Working Paper Series no. 5, Grafton, Ontario: Women in Global Science and Technology.

Benjamin, G. R. and James, E. (1993) 'Public and private schools and educational opportunity in Japan', in Shields, J. J. (ed.) (1993) *Japanese Schooling: Patterns of Socialization, Equality and Political Control*, University Park, PA: Pennsylvania State University Press, pp. 152–62.

Berger, S. (1996) 'Introduction' in Berger, S. and Dore, R. (eds) *National Diversity and Global Capitalism*, London: Cornell University Press, pp. 1–29.

Berger, S. and Dore, R. (eds) (1996) *National Diversity and Global Capitalism*, London: Cornell University Press.

Bergeron, S. (2001) 'Political economy discourses of globalization and feminist politics', *Signs*, 26 (4): 983–1006.

Booth, K. and Smith, S. (eds) (1995) *International Relations Theory Today*, Cambridge, Oxford: Polity Press.

Boyer, R. and Drache, D. (eds) (1996) *States Against Markets*, London: Routledge.

Brinton, M. (1989) 'Gender stratification in contemporary Japan', *American Sociological Review*, 4: 549–64.

Brinton, M. (1993) *Women and the Economic Miracle: Gender and Work in Postwar Japan*, Oxford: University of California Press.

Brodie, J. (1994) 'Shifting the boundaries: gender and the politics of restructuring' in Bakker, I. (ed.) (1994) *The Strategic Silence: Gender and Economic Policy*, London: Zed Books, pp. 46–60.

Brown, K. (1998) *Britain and Japan: A Comparative Economic and Social History since 1900*, Manchester: Manchester University Press.

Bruyn, S. T. (1966) *The Human Perspective in Sociology: The Methodology of Participant Observation*, Englewood Cliffs, NJ: Prentice-Hall, cited in May (1997: 145–6).

Bryman, A. and Burgess, R. (eds) *Analysing Qualitative Data*, London: Routledge.

Buckley, S. (1993) 'Altered States: The Body Politics of "Being Woman"' in Gordon, A. (ed.) *Postwar Japan as History*, Berkeley, CA: University of California Press, pp. 347–72.

Buckley, S. (1994) 'A short history of the feminist movement in Japan' in Gelb, J. and Palley, M. L. (eds) *Women of Japan and Korea: Continuity and Change*, Philadelphia, PA: Temple University Press, ch. 7, pp. 150–88.

Buckley S. (1996) *Broken Silence: Voices of Japanese Feminism*, Berkeley, CA: University of California Press.

BusinessWeek (1997) 'A big stink speeds Tokyo's Big Bang', 27 June.

Cabinet Office (2001a – downloaded date) *Labour Force Participation by Age Group: Changes and Predictions*, Tokyo: Cabinet Office, www8.cao.go.jp/hoshou/whitepaper.nenkin/5/siryou-e/4/3.html, downloaded 18 September 2001.

Cabinet Office (2001b) *FY 2001: Annual Report on the State of Formation of a Gender-Equal Society*, Tokyo: Cabinet Office, www.gender.go.jp/english_contents/index.html, downloaded 1 November 2002.

Carlile, L. and Tilton, M. (1998) *Is Japan Really Changing Its Ways? Regulatory Reform and the Japanese Economy*, Washington, DC: Brookings Institution Press.

Carney, L. and O'Kelly, C. (1990) 'Women's work and women's place in the Japanese economic miracle' in Ward, K. (ed.) *Women Workers and Global Restructuring*, New York: Cornell University Press.

Carr, M. and Chen, M. (2001) *Globalization and the Informal Economy: How Global Trade and Investment Impact on the Working Poor*, Cambridge, MA: WIEGO (Women in Informal Employment Globalizing & Organizing), www.wiego,org/papers/carrchenglobalization.pdf, downloaded 22 September 2002.

Castells, M. (1996) *The Information Age: Economy, Society and Culture; Volume 1: The Rise of the Network Society*, Oxford: Blackwell.

Cerny, P. (2000) 'Political globalization and the competition state' in Stubbs, R. and Underhill, G. (eds) *Political Economy and the Changing Global Order, 2nd edition*, Oxford: Oxford University Press, ch. 24, pp. 300–9.

Cerny, P. (2001) 'Financial globalization and the unravelling of the Japanese model' in Hook, G. and Hasegawa H. (eds) *The Political Economy of Japanese Globalization*, London: Routledge, ch. 6, pp. 104–87.

Chang, K. A. and Ling, L. H. M. (2000) 'Globalization and its intimate other: Filipina domestic workers in Hong Kong' in Marchand, M. H. and Sisson

Runyan, A. (eds) *Gender and Global Restructuring: Sightings, Sites and Resistances*, London: Routledge, ch.1, pp. 27–43.

Chin, C. B. N and Mittelman, J. H. (1997) 'Conceptualising resistance to globalisation', *New Political Economy*, 2 (1): 25–37.

China Rights Forum (1995) *Going to Beijing with Open Eyes: Preparing for the World Conference on Women*, New York: Human Rights in China.

Cho, L-J. and Yada, M. (eds) (1994) *Tradition and Change in the Asian Family*, Honolulu, Hawaii: East-West Center.

Choy, J. (1999a) 'Japan's educational system heads for reform', *US–Japan Link*, no. 46.

Choy, J. (1999b) 'Low Wages Hikes for FY1999: Just One of Japanese Workers' Concerns', *Japan Economic Institute, Report No. 15B*, Washington, DC: Japan Economic Institute Report, pp. 3–6.

Chun, L. (2001) 'Whither feminism: a note on China', *Signs*, 26 (4): 1281–6.

Cixous, H. (1992) 'The laugh of the Medusa' in Humm, M. (ed.) *Feminisms: A Reader*, Brighton: Harvester, pp. 196–202.

Clark, R. (1979) *The Japanese Company*, London: Yale University Press.

Clinical Geriatrics (2002) International Survey of Health Systems, www.mmhc.com/cg/articles/CG0005/internationalmonitor.html, downloaded 27 September 2002.

Cohen, R. and Rai, S. (2000) *Global Social Movements*, London: Athlone Press.

Convention of the Elimination of All Forms of Discrimination Against Women (CEDAW) (2000) *Test of the Convention*, New York: United Nations Division for the Advancement of Women, www.un.org/womenwatch/daw/cedaw, downloaded 30 September 2002.

Corbin, B. (1996) *Global Campaign Aims to End 'Seku Hara': Protests by U.S. and Japanese Feminists*, Merryfield, VA: NOW, www.now.org/nnt/11-96/mitsu.html, downloaded 30 September 2002.

Costa, L. (1999) Chiang Mai: APWLD (Asia Pacific Forum on Women, Law and Development) Conference Report: 'Rural and indigenous women speak out on the impact of globalization: conference report', Singapore: *Awareness*, 6 March, pp. 66–71.

Cowling, K. and Tomlinson, P. (2000) 'The Japanese crisis – a case of strategic failure?', *The Economic Journal*, 110 (464), June: F358-81.

Cox, K. (ed.) (1997) *Spaces of Globalization: Reasserting the Power of the Local*, New York: Guildford Press.

Cox, R. (1999) 'Civil society at the turn of the millennium: prospects for an alternative world order', *Review of International Studies*, 25 (1): 3–28.

Cox, R. (2000) 'Political economy and world order: problems of power and knowledge at the turn of the millennium' in Stubbs, R. and Underhill, G. (eds) *Political Economy and the Changing Global Order, 2nd edition*, Oxford: Oxford University Press, ch.1, pp. 25–37.

Dales, L. (2001) *Identifying Feminists and Feminisms in 3 Kansai Women's Groups*, paper prepared for GALE and EASH Joint Conference: *The Other Hokkaido: Gender, Diversity and Minorities*, 29–30 September 2001, Sapporo, Hokkaido.

Dedoussis, V. and Littler, C. (1994) 'Understanding the transfer of Japanese management practices: the Australian case' in Elger, T. and Smith, C. (eds) *Global Japanization? The Transnational Transformation of the Labour Process*, London: Routledge, ch. 6, pp. 175–95.

Dewan, R. (1999) 'Gender implications of the "new" economic policy: a conceptual overview', *Women's Studies International Forum*, 22 (4): 425–9.

Dex, S. (1988) *Women's Attitudes towards Work*, Basingstoke: Macmillan.

Dicken, P. (1998) *Global Shift: Transforming the World Economy, 3rd edition*, London: Paul Chapman Publishing.

Dilatush, L. (1976) 'Women in the Professions' in Lebra, J., Paulson, J. and Powers, E. (eds) (1976) *Women in Changing Japan*, Boulder, CO: Westview Press, ch. 9, pp. 191–208.

Diplomatic Bluebook (2000) *Toward the 21st Century – Foreign Policy for a Better Future*, Tokyo: Ministry of Foreign Affairs.

Doi, T. (1971) *The Anatomy of Dependence*, New York: Kodansha.

Dore, R. (1973) *British Factory-Japanese Factory*, Berkeley, CA: University of California Press.

Dore, R. (1986) *Flexible Rigidities: Industrial Policy and Structural Adjustment in the Japanese Economy 1970–1980*, London: Athlone Press.

Dore, R. (1996) 'Convergence in whose interest?' in Berger, S. and Dore, R. (eds) (1996) *National Diversity and Global Capitalism*, London: Cornell University Press, ch. 15, pp. 366–76.

Dore, R. (1998) 'Asian crisis and the future of the Japanese model', *Cambridge Journal of Economics*, 22: 773–87.

Dore, R. (2000) *Stock Market Capitalism: Welfare Capitalism: Japan and Germany versus the Anglo-Saxons*, Oxford: Oxford University Press.

Eades, J. S., Gill, T. and Befu, H. (eds) (2000) *Globalization and Social Change in Contemporary Japan*, Melbourne: Transpacific Press.

Economic Planning Agency (1995) *National Survey on Lifestyle Preferences*, Tokyo: Economic Planning Agency.

Economic Planning Agency (1997) *1997 National Survey on Lifestyle Preferences*, Tokyo: Economic Planning Agency.

Economic Planning Agency (1998) *Monetary Valuation of Unpaid Work in 1996: Japan*, Tokyo: Economic Planning Agency.

Economic Planning Agency (1999) *White Paper on the National Lifestyle (Fiscal Year (1999)): Towards A Society of Higher Quality of Life With Flexible Job Opportunities for People to Choose*, Tokyo: Economic Planning Agency.

Economist (1998) 'Japan's amazing ability to disappoint', 26 September–2 October, pp. 17–18.

Elger, T. and Smith, C. (1994) 'Global Japanization: convergence and competition in the organization of the labour process' in Elger, T. and Smith, C. (eds) *Global Japanization? The Transnational Transformation of the Labour Process*, London: Routledge, ch. 1, pp. 31–59.

Elson, D. (1999) 'Labor markets as gendered institutions: equality, efficiency and empowerment issues', *World Development*, 27 (3): 611–27.

Elson, D. and Pearson, R. (1981) 'The subordination of women and the internationalisation of factory production' in Young, K., Wolkowitz, C. and McCullah, R. (eds) *Of Marriage and the Market*, London: CSE, pp. 144–66.

Elson, D. and Pearson, R. (1997) 'The subordination of women and the internationalization of factory production' in Visvanathan, N., Duggan, L., Nisonoff, L. and Wiegersma, N. (eds) (1997) *The Women, Gender and Development Reader*, London: Zed Books, pp. 191–203.

English Discussion Society (1993) *Japanese Women Now I*, Kyoto: Shokado Publishers.

English Discussion Society (1996) *Japanese Women Now II*, Kyoto: Shokado Publishers.

Eschle, C. (2000) *Engendering Global Democracy*, edited version of paper produced as part of the seminar series, *New World Order Ten Years On*, Brighton: University of Sussex, 29 June.

Eto, M. (2001) 'Women's leverage on social policymaking in Japan', *PS*, June, pp. 241–6.

Evans, P. (1997) 'Eclipse of the state? reflections on stateness in an era of globalization', *World Politics*, 50, October, pp. 62–87.

Fagan, C. and O'Reilly, J. (1998) 'Conceptualising part-time work: the value of an integrated perspective' in O'Reilly, J. and Fagan, C. (eds) *Part-Time Prospects: An international comparison of part-time work in Europe, North America and the Pacific Rim*, London: Routledge, ch. 1, pp. 1–32.

Falk, R. (1997a) 'State of siege: will globalization win out?' *International Affairs*, 73 (1): 123–36.

Falk, R. (1997b) 'Resisting "Globalisation-from-above" through "Globalisation-from-Below"', *New Political Economy*, 2 (1): 17–24.

Featherstone, M. (1987) 'Lifestyle and consumer culture', *Theory, Culture and Society*, 4 (1): 55–70.

Featherstone, M. (ed.) (1990) *Global Culture: Nationalism, Globalization and Modernity*, London: Sage.

Feldman, S. (2001) 'Exploring theories of patriarchy: a perspective from contemporary Bangladesh', *Signs*, 26 (4): 1097–128.

Fernandez-Kelly, P. (1983) *For We are Sold, I and My People: Women and Industry in Mexico's Frontier*, Albany: SUNY Press.

Fernandez-Kelly, P. (2001) 'A Dialogue on Globalization', *Signs*, 26 (4): 1243–50.

Financial Times (2002a) 'Japan "faces bankruptcy threat"', 14 June, p. 12.

Financial Times (2002b) 'Tokyo prepares its citizens for the unthinkable – a tax rise', 14 June, p. 12.

Flew, F. with Bagilhole, B., Carabine, J., Fenton, N., Kitzinger, C. and Wilkinson, S. (1999) 'Introduction: local feminisms, global futures', *Women's Studies International Forum*, 22 (4): 393–403.

Foreign Press Center (2001) *People in the News: Managing Director, NPO (Non-profit Organisation) Fifty-Net, Yuko Moriya*, Japan Foreign Press Center, www.fpcj.jp/e/shiryo/person/docs/(2001)07_02.html, downloaded 6 February 2002.

Fox, C. M. (no date) 'Changing Japanese employment patterns and women's participation: anticipating the implications of employment trends', *The Manoa Journal of Fried and Half-Fried Ideas about the Future*, 3, www.soc.hawaii.edu/future/j3/fox.html, downloaded 4 December 1999.

Freeman, C. (2001) 'Is local:global as feminine:masculine? Rethinking the gender of globalization', *Signs*, 26 (4): 1007–37.

Frey, B. and Schneider, F. (2000) *Informal and Underground Economy*, www.economics.uni-linz.ac.at/Members/Schneider/informal.PDF, downloaded 22 September 2002.

Fucini J. and Fucini, S. (1990) *Working for the Japanese*, New York: The Free Press.

Fujieda, M. (1995) 'Japan's first phase of feminism' in Fujimura-Fanselow, K. and Kameda, A. (eds) (1995) *Japanese Women: New Feminist Perspectives on the Past, Present and Future*, New York: The Feminist Press, pp. 323–41.

Fujimura-Fanselow, K. (1993) 'Women's participation in higher education in Japan' in Shields, J. J. (ed.) *Japanese Schooling: Patterns of Socialization, Equality and Political Control*, University Park, PA: Pennsylvania State University Press, pp. 163–75.

Fujimura-Fanselow, K. and Kameda, A. (1994) 'Women's Education and Gender Roles in Japan' in Gelb, J. and Palley, M. L. (eds) *Women of Japan and Korea: Continuity and Change*, Philadelphia, PA: Temple University Press.

Fujimura-Fanselow, K. and Kameda, A. (eds) (1995) *Japanese Women: New Feminist Perspectives on the Past, Present and Future*, New York: The Feminist Press.

Fujita, K. (1987) 'Gender, state and industrial policy in Japan', *Women's Studies International Forum*, 10 (6): 589–97.

Fukai, S. (1999) 'The impact of changes in the international system on domestic politics: Japan in the 1990s' in Yamamoto, Y. (ed.) *Globalism, Regionalism and Nationalism: Asia in Search of its Role in the 21st Century*, Oxford: Blackwell, pp. 199–225.

Fukami, M. (1999) *Monetary Value of Unpaid Work in 1996: Japan*, paper presented at International Seminar on Time Use Surveys, Centre for Development Alternatives, 7–10 Dec 1999, Ahmedabad, India.

Fukuoka, Y. (2000) 'Koreans in Japan: past and present', *Saitama University Review*, 31 (1), www.han.org/a/fukuoka96a.html, downloaded 28 September 2002.

Fukuyama, F. (1992) *The End of History and the Last Man*, New York: The Free Press.

Gamble, A. and Payne, A. (eds) (1996) *Regionalism and World Order*, London: Macmillan.

Gelb (1998) 'The equal employment opportunity law in Japan: a decade of change for Japanese women', *Yale Asia-Pacific Review*, 1, pp. 41–5.

Gelb, J. and Palley, M. L. (eds) (1994) *Women of Japan and Korea: Continuity and Change*, Philadelphia: Temple University Press.

Gender Equality Bureau (2000) *Policies implemented in FY(1999) to Promote the Formation of a Gender Equal Society*, Tokyo: Cabinet Office, www.gender.go.jp/index2.html, downloaded 6 February 2002.

Gender Equality Bureau (2002) *Results of the Analysis of Time Spent on Care for the Elderly and Child Care*, Tokyo: Cabinet Office, www.gender.go.jp/women2000/n11.html, downloaded 28 September 2002.

Gerlach, M. L. (1992) 'The Japanese corporate network – a blockmodel analysis', *Administrative Science Quarterly*, 37(1): 105–39.

Gertler, M. C. (1997) 'Between the global and the local: the spatial limits to productive capital' in Cox, K. (ed.) *Spaces of Globalization: Reasserting the Power of the Local*, New York: Guildford Press, pp. 45–63.

Gibson-Graham, J. K. (1996) *The End of Capitalism (As We Knew It): A Feminist Critique of Political Economy*, Oxford: Blackwell.

Giddens, A. (1979) *Central Problems in Social Theory*, Berkeley, CA: University of California Press.

Giddens, A. (1984) *The Construction of Society*, cited in Kurani, K. (1999) *Social Marketing: Transportation Theory for the 21st Century*, California, www.ott.doe.gov/pdfs/kurani.pdf downloaded 22 September 2002.

Giddens, A. (1990) *The Consequences of Modernity*, Cambridge: Polity Press.

Gill, S. (2000) 'Knowledge, politics and the neo-liberal political economy' in Stubbs, R. and Underhill, G. (eds) (2000) *Political Economy and the Changing Global Order*, 2nd edition, Oxford: Oxford University Press, pp. 48–59.

Gill, S. (2002) 'The Political Economy of Globalization: The Old and the New', in Aksu, E. and Camilleri, (eds) *Democratizing Global Governance*, London: Palgrave.

Gills, D-S. (2001) 'Neo-liberal economic globalization and women's in Asia' in Gills, D-S. and Piper, N. (eds) *Women and Work in Globalizing Asia*, London: Routledge, pp. 1–12.

Gills, D-S. and Piper, N. (eds) (2001) *Women and Work in Globalizing Asia*, London: Routledge.

Gilpin, R. (2000). *The Challenge of Global Capitalism*, Princeton, NJ: Princeton University Press.

Goka, K. (1998) *Country Study: Japan: Development of private employment agencies and government policies*, Geneva: ILO, www.ilo.org/public/english/dialogue/govlab/admitra/papers/1998/japan/index.htm, downloaded 21 September 2001.

Goldblatt, D., Held, D., McGrew, A. and Perraton, J. (1997) 'Economic globalization and the nation-state: shifting balances of power', *Alternatives* 22: 269–85.

Gonzalez, L. (2001) 'Mexico/U.S. migration and gender relations: the Guanajuatense community in Mexico and the United States' in Kelly, R. M., Bayes, J. H., Hawkesworth, M. E. and Young, B. (eds) *Gender, Globalization and Democratization*, Oxford: Rowman & Littlefield, pp. 75–94.

Gordon, A. (ed.) (1993) *Postwar Japan as History*, Berkeley, CA: University of California Press.

Gordon, A. (1998) 'The invention of Japanese-style labor management' in Vlastos, S. (ed.) *Mirror of Modernity: Invented Traditions of Modern Japan*, London: University of California Press, ch. 1, pp. 19–36.

Gordon, D. (1988) 'The global economy: new edifice or crumbling foundations?', *New Left Review*, no. 168.

Graham, L. (1994) 'How does the Japanese model transfer to the United States? A view from the line' in Elger, T. and Smith, C. (eds) *Global Japanization? The Transnational Transformation of the Labour Process*, London: Routledge, ch. 4, pp. 123–51.

Gray, J. (1998) *False Dawn: The Delusions of Global Capitalism*, London: Granta.

Greater Manchester Low Pay Unit (1998) *Local Government and Homeworking: A Resource Pack*, Manchester: Greater Manchester Low Pay Unit.

Greer, G. (2000) *The Whole Woman*, London: Anchor.

Grown, C., Elson, D. and Çagatay, N. (eds) (2000) Special Issue on 'Growth, trade, finance and gender inequality', *World Development*, July, 27 (7).

Hadjicostandi, J. (1990) '"Facon": women's formal and informal work in the garment industry in Kavala, Greece' in Ward, K. (ed.) (1990) *Women Workers and Global Restructuring*, New York: Cornell University Press, pp. 64–81.

Hall, P. (1992) 'The movement from Keynesianism to monetarism: institutional analysis and British economic policy' in Steinmo, S., Thelen, K. and Longstreth, F. (1992) *Structuring Politics*, Cambridge: Cambridge University Press, pp. 90–113.

Hall, P. and Taylor, R. (1996) 'Political science and the three new institutionalisms', *Political Studies*, no. 444, pp. 952–73.

Hall, P. and Taylor, R. (1998) 'The potential of historical institutionalism: a response to Hay and Wincott', *Political Studies*, XLVI, pp. 958–62.

Halliday, F. (1995) 'The end of Cold War and international relations: some analytic and theoretical conclusions' in Booth, K. and Smith, S. (eds) *International Relations Theory Today*, Cambridge, Oxford: Polity Press, pp. 38–61.

Halmos, P. (ed.) (1966) *The Sociological Review Monograph: Japanese Sociological Studies*, Keele: University of Keele.

Hanami, T. (2000) 'Equal employment revisited', *Japan Labour Bulletin*, 39 (1), 1 January, www.jil.go.jp/bulletin/year/(2000)/vol39-01/05.htm, downloaded 1 August 2001.

Harrison, B. (1997) *Lean and Mean: The Changing Landscape of Corporate Power in the Age of Flexibility*, New York: Basic Books.

Hasegawa, H. and Hook, G. (1998) *Japanese Business Management: Restructuring for Low Growth and Globalization*, London: Routledge.

Hatch, W. and Yamamura, K. (1996) *Asia in Japan's Embrace: Building a Regional Production Alliance*, Cambridge: Cambridge University Press.

Hayashi, Y. (1996) 'Policies of the Japanese government towards women' in AMPO (eds) *Voices from the Japanese Women's Movement*, New York: M. E. Sharpe, ch. 6, pp. 82–9.

Headquarters for the Promotion of Gender Equality (1996) *Plan for Gender Equality 2000: The National Plan of Action for Promotion of a Gender-Equal Society*, Tokyo: Headquarters for the Promotion of Gender Equality.

Headquarters for the Promotion of Gender Equality (2000) 'Results of the analysis of time spent on care for the elderly and child care', *News from the Headquarters for the Promotion of Gender Equality, Women in Japan Today*, Tokyo: Prime Minister's office, January, p. 2.

Hein, L. E. (1994) 'In search of peace and democracy: Japanese economic debate in political context', *Journal of Asian Studies*, 53 (3), August, pp. 752–78.

Held, D. (1995) *Democracy and the Global Order. From the Modern State to Cosmopolitan Governance*, London: Polity Press.

Held, D., McGrew, A., Goldblatt, D. and Perraton, J. (1999) *Global Transformations*, Cambridge: Polity Press.

Helleiner, E. (1996) 'Post-globalization: is the financial liberalization trend likely to be reversed?' in Boyer, R. and Drache, D. (eds) *States Against Markets*, London: Routledge, pp. 193–210.

Higuchi, Y. (1993) 'Kohy-o Data ni yoru Kaikibunseki kara mita Nihonkigy-o to Gaishikeikigy-o no Chigai' ('On the difference between Japanese companies and foreign-affiliated companies by regression analysis'), *Ch-osa Kenky-u H-okokusho* (Research Report) 48: 146–82, cited in Watanabe, H. (1999) 'Recent trends of foreign affiliated companies in Japan' *Japan Labour Bulletin*, 38 (8), 1 August, www.jil.go.jp/bulletin/year/1999/vol38-08/05.htm, downloaded 30 September 2002.

Higuchi, Y. (trans. Priscilla Lambert) (1997) 'The effects of income tax and social security policy: married women in the Japanese labor supply', *US-Japan Women's Journal*, English Supplement, no. 13, pp. 104–29.

Hikita, M. (1996) 'The world agricultural crisis and Japanese rural women's challenge', *Women's Asia 21: Voices from Japan*, no. 2, August, pp. 28–31.

Hiroki, M. (1986) *In the Shadow of Affluence: Stories of Japanese Women Workers*, Tokyo: Asian Women Workers' Centre.

Hirst, P. and Thompson, G. (1996) *Globalization in Question: The International Economy and the Possibilities Of Governance*, Cambridge: Polity Press.

Hook, G. and Hasegawa H. (eds) (2001) *The Political Economy of Japanese Globalization*, London: Routledge.

Hook, G. and McCormack, G. (2001) *Japan's Contested Constitution: Documents and Anaylsis*, London: Routledge.

Hooper, C. (2000) 'Masculinities in transition: the case of globalization' in Marchand, M. H. and Sisson Runyan, A. (eds) (2000) *Gender and Global Restructuring: Sightings, Sites and Resistances*, London: Routledge, ch. 3, pp. 59–73.

Hossfeld, K. (1990) '"Their logic against them": contradictions in sex, race and class in Silicon Valley' in Ward, K. (ed.) (1990) *Women Workers and Global Restructuring*, New York: Cornell University Press, ch. 7, pp. 149–78.

Houseman, S. and Osawa, M. (1995) 'Part-time and temporary employment in Japan', *Monthly Labor Review*, October.

Houseman, S. and Osawa, M. (1998) 'What is the nature of part-time work in the United States and Japan?' in O'Reilly, J. and Fagan, C. (eds) (1998) *Part-Time Prospects: An International Comparison of Part-time Work in Europe, North America and the Pacific Rim*, London: Routledge.

Hughes, C. (1999) 'Japanese Policy and the East Asian Crisis: Abject Defeat or Quiet Victory?', *Working Paper No.24/99*, Warwick: Centre for the Study of Globalisation and Regionalisation (CSGR), University of Warwick.

Hulme, D. (1996) 'Temps catch on in Japan', *AsiaOne.Com*, www.web3.asia1.com.sg/timesnet/data/ab/docs/ab0964.html, downloaded 13 October 1999.

Humm, M. (ed.) (1992) *Feminisms*, Brighton: Harvester.

Hunter, J. (ed.) (1993) *Japanese Women Working*, London: Routledge.

Ikeda, M. (1998) 'Globalisation's impact upon the subcontracting system' in Hasegawa, H. and Hook, G. (eds) *Japanese Business Management: Restructuring for Low Growth and Globalization*, London: Routledge, pp. 109–28.

Ikenberry, G. J. (1988) 'Conclusion: an institutional approach to American foreign policy', in Ikenberry, G. J., Lake, D.A. and Mastanduno, M. (eds) (1988) *The State and American Foreign Economic Policy*, Ithaca, NY: Cornell University Press, pp. 222–3.

Ikenberry, G. J., Lake, D.A. and Mastanduno, M. (eds) (1988) *The State and American Foreign Economic Policy*, Ithaca, NY: Cornell University Press.

Imada, S. (1994) 'Female employment and ability development', *Japan Labour Bulletin*, 9 (33), 1 September.

Imada, S. (1996) 'Female labor force after the enforcement of the equal employment opportunity law', *Japan Labour Bulletin*, 1 August, pp. 5–8.

Imada, S. (1997) 'Work and family life', *Japan Labour Bulletin*, 36 (8), 1 August, p. 6, www.jil.go.jp/bulletin/year/1997/vol36-08/06.htm, downloaded 17 August 2004.

Imai, T. (2001) 'At the outset of the 21st century', *Monthly Keidanren*, January.

Imamura, A. (1993) 'Interdependence of family and education: reactions of foreign wives of Japanese to the school system' in Shields, J. J. (ed.) *Japanese Schooling: Patterns of Socialization, Equality and Political Control*, University Park, PA: Pennsylvania State University Press, ch. 2, pp. 16–27.

Imamura, A. (ed.) (1996) *Re-imaging Japanese Women*, Berkeley, CA: University of California Press.

Inoue, S. (1999) *Japanese Trade Unions and Their Future: Opportunities and Challenges in an Era of Globalization*, Geneva: International Labour Organization.

International Confederation of Free Trade Unions (ICFTU) (2001) *The Role of the International Financial Institutions in a Globalized Economy*, Washington, DC: Statement by the ICFTU, TUAC and ITS to the 2001 Annual Meetings of the IMF and World Bank, 29–30 September.

International Labour Organization (ILO) (1997) 'Perspectives: part-time work: solution or trap?', *International Labour Review*, 136 (4).

International Labour Organization (ILO) (1999) *Women and Training in the Global Economy, World Employment Report 1998–1999*, Geneva: ILO.

International Labour Organization (ILO) (2002) *National Agenda on OSH policies and Extension of Coverage to Home-based Workers*, www.ilo.org/public/english/region/asro/bangkok/asiaosh/country/thailand/hmworker/agenda.htm.

International Labour Organization/South-East Asian and the Pacific Multi-disciplinary Advisory Team (ILO/SEAPAT) (1998a) *Gender Issues in the World of*

Work: Emerging Gender Issues in the Asia Pacific Region, www-ilo.org/public/english/region/asro/mdtmanila/training/unit2/asiaatyp.htm, downloaded 16 August 2004.

International Labour Organization/South-East Asian and the Pacific Multi-disciplinary Advisory Team (ILO/SEAPAT) (1998b) *Gender Issues In The World Of Work: Effects Of Structural Adjustment Policies*, www-ilo-mirror.who.or.jp/public/english/mdtmanil/training/unit2/asiasap.htm, downloaded 21 October 1999.

International Monetary Fund (IMF) (1999) *IMF Staff Country Report no. 99/83 Japan: Staff Report for the (1999) Article VI Consultation*, Washington, DC: International Monetary Fund.

International Reform Monitor (2000) *Reforms: Japan: Reforms of Japanese Labor Market Regulations (revision of the Employment Security Law (ESL) and the Worker Dispatching Law (WDL))*, Bertelsmann Foundation, www.reformmonitor.org/index.php3, downloaded 21 September 2001.

International Reform Monitor (2001 – download date) *Reform on Equal Employment Opportunity Between Men and Women (1997) revision of Equal Employment Opportunity Law (EEOL)*, Bertelsmann Foundation, www.reformmonitor.org/httpd-cache/doc_reports_1-37.html, downloaded 19 July 2001.

Itoh, J. (1997) 'Time to rethink our nation – promoting reform at all levels', *Monthly Keidanren*, July, www.keidanren.or.jp/english/journal/jou9707/html, downloaded 24 June 2002.

Itoh, M. (2000) *The Japanese Economy Reconsidered*, Basingstoke: Palgrave.

Iwamoto, M. (2001) 'The madonna boom: the progress of Japanese women into politics in the 1980s', *PS*, June, pp. 225–6.

Iwao, S. (1993) *The Japanese Woman: Traditional Image and Changing Reality*, Cambridge, MA: Harvard University Press.

Japan Access (2002) *Social Security System: An Ageing Society and Its Impact on Social Security*, www.sg.emb-japan.go.jp/JapanAccess/social,htm, downloaded 30 September 2002.

Japan Airlines (JAL) Cabin Attendants' Union (1995) *Our View on Part-Time Cabin Crew*, campaign literature.

Japan Institute for Workers' Evolution (2001) *The Situation of Women in Japan: Working Women*, Tokyo: Institute of Workers' Evolution, www.jiwe.orijp/english/situation/working.html, downloaded 12 August 2004.

Japan Institute of Labour (1999) *Labour Situation in Japan (1999)*, Tokyo: Japan Institute of Labour.

Japan Institute of Labour (2001) *JIL Statistical Information: Recent Statistical Survey Reports (Friday, December 29–Wednesday, January 31) Survey on Situation of Preliminary offer of Hiring of New Graduates, Tuesday 16, released by Ministry of Health, Labour and Welfare*, Tokyo: Japan Institute of Labour.

Japan International Cooperation Agency (2001) *Japan's Official Development Assistance*, www.jica.go.jp/english/about/01.html, downloaded 11 July 2001.

Japan Labour Bulletin (1997) 'Overhauling the equal employment opportunity law', *Japan Labour Bulletin*, 36 (3), 1 March.

Japan Labour Bulletin (1999) 'The revised labour standards law enables recruitment of women', *Japan Labour Bulletin*, 38 (5), 1 May.

Japan Labour Bulletin (1999) 'Measures to prevent sexual harassment in the workplace', *Japan Labour Bulletin*, 38 (8), 1 August.

Japan Labour Bulletin (2001) 'Are Working Mothers Bad for Their Children?', *Japan Labour Bulletin*, 40 (7), 1 July.

Japan NGO Report Preparatory Committee (1999*) Japan NGO Alternative Report: Towards the Special Session of the UN General Assembly 'Women (2000): Gender Equality, Development, and Peace'*, Tokyo: Japan NGO Report Preparatory Committee.

Japan Statistical Yearbook (2001) *Statistical Handbook of Japan, 2001*, Tokyo: Statistics Bureau and Statistics Center, Ministry of Public Management, Home Affairs, Posts and Telecommunications,www.stat.go.jp/english/data/handbook/c04cont/ htm, downloaded 21 September 2001.

Japan Times (2000) 'Women's job bias suit fails: Sumitomo Electric's gender discrimination upheld', 1 August.

Japan Times (2001) 'Temp staff rise said worrisome', 4 April.

Japanese External Trade Organization (JETRO) (1997) *Foreign Direct Investment Inflow/Outflow for EU (12 States) (Flow, Excluding Intra-Regional Investment)*, Tokyo: Japan External Trade Organization.

Japanese External Trade Organization (JETRO) (2001) *Accelerated Corporate Realignment Through Mergers and Acquisitions* (White Paper on Foreign Direct Investment), Tokyo: Japan External Trade Organization.

Jessop, B., Bonnett, K., Bromley, S. and Ling, T. (1987) 'Popular capitalism, flexible accumulation and left strategy', *New Left Review*, no. 165, pp. 104–23.

Johnson, C. (1998) 'Economic crisis in East Asia: the clash of capitalisms', *Cambridge Journal of Economics*, no. 22, pp. 633–61.

Kakuyama, K. (1997) *Litigating Sexual Discrimination Employment Cases in Japan: Legal Developments*, Tokyo: Temple University Japan.

Kaneko Masaru (1999) *Han-gurobarizumu: Shijo kaikaku no senryaku-teki shiko (Antiglobalism: Strategic Ideas of Market Reform)*, Tokyo: Iwanami Shoten.

Kaneko, Masaru, Jinno, N. and Nomura, H. (2000) 'Stop the slide toward national bankruptcy', *Japan Echo*, 27 (6), www.japanecho.co.jp/sum/2000/b2706.html, downloaded 3 March 2004.

Kaneko, Masaru and Kaneko, Masaomi, K. (2003) 'Is there a tomorrow for a Japanese society without hope? A dialogue between Kaneko Masaru and Kaneko Masaomi', *Sekai*, no. 710, February, translated by Lorinda Kiyama, www. iwanami.co.jp/jpworld/text/Povertydialogue01.html, downloaded 3 March 2004.

Kashima, T. (1989) *Otoko to Onna Kawaru Rikigaku (The Dynamics of Changing Men and Women)*, Tokyo: Iwanami Shinsho.

Kato, T. and Steven, R. (1993) *Is Japanese Management Post-Fordist: An International Debate*, Tokyo: Madosha.

Katz, R. (1998) *Japan: The System that Soured*, Portland, OR: M.E. Sharpe.

Kawashima, Y. (1995) 'Female workers: an overview of past and current trends' in Fujimura-Fanselow, K. and Kameda, A. (eds) *Japanese Women: New Feminist Perspectives on the Past, Present and Future*, New York: Feminist Press, pp. 271–94.

Kaya, E. (1995) 'Mitsui Mariko: An avowed feminist assemblywoman' in Fujimura-Fanselow, K. and Kameda, A. (eds) *Japanese Women: New Feminist Perspectives on the Past, Present and Future*, New York: Feminist Press, pp. 384–92.

Keck, M. E. and Sikkink, K. (1998) *Activists Beyond Borders*, London: Cornell University Press.

Keira, T. (1996) 'Ainu women speak out: the situation of indigenous women in Japan', *Women's Asia 21: Voices from Japan*, no. 2, pp. 11–12.

Kelly, D. C. (1998) 'The Modern Japanese State-Society Complex and the Implications for Competing Constructions of Regionalism in East Asia: a Neo-Gramscian Reinterpretation', unpublished PhD thesis, Sheffield: University of Sheffield.

Kelly, R. M., Bayes, J. H., Hawkesworth, M. E. and Young, B. (eds) (2001) *Gender, Globalization and Democratization*, Oxford: Rowman & Littlefield.

Kelsky, K. (2001) *Women on the Verge: Japanese Women, Western Dreams*, London: Duke University Press.

Khor, D. (1999) 'Organizing for Change: Women's Grassroots Activism in Japan', *Feminist Studies*, Fall 1999, 25 (3), pp. 633–61.

Knipe Mouer, E. (1976) 'Women in teaching' in Lebra, J., Paulson, J. and Powers, E. (eds) *Women in Changing Japan*, Boulder, CO: Westview Press, ch. 8, pp. 157–90.

Kofman, E. (2000) 'The invisibility of skilled female migrants and gender relations in studies of skilled migration in Europe', *International Journal of Population Geography*, 6: 45–59.

Kofman, E. and Youngs, G. (eds) (1996) *Globalization: Theory and Practice*, London: Pinter.

Koike, K. (1995) *The Economics of Work in Japan*, Tokyo: LTCB Library Foundation.

Kojima, A. (1996) 'Japan's grave choice: 25 years after the Nixon Shock', *NIRA Review*, Summer, www.nira.go.jp/publ/review/96summer/kojima.html, downloaded 15 October 1999.

Kojima, A. (2000) 'Globalization and Japan', *Japan Echo*, 27 (5), www.japanecho.co.jp/sum/2000/270612.html, downloaded 28 February 2004.

Kondo, H., Takahashi, T. and Ito, A. (1999) 'Revised law on temporary workers', *The Global Employer: Global Labour, Employment and Employee Benefits Bulletin*, Chicago: The Global Employer.

Kuiper, E. and Sap, J. (eds) (1995) *Out of the Margins: Feminist Perspectives on Economics*, London: Routledge.

Kurani, K. (1999) *Social Marketing: Transportation Theory for the 21st Century*, paper prepared for Washington, DC: US Department of Energy.

Kuroiwa, Y. (2001) 'The Situation of non-standard employment in Japan and its Problems: From a women workers' perspective', *Centre for Transnational Labour Studies*, no. 6, February, pp. 2–9.

Lash, S. and Urry, J. (1987) *The End of Organised Capitalism*, Cambridge: Polity Press.

Lawton, T. C., Rosenau, J. N. and Verdun, A. C. (eds) (2000) *Strange Power: Shaping the Parameters of International Relations and International Political Economy*, Aldershot: Ashgate Publishing.

Lebra, J. (1976a) 'Women in service industries' in Lebra, J., Paulson, J. and Powers, E. (eds) *Women in Changing Japan*, Boulder, CO: Westview Press, ch. 6, pp. 107–32.

Lebra, J. (1976b) 'Conclusions' in Lebra, J., Paulson, J. and Powers, E. (eds) *Women in Changing Japan*, Boulder, CO: Westview Press, ch. 7, pp. 297–304.

Lebra, J., Paulson, J. and Powers, E. (eds) (1976) *Women in Changing Japan*, Boulder, CO: Westview Press.

Lebra, T. S. (1984) *Japanese Women: Constraint and Fulfilment*, Honolulu: University of Hawaii Press.

Lee-Cunin, M. (2004) *Student Views in Japan: A Study of Japanese Students' Perceptions of their First Years at University*, Rochdale: Fieldwork Publications.

Lehmann, J.-P. (2000) 'The dynamics of paralysis: Japan in the global era' in Lawton, T. C., Rosenau, J. N. and Verdun, A. C. (eds) *Strange Power: Shaping the Parameters of International Relations and International Political Economy*, Aldershot: Ashgate Publishing Company, ch. 16, pp. 295–320.

LeMaitre, G., Marianna, P. and van Bastelaer, A. (1997) *OECD Economic Studies No. 29, 1997/II: International Comparisons of Part-time Work*, Paris: OECD.

Lim, L. Y. C. (1997) 'Capitalism, imperialism and patriarchy: the dilemma of Third-World women workers in multinational factories' in Visvanathan, N. *et al.* (eds) *The Women, Gender and Development Reader*, London: Zed Books.

Lind, A. (2000) 'Negotiating boundaries: women's organizations and the politics of restructuring in Ecuador' in Marchand, M. H. and Sisson Runyan, A. (eds) (2000) *Gender and Global Restructuring: Sightings, Sites and Resistances*, London: Routledge, ch. 9, pp. 161–75.

Lipietz, A. (1987) *Mirages and Miracles*, London: Verso.

Lo, Jeannie (1990) *Office Ladies, Factory Women: Life and Work in a Japanese Company*, Portland OR: M. E. Sharpe.

Määttä, P. (1998) *Equal Pay Policies: International Review of Selected Developing and Developed Countries*, Geneva: International Labour Organisation, www.ilo.org/public/english/dialogue/govlab/legrel/papers/equalpay/1_2.htm, downloaded 9 July 2002.

McCormack, G. (1996) *The Emptiness of Japanese Affluence*, New York: M.E. Sharpe.

Mackie, V. (1999) 'Dialogue, distance and difference: feminism in contemporary Japan', *Women's Studies International Forum*, 22 (4), pp. 599–615.

Management and Coordination Agency (1999a) *Annual Report on Labour Force Survey (1999)*, Tokyo: Statistics Bureau, Management and Coordination Agency.

Management and Coordination Agency (1999b) *Labour Force Survey (1999) Changes in the Number of Employees by Industries*, Tokyo: Statistics Bureau, Management and Coordination Agency, www.mhlw.go.jp/english/wp/wp-l/fig42.html, downloaded 28 September 2002.

Mann, M. (1997) 'Has globalization ended the rise of the nation-state?', *Review of International Political Economy*, 4 (3): 472–96.

March, J. and Olsen, J. (1989) *Rediscovering Institutions*, New York: The Free Press.

Marchand, M. (1996a) 'Seeing NAFTA: gendered metaphors and silenced gender implications' in Kofman, E. and Youngs, G. (eds) (1996) *Globalization: Theory and Practice*, London: Pinter, ch. 18, pp. 253–70.

Marchand, M. (1996b) 'Reconceptualising "gender and development" in an era of "Globalisation"', *Millennium*, 25 (3): 577–603.

Marchand, M. (2000) 'Gendered representations of the "global": reading/writing globalization' in Stubbs, R. and Underhill, G. (eds) *Political Economy and the Changing Global Order, 2nd edition*, Oxford: Oxford University Press, pp. 218–28.

Marchand, M. and Runyan, A. S. (2000) 'Introduction: feminist sightings of global restructurings: conceptualizations and reconceptualizations' in Marchand, M. H. and Runyan, A. S. (eds) *Gender and Global Restructuring: Sightings, Sites and Resistances*, London: Routledge, pp. 1–22.

Marcos, S. (1999) 'Twenty-five years of Mexican feminisms', *Women's Studies International Forum*, 22 (4): 431–33.

Martin, L. and Tsuya, N. (1991). 'Interactions of middle-aged Japanese with their parents', *Population Studies*, 45: 299–311.

Martinez, D. P. (ed.) (1998) *The Worlds of Japanese Popular Culture: Gender, Shifting Boundaries and Global Cultures*, Cambridge: Cambridge University Press.

Maruo, N. (1997) *Social Security in Japan: Toward a Japanese Model of the Welfare State*, Tokyo: Ministry of Foreign Affairs, www.mofa.go.jp/j_info/japan/socsec/maruo/maruo_1.html, downloaded 21 August 2002.

Mason, J. (1994) 'Linking qualitative and quantitative data analysis' in Brynaan, A. and Burgess, R. (eds) *Analysing Qualitative Data*, London: Routledge.

Matsumoto, S. (1976) 'Women in factories' in Lebra, J., Paulson, J. and Powers, E. (eds) (1976) *Women in Changing Japan*, Boulder, CO: Westview Press, ch. 3, pp. 51–74.

Matsushima, S. (1966) 'Labour Management Relations in Japan', in Halmos, P. (ed.) (1966) *The Sociological Review Monograph: Japanese Sociological Studies*, Keele: University of Keele, pp. 69–82.

Matsui, Y. (1996a) 'Economic development and Asian women' in AMPO (eds) *Voices from the Japanese Women's Movement*, New York: M. E. Sharpe, pp. 55–64.

Matsui, Y. (1996b) 'The women's movement: progress and obstacles: dialogue with Kitazawa Yoko, Matsui Yayori and Yunomae Tomoko' in AMPO (eds) *Voices from the Japanese Women's Movement*, New York: M. E. Sharpe, pp. 23–37.

May, T. (1997) *Social Research: Issues, Methods and Process, 2nd edition*, Buckingham: Open University Press.

Mbire-Barungi, B. (1999) 'Ugandan feminism: political rhetoric or reality', *Women's Studies International Forum*, 22 (4): 435–9.

Meng, X. (1996) 'The economic position of women in Asia', *Asian-Pacific Economic Literature*, 10 (1): 23–41.

Menju, T. (1999) 'Globalization and grassroots networks: what do Japanese experiences suggest?', *Japan Editorial*.

Meyer, M. and Prugl, E. (eds) (1999) *Gender Politics in Global Governance*, Oxford: Rowman & Littlefield.

Mies, M. (1986) *Patriarchy and Accumulation on a World Scale*, London: Zed Books.

Mikami, H. (1999) *Time Use Survey in Japan*, conference paper prepared for Seminar on Time Use Survey, Ahmedabad, India, 8 December.

Mikanagi, Y. (2001) 'Women and political institutions in Japan', *PS*, June, pp. 211–12.

Mindry, D. (2001) 'Nongovernmental organization, "grassroot," and the politics of virtue', *Signs*, 26 (4): 1187–211.

Ministry of Economy, Trade and Industry (METI) (2001) *White Paper on International Trade (2001)* Tokyo: METI.

Ministry of Education, Culture, Sports, Science and Technology (2001) *Statistics: Universities and Junior Colleges*, www.mext.go.jp/english/statist/index11/html, downloaded 21 September 2002.

Ministry of Education, Science, Sports and Culture (1995) *Japanese Government Policies in Education, Science, Sports and Culture, 1995*, Tokyo: Ministry of Education, Science, Sports and Culture.

Ministry of Finance (1999) *Annual Report on Customs and Tariffs*, Tokyo: Ministry of Finance.

Ministry of Foreign Affairs (1996) *Policy Speech by Prime Minister Ryutaro Hashimoto to the 136th Session of the National Diet*, infojapan.org/region/n-america/us/security/alliance/ry_136.html, downloaded 21 September 2001.

Ministry of Foreign Affairs (2000) *Diplomatic Bluebook 2000: Towards the 21st Century: Foreign Policy for a Better Future*, Tokyo: Ministry of Foreign Affairs.

Ministry of Health, Labour and Welfare (1998) *Trends and Features of the Labour Economy in 1998*, Tokyo: Statistics and Information Department, Minister's Secretariat, www.mhlw.go.jp/english/wp/wp-1/1.1.html, downloaded 28 September 2002.

Ministry of Health, Labour and Welfare (1999) *White Paper: Annual Report on Health and Welfare 1998–1991: Social Security and National Life*, Tokyo: Ministry of Labour and Welfare.

Ministry of Health, Labour and Welfare (2000) *Abridged Life Tables for Japan 2000*, www.mhlw.go.jp/english/database/db-hw/lifetb00/part1.html, downloaded 28 September 2002.

Ministry of Health, Labour and Welfare (2001) *Basic Survey on Wage Structure*, Tokyo Statistics and Information Department, Minister's Secretariat, 20 June, jin. jcic.or.jp/stat/stats/18WME34.html, downloaded 19 September 2001.

Ministry of Health, Labour and Welfare (2002) *Summary of Vital Statistics*, Tokyo: Statistics and Information Department, Minister's Secretariat, jin.jcic.or.jp/ stat/stats/02VIT11.html, downloaded 25 September 2002.

Ministry of International Trade and Industry (MITI) (1998) *White Paper on International Trade*, Tokyo: Ministry of International Trade and Industry.

Ministry of Labour (1990) *Comprehensive Survey on the Actual Conditions of Part-time Employees*, jin.jcic.or.jp/insight/html/focus05/data/DATA022, downloaded 1 August 2002.

Ministry of Labour (1994) *General Survey on Diversified Types of Employment*, Tokyo: Ministry of Labour.

Ministry of Labour (1996) *White Paper on Labour, 1996: Summary*, Tokyo: Japan Institute of Labour.

Ministry of Labour (1999) *White Paper on Labour 1999: The Rapidly Changing Labour Market and Job Creation: Summary*, www.mhlw.go.jp/english/wp/wp-l/fig42.html, downloaded 7 June 2002.

Ministry of Public Management, Home Affairs, Posts and Telecommunications (2001) *Labour Force Survey*, Tokyo: Statistics Bureau and Statistics Center.

Ministry of Public Management, Home Affairs, Posts and Telecommunications (2002) *Employment Status Survey 2002*, Tokyo: Statistics Bureau, www.stat.go. jp/english/data/shugyou/2002/kakuhou/youyaku.htm#6, downloaded 6 March 2004.

Ministry of Public Management, Home Affairs, Posts and Telecommunications (2003) *Statistical Yearbook 2003*, Tokyo: Statistics Bureau, www.stat.go.jp/english/ data/handbook/c12cont.htm, downloaded 6 March 2004.

Ministry of Public Management, Home Affairs, Posts and Telecommunications (2004) *Japan Statistical Yearbook 2004*, Tokyo: Statistics Bureau, http://www.stat. go.jp/english/data/handbook/c04cont.htm, downloaded 6 March 2004.

Miura, M. (2001) *Globalization and Reforms of Labor Markets Institutions: Japan and Major OECD Countries*, Tokyo Institute of Social Science, Domestic Politics Project no. 4, July, Tokyo: University of Tokyo.

Moghadam, V. M. (2000) 'Economic restructuring and the gender contract: a case study of Jordan' in Marchand, M. H. and Sisson Runyan, A. (eds) *Gender and Global Restructuring: Sightings, Sites and Resistances*, London: Routledge, ch. 5, pp. 99–115.

Molony, B. (1993) 'Equality versus difference: the Japanese debate over "motherhood protection", 1915–1950' in Hunter, J. (ed.) *Japanese Women Working*, London: Routledge, ch. 6, pp. 122–48.

Molony, B. (1995) 'Japan's 1986 Equal Employment Opportunity Law and the changing discourse on gender', *Signs*, Winter, pp. 268–302.

Molony, B. (1999) *State and Women in Modern Japan: Feminist Discourses in the Meiji and Taisho Eras*, London: paper presented at the STICERD 20th Anniversary Symposium, The Suntory Centre, London School of Economics and Political Science.

Moore, D. (2000) 'Levelling the playing fields and embedding illusions: "post- conflict" discourse and neo-liberal "development" in war-torn Africa', *Review of African Political Economy*, 27 (83): 11–28.

Mori, N., Shiratsuke, S. and Taguchi, H. (2000) *Policy responses to the post-bubble adjustments in Japan: a tentative review, Discussion Paper No. 2000–E–1b*, Tokyo: Institute for Monetary and Economic Studies, Bank of Japan.

Moriki, K. (1997) 'Japanese women seek solidarity with Asian women' *Osaka Dawn, Newsletter of the Dawn Center* (Osaka Prefectural Women's Center), November, pp. 1–3.

Morito, H. (1999) '*Deregulation of Labor Law in Japan*', *Deregulation and Labor Law: in Search of a Labor Law Concept for the 21st Century, 1998*, JIL Comparative Labor Law Seminar, JIL Report, no. 8, Japan Institute of Labour, pp. 149–64.

Morrison, C. and Soesastro, H. (eds) (1998) *Domestic Adjustments to Globalization*, Tokyo: Japan Center for International Exchange.

Murata, N. (1996) 'The trafficking of women' in AMPO (eds) *Voices from the Japanese Women's Movement*, New York: M. E. Sharpe, pp. 115–19.

Nakajima, M. (1997) 'Has the Equal Opportunity Law brought equality?', *AMPO: Japan Asia Quarterly Review*, 27 (3): 8–10.

Nakamura, J. and Ueda, A. (1999) 'On the determinants of career interruption by childbirth among married women in Japan', *Journal of Japanese and International Economics*, no. 13, pp. 73–89.

Nakano, M. (1996) 'Ten years under the Equal Employment Opportunity Law', in *AMPO: Voices from the Japanese Women's Movement*, New York: M.E. Sharpe, pp. 11–14, 65–81.

Nakatani, I. (1987) *Bodaresu ekonomi (Borderless Economy)*, Tokyo: Nihon Keizai Shimbun.

Nakayama, M. (1996) *Sexual Harassment as Sex Discrimination – An Overview and Some Perspectives Offered*, Network Pacific Asia, http://law.rikkyo.ac.jp/npa/ng205.htm, downloaded 11 July 2001.

Nakura, Y. (1997) 'Japan's Part-Time Women Workers', unpublished MA dissertation, Warwick: University of Warwick.

National Institute of Employment and Vocational Research (1988) *Women Workers in Japan*, Tokyo: NIEVR.

National Organization for Women (NOW) (1996) *Global Campaign Aims to End 'Seku Hara': Protests by U.S. and Japanese Feminists*, www.now.org/nnt/11–96/mitsu.html, downloaded 31 January 2002.

New Japan Women's Association (no date given) *Women Workers Achieving Victory in Labor Disputes*, Tokyo: New Japan Women's Association, www.iijnet.or.jp/c-pro/shinfujin/eng/disputes.html, downloaded 14 February 2001.

New York Times (2001) 'Diploma at hand: Japanese women find glass ceiling reinforced with iron', 1 January, late edition – final, section A, p. 4, column 1.

Neysmith, S. and Chen, X. (2002) 'Understanding how globalisation and restructuring affect women's lives: implications for comparative policy analysis', *International Journal of Social Welfare*, pp. 243–53.

NHK Broadcasting Culture Research Institute (1998) *JPOLL – the Japanese Public Opinion Database*, hosted by the Roper Centre, roperweb.ropercenter.uconn.edu/cgi-bin/hsrun.exe/roperweb/JPOLL/.

Nikkei Keizai Shimbun (2004) *Employment Gap Widens between Large, Small Firms*, 1 May.

Nikkeiren (2001) 'Corporate welfare costs remain almost unchanged from previous year', Tokyo: Nikkeiren, www.keikyoweb.gr.jp/nikkeiren/english/01_news/019.htm, downloaded 17 August 2004.

Nikkei Weekly (2002) 'Women Getting Better Deal at Work', Tokyo: *Nikkei Weekly*.

Ochiai, E. (1997) *The Japanese Family System in Transition: A Sociological Analysis of Family Change in Postwar Japan*, Tokyo: LTCB Library Foundation.

Office for Gender Equality (1997) *The Present Status of Women and Measures* (White Paper on Women), abridged, www.sorifu.go.jp/danjyo/index2.html, downloaded 20 October 1999.

Office for Gender Equality (2001) *Women in Japan Today: Statistics*, January, www.gender.go.jp/index2.html, downloaded 30 September 2002.

Ogai, T. (2001) 'Japanese women and political institutions: why are women politically underrepresented?', *PS*, June, pp. 207–10.

Ogasawara, Y. (1998) *Office Ladies and Salaried Men: Power, Gender and Work in Japanese Companies*, Berkeley, CA: University of California Press.

Ogawa, M. (1997) 'The establishment of the Women's and Minors' Bureau in Japan', *U.S.-Japan Women's Journal, English Supplement*, no. 13, pp. 56–86.

Ohmae, K. (1995) *The Borderless World: Power and Strategy in the Interlinked Economy*, New York: Harper Perennial.

Okimoto, D. and Rohlen, T. (1988) *Inside the Japanese System: Readings on Contemporary Society and Political Economy*, Stanford, CA: Stanford University Press.

Okura, Y. (1996) 'Promoting prostitution', in AMPO (eds) (1996) *Voices from the Japanese Women's Movement*, New York: M. E. Sharpe, pp. 11–14.

O'Reilly, J. and Fagan, C. (eds) (1998) *Part-Time Prospects: An International Comparison of Part-time Work in Europe, North America and the Pacific Rim*, London: Routledge.

Organisation for Economic Co-operation and Development (OECD) (1991) *Employment Outlook*, Paris: OECD.

Organisation for Economic Co-operation and Development (OECD) (1997) *Employment Outlook*, Paris: OECD, www.hil.go.jp/bulletin/year/2000/vol39-01/05.htm, downloaded 9 February 2000.

Organisation for Economic Co-operation and Development (OECD) (2002a) *Employment Outlook*, Paris: OECD, www.oecd.org/dataoecd/36/7/17652667.pdf, downloaded 6 March 2004.

Organisation for Economic Co-operation and Development (OECD) (2002b) *Employment Outlook 2002: Statistical Annex*, p. 319, Paris: OECD.

Osawa, M. (1998) 'The feminization of the labour market' in Banno, J. (ed.) *The Political Economy of Japanese Society, volume 2: Internationalization and Domestic Issues*, Oxford: Oxford University Press, ch. 5, pp. 143–74.

Osawa, M. (2000) 'Government approaches to gender equality in the mid-1990s', *Social Science Japan Journal*, 3 (1): 3–19.

Osawa, M. and Kingston, J. (1995) 'Flexibility and inspiration: restructuring and the Japanese Labor Market', *Japan Labour Bulletin*, 35 (1), 1 January, www.jil.go.jp/bulletin/year/1996/vol35-01/04.htm, downloaded 30 September 2002.

Pan-Asian Chamber of Commerce (1999) 'Diversity seminar: what it means to be Japanese in corporate America', news release, 10 November, Washington, DC: Pan Asian Chamber of Commerce.

Passy, F. (2000) *Socialization, Recruitment and the Structure-agency Gap: A Specification of the Impact of Networks on Participation in Social Movements*, paper given 22–5 June, Social Movement Analysis: The Network Perspective, Ross Priory, Loch Lomond, Scotland.

Paulson, J. (1976) 'Evolution of the Feminine Ideal', in Lebra, J., Paulson, J. and Powers, E. (eds) *Women in Changing Japan*, Boulder, CO: Westview Press, ch. 1, pp. 1–24.

PBS online (2002a) *Commanding Heights: Japan*, www.pbs.org/wgbh/commanding heights/lo/countries/jp/jp_trade.html, downloaded 27 September 2002.

PBS online (2002b) *Japanese Women in Politics: Forging Ahead*, www.pbs.org/ttc/hottopics/jappolwom.html, downloaded 7 February 2002.

Pempel, T. (1999) 'Structural gaiatsu: international finance and political change in Japan', *Comparative Political Studies*, 32 (8): 907–32.

People's Daily online (1999) *MOFTEC Minister: China Welcomes Japanese Investment*, 25 November, http://english.peopledaily.com.ch/english/199911/25/eng/1991125 B110.html, downloaded 15 August 2004.

Peters, B. G. (1999) *Institutional Theory in Political Science: The 'New Institutionalism'*, London: Pinter.

Peterson, V. S. (forthcoming) Untitled piece on productive, reproductive and virtual economies, unpublished mimeograph.

Pfau-Effinger, B. (1998) 'Culture or structure as explanations for differences in part-time work in Germany, Finland and the Netherlands?' in O'Reilly, J. and Fagan, C. (eds) *Part-Time Prospects: An International Comparison of Part-time Work in Europe, North America and the Pacific Rim*, London: Routledge, ch. 9, pp. 177–98.

Pharr, S. (1981) *Political Women in Japan: The Search for a Place in Political Life*, Berkeley, CA: University of California Press.

Phelps, E. S. (1972) 'The statistical theory of racism and sexism', *American Economic Review*, 62, September, pp. 659–61.

Ping, H. (2001), 'Talking about gender, globalization, and labour in a Chinese context', *Signs*, Summer, 26 (4): 1278–81.

Piper, N. (2001) 'Global labour markets and national responses: legal regimes governing female migrant workers in Japan' in Gills, D-S. and Piper, N. (eds) *Women and Work in Globalizing Asia*, London: Routledge, pp. 188–208.

Polanyi, K. (1944) *The Great Transformation*, Boston, MA: First Beacon Press.

Porter, M. (1990) *The Competitive Advantage of Nations*, London: Macmillan.

Preston, P. W. (2000) *Understanding Modern Japan: A Political Economy of Development, Culture and Global Power*, London: Sage.

Pujol, M. (1995) 'Into the margin!' in Kuiper, E. and Sap, J. (eds) *Out of the Margins: Feminist Perspectives on Economics*, London: Routledge, pp. 17–34.

Pyle, J. (1990) 'Export-led development and the underdevelopment of women: the impact of discriminatory development policy in the Republic of Ireland' in Ward, K. (ed.) *Women Workers and Global Restructuring*, New York: Cornell University Press, ch. 5, pp. 85–113.

Radelet, S. and Sachs, J. (1998) 'The Onset of the East Asian Financial Crisis', *Working Paper 6680*, Cambridge, MA: National Bureau of Economic Research, http://papers.nber.org/papers/w6680.pdf, downloaded 30 September 2002.

Rai, S. (1996) 'Women and the state in the Third World: some issues for debate' in Rai, S. and Livesley, G. (eds) *Women and the State: International Perspectives*, London: Taylor & Francis, pp. 5–23.

Rai, S. (2002) *Gender and the Political Economy of Development*, Cambridge: Polity Press.

Rai, S. and Livesley, G. (eds) (1996) *Women and the State: International Perspectives*, London: Taylor & Francis.

Randall, V. and Waylen, G. (eds) (1998) *Gender, Politics and the State*, London: Routledge.

Rengo White Paper (1999) *The Spring Struggle for a Better Life, (1999): Invigorate Japan in All Aspects: Employment, Labor, Living and Economics*, Tokyo: JTUC-Rengo.

Renshaw, J. R. (1999) *Kimono in the Boardroom: The Invisible Evolution of Japanese Women Managers*, Oxford: Oxford University Press.

Rinehart, J., Robertson, D., Huxley, C. and Wareham, J. (1994) 'Reunifying conception and execution of work under Japanese production management? A Canadian case study' in Elger, T. and Smith, C. (eds) (1994) *Global Japanization? The Transnational Transformation of the Labour Process*, London: Routledge, ch. 5, pp. 152–74.

Roberts, G. S. (1994) *Staying on the Line: Blue-Collar Women in Contemporary Japan*, Honolulu: University of Hawaii Press.

Robertson, J. (1998) *Japanese Working Class Lives: An Ethnographic Study of Factory Workers*, London: Routledge.

Rohlen, T. (1988) 'Permanent employment policies in times of recession' in Okimoto, D. and Rohlen, T. *Inside the Japanese System: Readings on Contemporary Society and Political Economy*, Stanford CA: Stanford University Press, pp. 139–43.

Rowley, A. (1998) 'Japan finance: fear of foreign domination', *Capital Trends*, November, 3 (12), http://gwjapan.com/ftp/pub/nrca/ctv3n12c.html, downloaded 21 September 2001.

Ruigrok, W. and van Tulder, R. (1995) *The Logic of International Restructuring*, London: Routledge.

Ryuugaku Taikenki (1992) 'OL Ryuugaku watashi no baai' ('OL Study Abroad, My Case') *URASHIMER*, 6–7 September.

Saeki, K. (2000) 'How Japan lost sight of its strengths', *Japan Echo*, 27 (6): 34–40.

Sakai, K. (1999) 'Deregulate labor standards', *AMPO: Japan Asia Quarterly Review*, 28 (4): 24–7.

Sako, M. and Sato, H. (1997) *Japanese Labour and Management in Transition*, London: LSE/Routledge.

Sasaki, Y. (1995) 'Three steps behind', *Look Japan*, December, p. 33.

Saso, M. (1990) *Women in the Japanese Workplace*, London: Hilary Shipman.

Sassen, S. (1996) *Losing Control? Sovereignty in an Age of Globalization*, 1995 Columbia University Leonard Hastings Schoff Memorial Lectures, New York: Columbia University Press.

Sassen, S. (2001) *Towards a Feminist Analysis of the Global Economy*, http://ijgls.indiana.edu/archive/04/01/sassen.shtml, downloaded 19 April 2002.

Sato, H. (2000) 'The current situation of "family-friendly" policies in Japan', *JIL Bulletin*, 39 (2), 1 February, www.jil.go.jp/bulletin/year/(2000)/vol.39-02/04.htm, downloaded 6 June 2001.

Scholte, J. A. (2000) *Globalization: A Critical Introduction*, Basingstoke: Palgrave.

Schultz T. P. (1995) *Investment in Women's Human Capital*, Chicago: University of Chicago Press.

Schwartz, H. M. (2000) *States versus Markets: The Emergence of a Global Economy*, 2nd edition, London: Macmillan.

Scott, J. (1990) *Domination and the Arts of Resistance: Hidden Transcripts*, New Haven, CT: Yale University Press, pp. 183–201.

Sedgwick, M. (2000) 'The globalizations of Japanese managers' in Eades, J. S., Gill, T. and Befu, H. (eds) *Globalization and Social Change in Contemporary Japan*, Melbourne: Transpacific Press, pp. 41–54.

Seguino, S. (2000) 'The effects of structural change and economic liberalisation on gender wage differentials in South Korea and Taiwan', *Cambridge Journal of Economics*, 24: 437–59.

Sellek, Y. (2001) *Migrant Labour in Japan*, Basingstoke: Palgrave.

Sen, G. and Correa, S. O. (2000) *Gender Justice and Economic Justice: Reflections on the Five Year Reviews of the UN Conferences of the 1990s*, a paper prepared for UNIFEM in preparation for the five-year review of the Beijing Platform for Action: DAWN, www.dawn.org.fj/beijing+5/gender_justice.html, downloaded 20 May 2000.

Shalev, M. (ed.) (1996) *The Privatization of Social Policy? Occupational Welfare and the Welfare State in America, Scandinavia and Japan*, London: Macmillan Press.

Shea, G. (2001) *The Japanese Recovery from War and Transition to High Growth*, St Andrews: St Andrew's University, www.st-and.ac.uk/~gss/ec2006/ec2006lecture6.pdf, downloaded 27 September 2002.

Shields, J. J. (ed.) (1993) *Japanese Schooling: Patterns of Socialization, Equality and Political Control*, University Park, PA: Pennsylvania State University Press.

Shinotsuka, E. (1994) 'Women workers in Japan: past, present, future' in Gelb, J. and Palley, M. L. (eds) *Women of Japan and Korea: Continuity and Change*, Philadelphia, PA: Temple University Press, pp. 95–119.

Shiozawa, M. and Hiroki, M. (1988) *Discrimination against Women Workers in Japan*, Tokyo: Asian Women Workers' Center.

Shohat, E. (2001) 'Area studies, transnationalism, and the feminist production of knowledge', *Signs*, 26 (4): 1269–72.

Shosha ni hataraku josei no kai (1989) *A Perspective on Equality: A Nongovernmental Evaluation of the Efficacy of Japan's 1986 Law of Equal Opportunity*, Osaka: Shosha ni hataraku josei no kai.

Sievers, S. L. (1987) *Flowers in Salt: The Beginnings of Feminist Consciousness in Modern Japan*, Stanford, CA: Stanford University Press.

Sil, R. (2002) *Negotiating a Fruitful Convergence between the Formal and Informal: Institutions of Work in Japan and Soviet Russia*, paper prepared for Informal Institutions and Politics in the Developing World conference, Harvard University, 5–6 April.

Siim, B. (2003) 'Globalization, democracy and participation: dilemmas of the Danish gender model', in Andersen, J. and Siim, B. (eds) *Politics of Inclusion and Empowerment: Gender, Class and Citizenship*, Basingstoke: Palgrave.

Sircar, A. and Kelly, R. M. (2001) 'Globalization and Asian immigrant women in the United States' in Kelly, R. M., Bayes, J. H., Hawkesworth, M. E. and Young, B. (eds) *Gender, Globalization and Democratization*, Oxford: Rowman & Littlefield, pp. 95–120.

Sisson Runyan, A. (1996) 'The places of women in trading places: gendered global/regional and inter-nationalized feminist resistance' in Kofman, E. and Youngs, G. (eds) *Globalization: Theory and Practice*, London: Pinter, ch. 17, pp. 238–52.

Sklair, L. (1997) 'Social movements for global capitalism: the transnational capital class in action', *Review of International Political Economy*, 4 (3), Autumn: 514–38.

Soni-Sinha, U. (2001) 'Income control and houshold work-sharing' in Kelly, R. M., Bayes, J. H., Hawkesworth, M. E. and Young, B. (eds) *Gender, Globalization and Democratization*, Oxford: Rowman & Littlefield, pp. 95–120.

Sperling, V., Marx Ferree, M. and Risman, B. (2001) 'Constructing global feminism: transnational advocacy networks and Russian women's activism', *Signs*, 26 (4): 1155–85.

Standing, G. (1989) 'Global feminisation through flexible labour', *World Development*, 17 (7).

Standing, G. (1999) 'Global feminization through flexible labor: a theme revisited', *World Development*, 27 (3): 583–602.

Staudt, K., Rai, S. and Parpart, J. (2001) 'Protesting world trade rules: can we talk about empowerment?' *Signs*, 26 (4): 1251–7.

Steans, J. (1999) 'The private is global: feminist politics and global political economy', *New Political Economy*, 4 (1): 113–28.

Steinmo, S., Thelen, K. and Longstreth, F. (1992) *Structuring Politics*, Cambridge: Cambridge University Press.

Steven, R. (1996) *Japan and the New World Order: Global Investments, Trade and Finance*, London: Macmillan.

Stienstra, D. (2000) 'Dancing resistance from Rio to Beijing: transnational women's organising and United Nations conferences, 1992–6' in Marchand, M. H. and Sisson Runyan, A. (eds) *Gender and Global Restructuring: Sightings, Sites and Resistances*, London: Routledge, ch. 12, pp. 209–24.

Stockman, N., Bonney, N. and Xuewen, S. (1995) *Women's Work in East and West: The Dual Burden Of Employment And Family Life*, Portland, OR: M. E. Sharpe.

Strange, S. (1996) *The Retreat of the State: The Diffusion of Power in the World Economy*, Cambridge: Cambridge University Press.

Strange, S. (2000) 'World order, non-state actors, and the global casino: the retreat of the state', in Stubbs, R. and Underhill, G. (eds) *Political Economy and the Changing Global Order, 2nd edition*, Oxford: Oxford University Press, pp. 82–90.

Stubbs, R. and Underhill, G. (eds) (2000) *Political Economy and the Changing Global Order, 2nd edition*, Oxford: Oxford University Press, pp. 218–28.

Suehiro, A. (1999) 'The road to economic re-entry: Japan's policy toward Southeast Asian development in the 1950s and 1960s', *Social Science Japan Journal*, 2 (1), April: 85–105.

Sugeno, K. and Suwa, Y. (1997) 'Labour law issues in a changing labour market' in Sako, M. and Sato, H. *Japanese Labour and Management in Transition*, London: LSE/Routledge, pp. 55–78.

Suriyamongkol, M. (2002) *Women and Gender on Regional and International Agendas: Significance of the Beijing Platform for Action and 'Beijing Plus 5'*, paper prepared for presentation at the Annual Meeting of the International Studies Association, New Orleans, Louisiana, 23–27 March, 2002.

Takahashi, H. (1998) *Working Women in Japan: A Look at Historical Trends and Legal Reform*, Japan Economic Institute Report, No. 42, 6 November, Washington: Japan Economic Institute, www.jei.org/Archive/JEIR98/9842f.html#footnote14, downloaded 26 August 2002.

Takahashi, M. (1994) ' The issues of gender in contemporary Japanese working life: a Japanese "vicious circle"', *Feminist Issues*, Spring, pp. 37–55.

Takanashi, A. (1989) *A Challenge to Economic Progress: Changing Aspirations and Labour Market Problems*, Paris: paper for OECD workshop: 'The challenge of economic progress: changing aspirations and labour market problems'.

Takeda, H. (2002) 'The Political Economy of Reproduction in Japan from the 1870s to 1970s: Between Nation-State and Everyday Life', PhD thesis, University of Sheffield.

Takeishi, E. (2000) *The Diversification of Types of Employment in the Retail Industry*, NLI Research Institute, Report no. 142.

Takenaka, H. and Chida, R. (1998) 'Japan', in Morrison, C. and Soesastro, H. (eds) *Domestic Adjustments to Globalization*, Tokyo: Japan Center for International Exchange, ch. 4, pp. 76–102.

Tamura, K. (1999) 'Gender roles in Japan and Singapore', *Journal of Asian Women's Studies*, vols. 6 and 7, pp. 103–12.

Tanaka, K. (1995) 'The new feminist movement in Japan, 1970–1990' in Fujimura-Fanselow, K. and Kameda, A. (eds) *Japanese Women: New Feminist Perspectives on the Past, Present and Future*, New York: The Feminist Press, pp. 343–52.

Tate, J. (2000) 'Giving homebased workers a voice', *IFWEA Journal*, February, www.ifwea.org/journal/0200/giving_homebased_workers_a_voice. html, downloaded 30 September 2002.

Terry, E. (1995) *How Asia Got Rich: World Bank vs. Japanese Industrial Policy*, JPRI Working Paper, no. 10, Tokyo: JPRI.

Thelen, K. and Steinmo, S. (1992) 'Historical institutionalism in comparative politics' in Steinmo, S., Thelen, K. and Longstreth, F. *Structuring Politics*, Cambridge: Cambridge University Press, pp. 1–32.

Todd, E. (1988) *L'illusion économique: Essai sur la stagnation des sociétés developpés*, Paris: Gallimard.

Tokyo Josei Union (1999), *Tokyo Josei Union Newsletter*, Tokyo: Tokyo Josei Union.

Toyoda, S. (1997) *Introduction to 'Request for Deregulation'*, *Nikkeiren* Policy Proposal, Tokyo: *Nikkeiren*, January.

Trends in Japan (1997) *Looking for Work: Unemployment Rate Remains at Highest Ever*, http://jin.jcic.or.jp/trends98/honbun/ntj971009.html, downloaded 24 July 2001.

Tripp, A. M. (1994) 'Gender, political participation, and the transformation of associational life in Uganda and Tanzania', *African Studies Review*, 37 (1): 107–31.

Tripp, A. M. (1997) 'Deindustrialization and the growth of women's economic associations and networks in urban Tanzania' in Visvanathan, N., Duggan, L., Nisonoff, L. and Wiegersma, N. (eds) *The Women, Gender and Development Reader*, London: Zed Books, ch. 21, pp. 238–50.

Tripp, A. M. (2000) *Women and Politics in Uganda*, Oxford: James Currey.

True, J. (2000) 'Gendering post-socialist transitions' in Marchand, M. H. and Sisson Runyan, A. (eds) *Gender and Global Restructuring: Sightings, Sites and Resistances*, London: Routledge, ch. 4, pp. 74–93.

True, J. and Mintrom, M. (2001) 'Transnational networks and policy diffusion: the case of gender mainstreaming', *International Studies Quarterly*, 45: 25–57.

Tsukaguchi-le Grand. T. (1999) *The 'Japanese Employment System' Revisited: Gender, Work and Social Order*, Stockholm: Stockholm University.

Uchida, T. (1998) 'Discussion: the future of women in the workplace', *Women's Asia 21: Voices from Japan*, 4, pp. 2–14.

Umezu, I. (2000) 'Japan has faced its past', *Far Eastern Economic Review*, 10 August, www.mofa.go.jp/j_info/japan/opinion/umezu.html, downloaded 27 April 2002.

United Nations (UN) (2001) Convention of the Elimination of All Forms of Discrimination Against Women, New York: United Nations, www.un.org/womenwatch/daw/cedaw/, downloaded 28 September 2002.

United Nations Conference on Trade and Development (UNCTAD) (2000) *World Investment Report (2000) Cross-Border Mergers and Acquisitions and Development*, Geneva: UNCTAD.

United Nations Conference on Trade and Development (UNCTAD) (2001) *World Investment Report (2000): Promoting Linkages: The Geography of International Production*, Geneva: UNCTAD.

United Nations Department of Economic and Social Affairs (1999) *1999 World Survey on the Role of Women in Development: Globalization, Gender and Work*, New York: United Nations.

United Nations Development Programme (2000) 'Gender Empowerment Measure' in *Monitoring Human Development: Enlarging People's Choices*, www.undp.org/hdr2000/english/presskit/gem.pdf, downloaded 30 September 2002.

Uno, K. (1993) 'The death of 'good wife, wise mother'?' in Gordon, A. (ed.) *Postwar Japan as History*, Berkeley, CA: University of California Press, pp. 293–321.

Uno, S. (1997) 'What are women's centers in Japan?' *Osaka Dawn: Newsletter of the Dawn Center* (Osaka Prefectural Women's Center), January: 6–8.

Upham, F. (1996) 'Retail convergence: the structural impediments initiative and the regulation of the Japanese retail industry' in Berger, S. and Dore, R. (eds) *National Diversity and Global Capitalism*, London: Cornell University Press, ch. 11, pp. 263–97.

Visvanathan, N., Duggan, L., Nisonoff, L. and Wiegersma, N. (eds) (1997) *The Women, Gender and Development Reader*, London: Zed Books.

Vlastos, S. (ed.) (1998) *Mirror of Modernity: Invented Traditions of Modern Japan*, London: University of California Press.

Wade, R. (1996) 'Globalization and its limits: reports of the death of the national economy are greatly exaggerated' in Berger, S. and Dore, R. (eds) (1996) *National Diversity and Global Capitalism*, London: Cornell University Press, ch. 2, pp. 60–88.

Wade, R. (2000) 'Out of the box: rethinking the governance of international financial markets', *Journal of Human Development*, 1 (1), February: 145–58.

Wakisaka, A. (1997) 'Women at work' in Sako, M. and Sato, H. *Japanese Labour and Management in Transition*, London: LSE/Routledge, pp. 131–50.

Wakisaka, A. and Bae, H. (1998) 'Why is the part-time rate higher in Japan that in South Korea?' in O'Reilly, J. and Fagan, C. (eds) *Part-Time Prospects: An International Comparison of Part-time Work in Europe, North America and the Pacific Rim*, London: Routledge, ch. 13, pp. 252–64.

Walby, S. (1986) *Patriarchy at Work*, Cambridge: Polity Press.

Walby, S. (2000) 'Gender, globalisation and democracy', *Gender and Development*, 8 (1): 20–8.

Walby, S. (2001) 'From community to coalition: the politics of recognition as the handmaid of the politics of equality in an era of globalization', *Theory, Culture and Society*, 18 (2–3): 113–35.

Walby, S. (2003) *Modernities/Globalization/Complexities*, paper presented to the conference of the British Sociological Association, York: University of York, April.

Wallace, I. (1990) *The Global Economic System*, London: Unwin Hyman.

Wallerstein, I. (2000) 'Globalization or the age of transition? A long-term view of the trajectory of the world system', *International Sociology*, 15 (2): 249–65.

Ward, K. (1990) 'Introduction and overview' in Ward, K. (ed.) *Women Workers and Global Restructuring*, New York: Cornell University Press, pp. 1–22.

Ward, K. (ed.) (1990) *Women Workers and Global Restructuring*, New York: Cornell University Press.

Watabe-Dawson, M. (1997) 'An overview: status of working women in Japan under the Equal Employment Opportunity Law of 1985', *Waseda Journal of Asian Studies*, 19: 41–58.

Watanabe, H. (1999) 'Recent trends of foreign affiliated companies in Japan', *Japan Labour Bulletin*, 38 (8), 1 August, www.jil.go.jp/bulletin/year/1999/vol3808/05.htm, downloaded 30 September 2002.

Waters, M. (1995) *Globalization*, London: Routledge.

Waylen, G. (1998) 'Towards a gendered political economy', *New Political Economy*, 3 (2): 181–8.

Waylen, G. (1999) 'International political economy, development and gender', *Journal of International Relations And Development*, 2 (4): 435–46.

Waylen, G. (2002) *Gendering globalisation: towards a framework*, paper prepared for ESRC Seminar Series on Gender, Globalisation and Governance, University of Sheffield, 20 June.

Weir, M. (1992) 'Ideas and the politics of bounded innovation' in Steinmo, S., Thelen, K. and Longstreth, F. *Structuring Politics*, Cambridge: Cambridge University Press, pp. 188–216.

Weiss, L. (1998) *The Myth of the Powerless State: Governing the Economy in a Global Era*, Oxford: Polity Press.

Went, R. (2000) *Globalization: Neoliberal Challenge, Radical Responses*, London: Pluto Press.

Whipple, C. (1996) 'Interview with the feminist', Index of *People* articles, www.charlest.whipple.net/ueno.html.

Whittaker, D.H. (1990) *Managing Innovation: A Study of British and Japanese Factories*, Cambridge: Cambridge Studies in Management.

Women in Informal Employment Globalizing and Organizing (WIEGO) (no date on website) *Women in Informal Employment Globalizing and Organizing*, www.wiego.org/textonly/membersoth.shtml, downloaded 30 September 2002.

Wings (2001) *The Catchphrase is 'To Have Fifty Percent of Women in Decision Making!'* Kyoto: Kyoto Wings, web.kyoto-inet.or.jp/org/wings262/human/maintheme/sankaku_1_e.html, downloaded 6 February 2002.

Wolf, D. (1996) 'Situating Feminist Dilemmas in Fieldwork', in Wolf, D. (ed.) (1996) *Feminist Dilemmas in Fieldwork*, Oxford: Westview Press, pp. 1–55.

Wolf, D. (ed.) (1996) *Feminist Dilemmas in Fieldwork*, Oxford: Westview Press.

Wolfensohn, J. (2002) *A Partnership for Development and Peace*, Keynote Address delivered at the Woodrow Wilson International Center, 6 March, Washington, DC, www.worldbank.org/html/extdr/extme/jdwsp030602.htm, downloaded 16 March 2002.

Womack, J., Jones, D., and Roos, D. (1991) *The Machine that Changed the World*, New York: HarperCollins.

Woolf, V. (1993) *A Room of One's Own*, London: Penguin.

Working Women's International Network (WWIN) (2000) *A Message from Japan*, Osaka: Working Women's International Network, 10 March.

Working Women's International Network (WWIN) (2001a) *Visited to the ILO*, www.ne.jp/asahi/wwn/wwin/frameen.html, downloaded 1 February 2002.

Working Women's International Network (WWIN) (2001b) *1999 Statement of Dr. Marsha Freeman*, www.ne.jp/asahi/wwn/wwin/frameen.html, downloaded 1 February 2002.

Working Women's Network (WWN) (1996) 'Why are women's wages half that of men's', *Journal of Asian Women's Studies*, 5 (3): 85–8.

Working Women's PAW (Part-Time Work Research Group) (1999) (*Josei no waakinggu raifu o kangaeru paato kenykuukai*) *Shigoto wa hitori mae atsukai hannin mae nan de! Kintou taiguu o kangaeru 2319 nin no ankeeto chousa oyobi kakugiyushu no hiaringu* Tokyo: Josei no waakinggu raifu o kangaeru paato kenykuuka.

World Development (1999) 'Gender, adjustment and macroeconomics', *World Development*, 23 (11), special issue.

World Economic Forum (1996) *The Global Competitiveness Report*, Geneva: World Economic Forum.

World Trade Organization (WTO) (2001) *The Marrakesh Agreement*, www.jurisint. org/pub/06/en/doc/02.htm, downloaded 7 March 2002.

Worldwide Organisation of Women's Studies (2000) *Women's Studies Association of Japan*, www.fss.uu.nl/wows/start.html, downloaded 30 September 2002.

Woronoff, J. (1982) *Japan's Wasted Workers*, Tokyo: Lotus.

Yamamoto, Y. (ed.) (1999) *Globalism, Regionalism and Nationalism: Asia in Search of its Role in the 21st Century*, Oxford: Blackwell.

Yamashita, Y. (1993) 'The international movement toward gender equality and its impact on Japan', *U.S.-Japan Women's Journal, English Supplement*, no. 5, pp. 69–85.

Yashiro, N. (1998) 'Globalization and the Japanese economy', *Japan Review of International Affairs*, Fall, pp. 178–98.

Yoon, B-S, L. (2001) 'Democratization and gender politics in South Korea' in Kelly, R. M., Bayes, J. H., Hawkesworth, M. E. and Young, B. (eds) *Gender, Globalization and Democratization*, Oxford: Rowman & Littlefield, pp. 171–93.

Yoshida, M. (2002) 'Social care for older people in Japan', unpublished PhD thesis, Sheffield: University of Sheffield.

Young, B. (2001) 'Globalization and gender: a European perspective' in Kelly, R. M., Bayes, J. H., Hawkesworth, M. E. and Young, B. (eds) *Gender, Globalization and Democratization*, Oxford: Rowan & Littlefield, pp. 27–47.

Youngs, G. (2000) 'Breaking patriarchal bonds: demythologizing the public/private' in Marchand, M. H. and Sisson Runyan, A. (eds) (2000) *Gender and Global Restructuring: Sightings, Sites and Resistances*, London: Routledge, ch. 2, pp. 44–58.

Zenroren, (1996) 'Part-timers set up union at Matsushita Electric Industrial Ltd.', *Zenroren Newsletter*, June, no. 58, www.zenroren.gr.jp/english/news/aa_e_news. html, downloaded June 2004.

Zenroren (1997a) 'Both women and men fight against abolition of women protection in Labor Standards Law', *Zenroren Newsletter*, no. 68, April, www.zenroren. gr.jp/english/news/aa_e_68/68_doc1.html, downloaded 28 September 2002.

Zenroren (1997b) 'Final report on review of labor laws published by Central Labor Standards Council', *Zenroren Newsletter*, no. 75, December, www.zenroren.gr.jp/ english/news/aa_e_75/75.html, downloaded 1 February 2002.

Zenroren (2001a) 'Part-Timers Sets Up Union at Matsushita Electric Industrial Ltd', Tokyo: *Zenroren Newsletter*, March, no. 90, www.zenroren.gr.jp/english/news/ aa_e_58/aa_e_58_doc1.html, downloaded 19 June 2002.

Zenroren (2001b) 'National Conference of Homeworkers to Promote Adoption of ILO Convention on Home Work', *Zenroren Newsletter*, no. 90, March, www. zenroren.gr.jp/english/news/aa_e_58/aa_e_58doc1.html, downloaded 19 June 2002.

Index